In the Tomb of the Soul

Copyright ©2017 by Herbert Meyer

Design Copyright ©2017 by Dan Roth, Athens Creative Design, LLC

All rights reserved. No part of this book may be used or reproduced by any means, graphic, electronic, or mechanical including photocopying, recording, tape or by any information storage retrieval system without the written permission of the publisher except in the case of brief quotations embodied in critical articles and reviews.

Bilbo Books Publishing
www.BilboBooks.com

ISBN 978-0-9981627-2-0
ISBN 0-9981627-2-8

Printed in the United States of America

All rights reserved. Published in the United States of America by Bilbo Books Publishing. Athens, Georgia.

Table of Contents

5	Dedication
7	Foreword
9	Introduction (from "The Melea Diary")
21	Chapter Two – *"Let Us Go Then"*
47	Chapter Three – *"Bewitched, Bothered"*
65	Chapter Four – *"I Can't Get No Sat-is-faction"*
81	Chapter Five – *"Young Heirs and Alchemists"*
97	Chapter Six – *"A Bundle of Memories"*
103	Chapter Seven – *"Slings and Arrows"*
117	Chapter Eight – *"History of Grief"*
129	Chapter Nine – *"Into the Breach"*
135	Chapter Ten – *"Young and Easy"*
143	Chapter Eleven – *"Let Things Slip"*
161	Chapter Twelve – *"Pranks and Coyotes"*
169	Chapter Thirteen – *"Could Not Stop"*
177	Chapter Fourteen – *"Two Roads Diverged"*
189	Chapter Fifteen – *"The King"*
203	Chapter Sixteen – *"Don't Need No Salvation"*
213	Chapter Seventeen – *"In Xanadu"*
229	Chapter Eighteen – *"I Have Known Them All"*
237	Chapter Nineteen – *"Ware's Café"*
251	Chapter Twenty – *"Sad Tales"*
257	Chapter Twenty-one – *"Death's Second Self"*
265	Chapter Twenty-two – *"My Youth Is Bent"*
287	Chapter Twenty-three – *"She Kills with Cruel Pride"*
299	Chapter Twenty-four – *"The Widening Gyre"*
307	The Melea Diary
349	Chapter Twenty-five – *"In All My Dreams"* Melea Diary
359	Chapter Twenty-six – *"What Foul Beast"*
367	Chapter Twenty-seven – *"The Way the World Ends"*
375	Chapter Twenty - eight – *"The Hapless Man"*
381	Chapter Twenty - nine – *"Certainly We Should Have..."*
387	Epilogue – *"What Place is This?"*
399	Glossary of Terms
405	Acknowledgments

Dedication

In the Tomb of the Soul is dedicated to the memory of Lt. Col. Robert (Bobby) Alford, originally from Milledgeville, Georgia, a soldier and friend.

Col. Alford lived in Irmo, S.C., with his wife and was the father of two children. I knew Bobby all my young life as classmate and friend. We grew up together at Georgia Military College, drove cars, loved the girls and laughed a lot. His ebullient personality, terrific smile, and fabulous dance moves, endeared him to many throughout his life. GMC was high on his list of favorite places to visit during and after his service. I saw him many times at reunions over the last twenty years. Bob was not a sentimentalist, but a strong and determined leader, and big story teller. Most of them were funny stories and memories; others were grim and cathartic for him.

Bob served for more than 30 years in the US Army. He was a graduate of the University of Georgia and received military education in Infantry Officers Advance Course, Command and General Staff College, and the Army War College. He had an MA in business management from Webster University. He served in Germany, South Korea, several posts throughout the US, and two tours in Vietnam. He received numerous decorations to include the Legion of Merit, the Bronze Star with V device for Valor, two Army Commendation Medals, the Air Medal, the Vietnam Cross for Gallantry, and the Vietnam Service Medal with four bronze service stars, a combat Infantryman's Badge and the Parachutist Badge. He was wounded in Vietnam and awarded the Purple Heart. Col. Alford died from complications from Agent Orange in 2015.

An Loc

Foreword

In the Tomb of the Soul took 16 years to complete. The combination of issues confronted in the book took a long time to process: the Vietnam War's impact on our culture and society, gender awareness and gay rights, and institutional unawareness, especially in schools, both public and private. In the 21st century American society has faced a number of civil rights issues not in the public arena in 1965. The pervasive silence regarding sexual issues gripped our culture. Gay men and women suffered in all arenas. *In Tomb of the Soul*, the suffering of a gay man in the military, and as a coach in a private school goes unnoticed.

I had to confront my own understanding of issues raised by characters in the book. As Nathan Kuballe evolved, I began to understand how cultural silence contributes to the misery and madness of an individual afraid to divulge his sexual preferences, how traditional marriage and family tormented him, and how sexual choices affected work-place relationships. As I wrote about these matters, I came to see the difficulty and confront the silence to a degree.

I had a lot of help creating this book, beginning with a class of 16-17 honor English students in 1997 at Athens Academy. They were tasked with writing their own short stories. I chose to spend a week with them in a new computer lab writing my own story. So I have to thank them for their diligence. I took my own story forward for the next 16 years! Becoming lost in the content, I had to work to understand the behavior of my characters.

Long talks with associates and editors helped clarify the central themes in the story. I wrote of the misery of Nathan, conveyed the silence and ignorance of his workplace relationships, and the misery of Emmett, a decorated Vietnam veteran ravaged by PTSD. Both were warriors and had different orientations, yet were bound together by teaching and coaching.

Herb Meyer, 2017
Athens, Georgia

Introduction

(From "The Melea Diary, 1969")

I'll never forget that patch of jungle ditch, or the ridge that ran down from a knoll, crowned by two large, abandoned termite mounds, like breasts of a woman, above a ravine overgrown with lacy, tropical vine. The squad of eleven guys had spread itself out at intervals of about twelve meters and moved slowly forward, letting Racine, an Indian from South Dakota, take the point. He slipped into the drainage depression and inched his way up the knoll like a silent, slithering snake toward the two mounds.

I kept myself low, feeling my heart begin to pound steadily in my throat and fixing my eyes without blinking on the serpentine crawling of Racine, then cutting them sharply to his objective, the two termite mounds, and, then, back to him. I slid my M-16 weapon to a more comfortable position, wound my arm inside the sling and pushed it up hard to the upper swivel. The stock settled into the ridge in my shoulder. I slipped off the safety, just in case Racine's movement drew fire. The set-up was perfect for an ambush. The two mounds were made for a gun emplacement. Our movement was slow and cautious.

Racine slithered along. The only sounds were the calls of birds and the ever-present dripping of jungle leaves, heavy from the predawn rain.

We had been returning from a recon patrol, when the radio had crackled that we may be walking right into a VC patrol as we crossed the ridge outside of Loc Ninh.

"Alpha Charlie, this is Jerry. Do you copy?"

"This is Alpha Charlie. Copy. Adjusting. Over."

Racine was twenty meters from the right-hand mound. The silence was oppressive. When the first burst came, I squinted up the rise ahead. Shots raked and kicked up the underbrush to my right in the ravine where Racine was working.

"Get down," someone yelled.

It was Sgt. Parker. No one moved. Racine froze.

Another burst. My heart raced wildly, yet my mind remained clear and sharp as a crystal. All was still. No sound at all, even cicadas were quiet. We were frozen.

A third burst licked the area. I could hear the bullets whizzing into the growth of trees behind me ripping leaves. Because the hits were over us and behind us, we knew we were too far below them for a clear shot from above. They really couldn't see us.

What followed was typical of our unit. A high pitched squealing began, a squeal that contained the essence of all human pain and terror, Roscoe's pig's squeal. This guy from Oklahoma could squeal like a tortured pig The sound was wild and terrible, slicing through the silence and timed perfectly following the shots. A scream from the edge of hell itself. Many times in a fire fight Roscoe would let loose his pig's scream. The first time we heard it, we thought he was wounded. The lieutenant had sent the medic into a frenzy to find the source, but soon enough we learned Roscoe's scream was one of our best weapons against surprise. I guess he held off his own fear by screaming like a pig, or he summoned strength. It would slice the air above the racket and have wicked effect on the enemy. A VC machine gunner got as frightened as any American, no matter how many times he had experienced the rush of combat. The scream was our battle cry.

To the VC, Roscoe's scream seemed to signal someone was hit. Usually another burst of fire came, then we would wait. We'd hear them check their weapons. We'd smell 'em, then open up on them.

It was no different this time. Roscoe's screams warbled and crippled the silence. Racine lay quiet, listening, catching the scent. The next burst kicked up debris behind him, while off to the left Roscoe made like a pig. It gave Racine the opening he needed. He slithered forward another six meters and paused again.

I lifted my weapon, aiming it at the opening between the two termite mounds. I knew the routine. Racine would, after a count of twenty, if there were no more bursts of enemy fire, heave a grenade over the two mounds. When it detonated, we would charge up the knoll with Roscoe's scream piercing our ears.

It worked. We fired round after round.

Racine's butt must have been in high gear. He gave a long scream, punctuating it with warbling yodels. "Mother fuckers!"

We heard voices of the VC's nervous chatter over the hill beyond us. Racine launched a grenade. An explosion shook the trees, and we charged again, firing and screaming up the embankment.

I ran scrambling up the knoll, digging out with my boots globs of leaves and soil. I could actually see the raking fire of my own weapon knocking out chunks of soil on the sides of the mounds.

Racine reached the right edge before I did as the others fanned out to cover the flanks. We dipped behind the knolls and emptied our clips into the brush pile that concealed the position. Four troopers crashed in the brush behind the nest area to secure a perimeter, while Racine and I checked things out. Three more remained below, covering our rear and flanks.

Inside the shallow, dugout bunker lay the mangled bodies of two dead VC, young boys, maybe about fifteen or sixteen, thin, pale and very dead. The grenade had gotten them. One had been wearing a GI helmet, the side of which was dented as though it had been struck by an heavy object. Part of his shoulder, the one who had manned the machine gun, was completely gone. Bone stuck out. Bowels spilled out on the ground in a brown, lumpish pool, where the grenade's impact had shredded them. The machine gun emitted blue smoke. An ammo can was tipped over, shells spilling on the ground. AK-47's lay on the ground. Only one layer of shells remained folded inside the ammo can. These boys were almost out of ammunition. If there were others around, they had retreated far away.

"Reckon, I hit the motherfuckers in the head with that grenade," said Racine. "I heard it go 'donk!'"

"You win the Cy Young for Viet Nam!"

I was checking the bunker for anything, documents, maps, other cashes of ammo or weapons. There was nothing, only the sight of bloody boys, one without an arm and shoulder, and the other like a gutted deer. My heart was no longer pounding. I felt absolutely nothing, pure numbness, only the weakness in my legs as if I had done wind-sprints up and down the hill we had just ascended.

"Chalk up two more crispy critters!" Racine sang out. "Bloody bastards! Oh, Jesus!"

There was this thumping sound.

Racine looked at me, gave a thumbs up, just as the area grew hot with fire.

Racine went flashing across my vision as I dove to my right. I don't know what made me clear the brush position as I did, but instinct drove me hard away from the fallen boys to a covering position a few meters from where Racine had dashed.

Were we surrounded? I felt hair on my neck wrinkle and burn. My heart rate increased, as it thumped in my throat. My weapon was primed. I was a warrior. Rampage 101.

If VC lurked in the bush, they'd pay for messing with me, I swore.

From down the ravine I heard the scrambling shouts of the guys in front of me as they tried to return fire, but the shots seemed heaviest to my rear, as though we had been encircled.

I had to get off the ridge and away from the two mounds. Forcing my way ahead, I fired in bursts as I hurried in a low squatting run down hill.

I was watching the ground, when I hit something very hard, and felt it give way. My helmet flew off, my rifle was ripped from my hand. I felt the quiver of a blow on my shoulder as though I had made a hard hit in a football game. I fell to the side.

I remember scrambling up again, as the firing raked the area. I dove. I hit the legs of another person, legs straining to run. They tangled in my own. I heard a grunting sound, as though a person struggled to get his breath. Focusing to keep my feet under me, I drove ahead blindly. For a minute, I thought I might have blasted into one of my squad members. It wasn't.

It was a VC.

I had bolted straight into the guy, caught him flush on his chest, knocked him down. The wind flew out of him.

I struggled with my knife, crawled up on his body, and blocked his movement with my forearm. He squirmed beneath me. Automatically, I struck him with my elbow, a forearm shiver across his jaw, and he went limp. My knife hand was poised above him, ready to strike.

I couldn't bring it down.

The bursts of fire had stopped. I rolled off the man, scrambled back a few feet, picked up my weapon, crammed a new clip into the magazine, and whirled around, nauseous and the gulping for air.

The man lay lifeless.

"Peterson!" came the shout. "Peterson, are you hit?"

My mouth was dry. I could hardly answer. I heard the sound of my own gasping.

"No!" I rasped, "but there is a guy here! I think he is unconscious."

Down from the knoll scrambled Roscoe and Sgt. Parker. Parker didn't stop to look at my quarry, but set up a perimeter.

"Stay down, be quiet. Take cover. We wait. If there's more in the area, they'll move."

We obeyed, finding the earth cool and the leaves thick. We sort of dug our own separate holes.

In a minute Parker whispered, "Three guys bought the farm. Racine has disappeared. God-damn motherfuckers!"

Roscoe put his fingers to his mouth sharply in a warning gesture that said, "Stow it!" and moved out from where I lay to check the VC I had belted. He was dead, neck broken. He crawled back a few yards toward me and said, "Goddamn, you hit him with a bat?" Roscoe said. "Fucker's neck is out of socket!"

I sort of heaved and felt the collision again, how I had used my forearm to shiver him.

We stayed quiet for about twenty minutes. Originally, eleven of us had begun the mission. The two firefights had not lasted more than two minutes total. The second one was especially short, yet there was no sign of the others. Our radioman was gone. Racine wasn't in sight. Three other guys might be dead, or scattered all over the place.

We inched our way back down past the two mounds where the bodies of the VC lay. We had crept a few meters away when Roscoe gave a birdlike whistle. We listened again for what seemed like ten minutes. Racine should have checked in, if he heard it. No sound at all, so we resumed our pace, spreading out about ten meters apart. We backtracked. Sgt. Parker led with Roscoe in the middle of two other guys. I came last, watching our rear.

Shit! Of our eleven guys, six were missing and three might be dead.

We had come up toward the knoll beside a trail the lieutenant had drawn for us on a lousy French map, a nondescript trail, maybe an animal path, because it was partly overgrown. It had led from our LZ in a serpentine fashion into the jungle where a report had been given out about a major crossing point over to Laos beside the Ho Chi Minh Trail.

Without a radio we could only hope that we could find our LZ and wait for the chopper. Our best guess was three of us had been hit in the firefight, and maybe Racine too. We should have looked, but the area was too hot. Roscoe and Sgt. Parker ordered us back.

Approaching the line of trees near a clearing, we recognized the place the chopper had set us down. The grass was blown around in every direction. The outline of trees gave us good cover and shade from the afternoon sun. Roscoe readied his smoke. We established a firing line to watch the clearing and our rear. When we heard the thump of the approaching chopper, Roscoe would light smoke.

In the back of my mind, I wanted to see Racine come running out of the bush. He didn't appear.

"Shouldn't we go back and give a look for the others?' I asked.

"You want to get the shit shot out of you, stupid?" hissed Sgt. Parker. "Stay put. Charlie might spot you, follow you back here, and hit the rest of us. Cool off. They're wasted. Anyway, if they ain't, they still got the coordinates on their map and a radio. They can find the LZ. They can radio TAC (Tactical Command Post) who can pull 'em out later."

We had only a minute to ETA. We were accustomed to making some contact with the in-coming helicopter, but without a radio, it was always a little touch-and-go. Pilots didn't like coming in blind, didn't like fly-overs either, but they also knew our plan of movement. Maybe they'd spot the other guys. Relying strictly on the smoke was nerve-wracking for them and for us - but it would have to be that - red for a hot area, yellow for caution, and white, for a free-wheel. We had the willie-peter ready (white phosphorous smoke) and red just in case.

If the VC had knocked out the others, they might have trailed us, I thought. Maybe they hoped to hit the chopper in one massive sweep when we set off the smoke.

This was a pisser.

I had no time to be scared. Like hawks we watched the tree line. We had a password, "Sadie Mack." Maybe Racine would come running. There was no sign of him or anybody else.

I gave a glance at my watch. 1300 hours. The chopper came in low. I glanced at my weapon. I hadn't taken time to wipe any of the stuff off of it from the ground where I had hit the guy. In fact, I had avoided looking him. I focused on how I needed to wipe off my weapon. Would it fire? I had a sense of fatigue, like a football game. I had thrown that forearm. I was bruised from my elbow to my wrist. My shoulder hurt, my right thigh throbbed.

In a combat situation you are so intent on the exterior events that you give little attention to your own feelings. Sensations seemed to double. The tension is automatic; muscles constrict and you don't know it until afterwards. Fatigue becomes exaggerated; aches throb and burn more intensely.

I felt all of that lying there, and I kept hearing the thud of my collision and the gurgling of that guy's breath. I only had glanced at those two bloody boys on the jungle floor, one with his shoulder gone, the other with his bowels spilling out.

In high school my buddy, Raymond Kingsley, the guy I idolized the most, had made me laugh. "You a regular hit-man. Hammer them mothers! Peterson the Hammer! Hey, we call you Hammer!"

My whole life had been one covert episode after another. All that stuff at Longstreet Military School - one covert operation after another. In the jungle I lay covered in dirt like an animal, having maybe shot two people and killed another with my bare hands . . . no adventure, only exquisite pain and pure agony covered me with maybes.

I remember letting my mind float, trying not to wonder if the other guys were like me, praying to be picked up. Did our run and leap into the door of the rumbling chopper mean we were abandoning the other men who hadn't come in? It stunk.

Crazy Racine was my friend, the indian warrior.

Nevertheless, when I heard the rumble of the helicopter, I saw home, base camp, and felt a sagging relief of tension. We were swept above the jungle to relative safety. The pain was more for my own bruises, the experience of striking the man ("Hell fire, Peterson, he was gonna waste you."), and stiffness. My incredible stiffness.

I remember Roscoe down the line, yelling, "Hey, it's Halloween! Firefight! Every night! War dance, man! That's how you know you are alive."

Two days later they found our guys. A patrol had been sent back. The bodies of our two with Racine and the two other guys were huddled together to fend off attacks that came at them. Three that lay dead about thirty meters away had probably been covering the opposite flank of the knoll when they got theirs. We had heard the shots during our flight. Racine said they hid out from roving groups of VC for several hours. They heard the chopper come in and get us out, but they couldn't move. They stayed in that shit-hole for 30 hours. They pulled them out two days later.

Racine was transferred two days later. Never saw him again.

Roscoe had to see the Captain to explain why he decided to split - he told him that we were taking a lot of fire and felt that pulling out was the best choice. We had not gone back to hunt because we were used up and unable to determine the size of the force we were up against.

The Captain bought his story, so we moved on . . . but there had been dead guys out there, ghosts in the night. I knew we should have tried to track them down, but we hadn't. It was the end of the hunt for us. . . Racine left.

– *Emmett Peterson, 1969*

In war, in combat, you kill people. Some kill directly, guns and knives; others kill indirectly, bombs or long shot artillery (arty stuff). None of it is art, none of it is glorious.

For Emmett Peterson, Infantry Operations Specialist had seemed exciting when he was twenty. It meant learning skills for tracking, and close combat. Just the sort of stuff he thought a jock would like. He was strong, understood leverage and contact.

He also had some feelings he hadn't really faced, the impact of his youth, his parents' decision to send him off to Longstreet Military School at fourteen to board and grow. He took refuge in football and antics with his friends. Later, he married, and the war came to him. He applied his skills. He took human life. He saw others die. When war was over, he was emotionally spent, having suddenly entered a world, not of battle, but of relationships: marriage, work, and colleagues. Certain events touched him in places he didn't know existed, mental places, dark places, even death-inviting places.

How could he have known?

Books tell stories in black and white. Characters have a paper life. One can absorb a story, but it is a story only, not the real reality of others, who look at you with all-consuming eyes, who breathe on you, or lie with you, and die on you...or *because of you*.

The trick is to go about your business, holding at bay some of the real stuff, which lurks like apparitions tucked in shadows. One can visit them sometimes, but not really - they reside in the crevasses and recesses - in the tomb of the soul. If they come, the unexpected, the acutely sentimental, the coincidental, the harsh, grotesque and violent aspects of life animate. We call them nightmares, dreams, hallucinations, bad trips, even mental anguish, The Hag of Vietnam. Modern science buffers the reality of them with clinical diagnosis: Post Traumatic Stress Disorder (PTSD). Emmett didn't define them. He lived with them.

Emmett knew of compassion bred of friendship and young love. He could be ebullient and funny. He could, however, become fumblingly lost, tell you of the incubus who comes in the night, the Hag of Vietnam. She destroys the light of normal living and reintroduces the jaded scenes to a candelabra of suffering, of killing, and dying. The Hag can hiss and twist the truth and mix a cauldron of guilt with the stuff of goodness to wring out the soul.

After the war, Emmett had a colleague who knew the vagaries of war in Vietnam, a man who possessed his own demons. His name was Nathan Kuballe. Nathan's war experience was of the indirect sort. Some called him a bean counter, one who tallied the score of ground fighting. Nathan would never dwell on the numbers he drew from his visits to the battle zones. He dwelt on fear, a two-fold fear: his own incubus, and his rising sense of self-hate, because he was an outsider, a gay man, who fought two battles, the enemy of the state, and the enemy of his own identity. He became a master of deception, an impersonator, an actor. His sense of love was deep, yet resentment lurked close at hand when certain boundaries were crossed. He was like a fish at the surface of the water, who preferred a water-world and not the strange airy world of others, who understood what he could not. He could not have what he wanted. It gnawed him and sucked life from him.

When the two, Emmett Peterson and Nathan Kuballe, met and tried to work together, all the candles were lit. All the desires were animated. All their deeds were quickened by the shadows that resided in their souls. What comes to dance for Emmett instigates guilt and war pain. Those candles for Nathan proclaim his difference, his alienation, his crumbling sense of self worth, and ultimately his hatred.

War and chance meeting sets everything in motion.

Two

Let us go then, you and I
When the evening is spread out against the sky
Like a patient etherized upon a table.
— TS Eliot

In the early spring of 1971, the rain had intensified and the wind had picked up. Robert Hughes and his wife, Sarah, decided not to go out for pizza. Sarah made sandwiches. The television evening news assured them that Nixon's administration was unraveling the mess at Kent State. Interdiction in the northern sector just below the DMZ in Vietnam was working. Poor people were marching on Washington. Atlanta was intense racially.

The doorbell seemed a compliment to the TV and rang twice before Sarah said, "Can't you see who is at the door, Rob?"

Robert, the lanky blonde haired teacher, peered into the eye-hole in the door. Rain drops obscured the stranger without. Robert opened the door slightly, "Can I help you?"

"It's me, Robert, Emmett Peterson," a familiar voice said. "Been awhile."

In the dim glow of a porch light, dressed in a dampened corduroy jacket, the apparition of Emmett Peterson stood in the shadows, a thin, gaunt figure, nothing like the strapping, robust friend that Robert Hughes knew from years earlier.

"I should have called first. Found your address in the phone book at the Atlanta airport. I...I just got in." He didn't move, but peered at Robert. "Didn't have the key to your flagpole."

"Emmett? My, god, Peterson! I'm not believing this. Get in here!" He snatched Emmett's arm. He was face-to-face with a living ghost. He embraced him anyway.

"Sarah, come here! Meet an old friend! Emmett Peterson, my best buddy at Longstreet. I don't know what to say. Come out of the rain." Words tumbled out of him.

Subdued, but not hesitant, Emmett stepped into the hallway and gazed at his tall, lanky friend. "I'm soaked to the bone, man," he said. He was stooped and tired from a several days of travel merged with fatigue accumulated over fourteen months in Vietnam.

"Doesn't matter. Get out of that coat. Come get a beer or something to eat. This is just a great surprise. It has been a long time, Peterson. A long time."

To Emmett, Hughes seemed deeply moved.

Sarah took his wet jacket and made him take off his soaked shoes. Robert ushered him into the living room. Sarah scurried around straightening pillows and picking up newspapers, switching off the TV. Emmett stood looking around, lost.

She was as slim as Robert, and beautiful. Her movements were natural, easy, and calm.

Emmett Peterson, athlete, midnight rambler, prankster seemed like the hollow man to this domestic couple. To Robert, Emmett appeared as an old gray ghost emerging from the wild, wet night, befuddled and exhausted.

"I had that jacket stuffed in my duffel bag. Didn't have a rain jacket. Just got off a plane from San Francisco. I been flying for nine hours."

"Well, sit down, Peterson. A beer and sandwich will make you feel better. Come on. I'm at a loss for words. You are just out of Vietnam?"

"I am. Still got the mud to prove it." Emmett sat down.

"We have to catch up. You are just back. God in heaven!" said Robert.

Sarah rustled bread and ham from the refrigerator. She put a six pack of beer in the freezer, and heard Robert say, "I married Sarah two years ago."

"Eighteen months, Robert!" she yelled from the kitchen. "I'm making another ham on rye. Is that okay, Emmett?"

"Sure, anything," he said, "I had peanuts on the plane and a baby crying all the way from the Denver layover. This is my first official landing spot in fourteen months. I was in Nam."

"And you just flew in? God, you didn't go home first? We heard you married," said Robert. He felt himself fumbling.

"Yeah, that," Emmett said. "It's a story."

Sarah brought a tray of ham sandwiches and three cans of beer. "Is PBR okay? Rob goes cheap."

"Always did," smiled Emmett, and took a long swig. "Oh, man," he sighed. "It's just good to sit in a quiet place for a change. I've been moving for a whole year."

Sarah slipped a tape on the tape deck.

Emmett slumped in his chair. "I feel like a snowflake. Must be the beer. I'm glad you were here. Haven't slept much in the last 50 hours."

"50 hours!" exclaimed Robert.

"Left Tans San Nhut for Gaum to Pearl to San Francisco four days ago. We drank all the way to Pearl, and tried to sleep to San Francisco. Just a lot of flying."

"Didn't your wife meet you?" asked Sarah.

"Sure, she was there. She had to get to New Orleans to do a show." He looked off to the living room wall with a picture on it. "She was a singer and on the road a lot."

"But, geez, Vietnam. Homecoming. She should have stayed. Still, I'm glad you came here. She didn't stay with you?"

"She did, brother. She stayed. One night."

"Ah," Robert said. "I was worried. So you just walked in here out of the night."

"Hey, I took a cab, Robert!" He smiled at his own joke. "Yeah, that's me. I'm still Peterson, the Night Rider - a ghost who walks."

"Well, we are glad you picked us, Emmett," Sarah said, and she left them to get more beer and putter around in her kitchen.

The moment was awkward.

Robert was a school teacher, a benign occupation, he thought, compared to other friends from Longstreet who enlisted or waited to be drafted. Robert had poor eyesight. He had learned that at Longstreet. They didn't take him in the draft.

"I can't see a damn thing," Robert had told an instructor on the rifle range. "I think I'm blind as a damn bat, Sergeant!"

Emmett had teased him back then. "You are one scant, son-of-a-bitch. At least, a blind dirtbag like you can study for us all!" Robert graduated at the top of their class, 1964.

A heavy crack and rattle of thunder shook the windows in the house, causing every one to startle. Emmett bent low, almost leaving his chair.

"That was close one," said Robert, as the rumble continued for a moment and died away.

"You want to know what thunder is, I could tell you. If I drink enough beer," said Emmett, "I'll tell you what happened." He swigged a second beer without breathing.

"We are not prying," said Sarah, coming back, straightening her hair behind her neck. "You just stay as long as you like." She smiled warmly at two old friends.

Robert had mentioned Emmett Peterson as being a great friend. She put a bowl of potato chips on a TV table.

"Saigon, Rob! I left last Sunday, duffel bag in hand. I was in-country for exactly 372 days. They choppered us out of the field, processed us out in a couple of weeks, then onto the tarmac, into a silver bird, and off we went. Nam in the rear view. Stewardesses on American Airlines carried just under the limit of cases of scotch to allow the plane to take off. Everybody got drunk. Hung over in Guam for six hours, then a jump to Pearl, refuel, and another six hours to Frisco Bay. That's where I met Gina, the wife."

"Gina. I'd love to meet her," said Sarah.

"Yeah," said Robert, "I can't get over that she isn't with you, man. I mean, what gives?"

"She works, Robert. She was doing a show in St. Louis, and on to New Orleans, and flew out to meet me. We spent the night, and I flew here." The waver in his voice made it apparent that he was uneasy.

"Well," said Sarah, "we sure need to catch up. But, if you want to sleep that's okay."

Emmett smiled at her. "You're really nice to let a swamp rat like me wander in here. I couldn't think of anyone else who might be in Atlanta. Hughes and I were close in high school. I'll sit here and enjoy you guys for a few more minutes."

Sarah smiled at him. "As long as you like. Robert's been teaching at the high school, and I've been teaching at the elementary school. I guess we are pretty settled in for a while."

Emmett shifted his seat. "That's a very good thing. I'm just gonna relax."

Robert was watching Emmett, expecting to find some spark of the old guy he knew, striving to understand more about his surprise guest.

"Do that. Your feet don't stink do, they? They used to be really bad."

Emmett laughed. "It was a great weapon. Stick my hot foot in the air, and the VC cleared the area." He wrinkled his toes. "God, is there a better feeling than your feet breathing?"

"Just sit back, partner. Let 'em breath Atlanta air. Get the spray can, Sarah. We might need to disinfect."

Sarah laughed and her nose wrinkled. Emmett could see why Robert had picked her. She seemed perfect. It was good, the time between them.

"Well, what's next for you? You got plans? Where will you head?" asked Robert.

The long pause was unsettling. The quiet became awkward before Emmett answered.

"I feel like I'm headed to the gallows-maker. You know me. I need a good gallows to climb to get a view of things. Has to be a gallows because that's a place where living and dying meet. I need to see the living part of things. Or else, jump off and hang myself because I don't like it! Kind of like that, right now."

That remark caused another long silence among the three of them.

"I think I'll be just fine single again," he finally said, and exhaled heavily. "For now, I just keep on being what I was in Vietnam. I thought I was married to Gina, the wonderful gift of my youth, my generic bride. Maybe they issued me a wife when I was in basic training. She didn't feel married to me, she said. That was a kick in the head.

"Remember that poem we studied in Major Burke's class our senior year he read to us: '...when I am pinned and wriggling on the wall/ Then how should I begin...' It said something about 'the butt-ends of my days?'

"Let me tell you guys I've come to understand those lines completely. I'm seeing some of the 'butt ends of ...days.'"

"Tough tour, then?" asked Robert, knowing it was an awkward question.

"You might say that. Best thing about Nam is I wasn't shot up. Every guy who gets to meet the Hag of Vietnam has a tough tour. I come back, and the tour doesn't end."

"Meaning what...?" asked Robert. His forehead wrinkled as Emmett remembered when Hughes was being serious.

Emmett shifted the focus of the conversation from himself and smiled.

"Meaning, why did you become a teacher?"

The shift wasn't lost on Robert. He sensed the hesitancy in his old friend to talk personally. He had always deflected talk about love-life, even though he was smitten in high school with an older girl.

"It was what I enjoyed," Robert said, "I liked to study. It's how I met Sarah."

"I'll bet you met her in the library," laughed Emmett.

"We did," said Sarah. "He was sitting at a table reading some dull book. I was with a girl friend, and saw this egghead blonde guy. He saw me. That's history."

"Yeah, she was forward," Robert said.

"I was not forward! You stared at me. I stared back."

"Look," said Emmett, "I know Hughes. Sometimes it took a grenade to get him out of a book. You loved it, Hughes. Saved us all in algebra because he did homework. Not a surprise you picked a girl who noticed you first, and she picked you because you were a serious student.

"So answer me. How did you get to be a teacher?"

Hughes was enjoying the old Emmett tease.

Robert pushed his hair out of his face and answered, "One day a professor said, 'Hughes, ever think of teaching? It's a good insurance policy, a teaching certificate. Make some money until you find something better.'

"So that's what I did, took a few courses, practice-taught, and landed a job teaching English at Crest High School. Been there for four years, working on a Masters Degree in the summertime. Not exciting, but it is fulfilling at times. I like the kids. They seem to like having a blind English teacher. Plus I could show Sarah I wasn't going to sit on my mother's porch and wait for a job to happen. She was aimed at teaching herself. It just came. Two together make a pretty nice, simple living. We can continue to do homework."

Emmett's melancholy was still apparent. "Is that all you do? Read and teach?"

"I can still hit a golf ball. Just can't see it land. Thought about coaching a little baseball, actually, but never volunteered."

"You can't catch, Rob!" Emmett laughed, and Sarah joined him.

"He should have been a pole vaulter," she exclaimed.

"He tried," laughed Emmett. "Fell on his head twice. Good thing he taught."

There was a long pause.

"You're a lucky man!" Emmett sighed, and reached for another beer. "I'm not calling you by your high school nickname. We thought you didn't do anything and teased your ass off, didn't we?"

"That you did. It was okay. I am a pretty square guy." Robert popped open his second can.

Emmett began to reflect, feeling more at ease.

"You know what?" said Emmett, "In all that Longstreet Military School crap with Rodman, you never ratted. You were solid as a rock. You stayed the course. I played football and roared around the school, getting in trouble, raising Cain, and you were there taking it all in, studying, being a good, loyal buddy. Like a brother in the middle of it all. It's a beautiful thing, Robert. Beautiful.

"Best of all you didn't have to know the steel or the shell. Really a lucky guy. Good wife, who can fix a mean ham on rye, nice house, and a job that has some meaning. I won't ever call you Aunt Scanty again.

"I am all about honesty now. War leads to that for some who make it through. Gina has led me to a sense of that, it's for sure. Truth can be painful as hell."

Robert didn't respond, but he felt like he wanted to. He wanted Emmett to show himself again, so Sarah could see what he knew lying behind the hollow eyes, to know the bright, electric Emmett, a man of deep passion and creative zest. This Emmett was pensive. He just wanted to talk, Robert thought, and that was okay.

"Tell you what Robert," Emmett said, "life is a series of blows you got to learn to absorb. Sort of like football. You can't get confused between yourself as player and the ball. You can get knocked around. I was that a few times, but I got up. At least I think I did. I'm sort of alive, still.

"Coming home reminds me of a game. The war reminded me of the game, but coming home - wow, it's a fifth quarter, it seems."

"Fifth quarter?" asked Sarah. "Sounds fatalistic to me." She watched Emmett's tired eyes.

"Yeah, extra playing time, and football don't have all that much overtime. You get all beat up, and suddenly the game ends. You can go to the shower or the hot tub. You don't have to take the pounding for another round. Over and done.

"Now, this time coming home, it feels like I'm in a fifth quarter. It ain't over, and more blows are coming. Sort of like that in Nam. Blows coming. Not knowing when."

He sighed again, a long heaving exhalation.

"Did you know my parents were separated four years ago?"

He lifted his glassy eyes, red from sleep deprivation and beer drinking. "You know I had this big fight with my dad before I left, so we haven't been in touch exactly. They know I'm headed home. At least mom knows. I sent them a few cards and a cable from Saigon, saying I had to go down to Fort Benning to process out. That was buying time. Told them I'd call when I got to the States. Haven't called. Thought maybe you'd give me a lay-over. Found your name in the phone book. Bizarre, ain't it? Midnight rambler riding in."

"You want to call your folks. Tell 'em you are here with us?" asked Sarah. She glanced at the phone on a nearby table." We got a jack in the spare bedroom. You can be private."

"Not just yet," said Emmett. "I need some shut-eye."

"Well, you just stay here with us." She spoke quickly, without hesitation, and Robert smiled at her. "We got room, and we leave early. You can sleep all day if you want. Ham and eggs in the refrigerator. Just plan on it."

Emmett smiled. "You better know what you are getting into."

Sarah got up and picked up the plates and switched off the music.

"You are no stranger in this house, Peterson," said Robert. "She is exactly right. Now talk to me. What happened with Gina?"

"Oh, Robert, let him go to bed. We can talk tomorrow," she said.

"It's okay. I need to tell you about Gina. We got married, me and Gina Marlowe, three and a half years ago. She's an actress, a singer, a good one. Funny, when I was at college, how I met her. I always had a way meeting girls at movies, like in high school.

"It is along story from Gina to Vietnam and back to Gina. Anyway, I need to tell you, so I have one friend who knows.

"I got dragged to a dinner theatre by this couple. Some musical called, 'A Funny Thing Happened on the Way to the Forum.' The funny thing that happened to Emmett was this girl in the show, the one who plays the whore. She was the best looking woman I ever saw. Great figure, full lips and the sultry singing voice.

"I got my friend's girlfriend to introduce me to my dance-hall girl. That was it. We dated up to Christmas my last year in college."

Sarah slipped back into her chair after tossing beer cans. Emmett continued his story.

"About that time the school I was attending announced it was closing - just going out of business and shutting down in January! The war was on, all hell breaking loose on college campuses and in cities. Unrest everywhere. Suddenly, I was draft bait.

"There were other factors. Hippies moved in on the campus, and a few athletes got into fights with them and tore-up some of their stuff. I had enough sense to stay out of it, but there was a lawsuit. Gina wanted to hit the road. She took a lot off my mind. Our football team was terrible. We lost eight games. Rumors that the program would be scrapped were circulating. They cut our scholarships. It was pretty chaotic.

"Your life can get screwed up in a situation like that. Happened at Longstreet, wrong place at the wrong time, that Rodman stuff. Lousy ending to a senior year.

"Gina said we ought to clear out. She was a roadie at heart, anyway. I had moved into her apartment, so we decided to get married, one of those quick jobs, and hit the road together. I wasn't speaking with the parents at the time.

"Story of my other life.

"We drove up to Gatlinburg, Tennessee, for a weekend, then called my parents. She even called her folks. Everybody seemed elated. Mine were really not. No surprise. I think they were embarrassed. I know my dad has never been happy with anything I've done. It's mom who supported me.

"Anyway, we had done it. Gina found a job in Gatlinburg for the summer, so I got a job as a weight trainer in a membership gym. I made a huge mistake when I failed to notify the Blakely County Draft Board. I was moving, and my college days were over. They reclassified me, 1-A. My number came up. Mom called, then Dad called. It was like running at a dog-track, all of us chasing some kind of carrot, but nobody knowing where the finish line was. I was rejecting them because they couldn't get along with each other, and they were giving me hell because I ran off and married Gina. Everybody was hurt and angry. I had to report to the military.

"We decided to give it up. Draft notices can bring things into perspective for a few moments. I was headed to do something that seemed to have a purpose, though it was risky, and inconvenient. Marriage to Gina was convenient, you know, at the time.

"I drove with her to Macon to meet my parents, let them know her before I reported for duty. I had a month. It was a mess.

"We got in for dinner. It was a helluva time.

"The new daughter-in-law, Gina, as usual, glowed. She was a beautiful woman. We were the happy couple!

"Mom and Dad put on this show. Dad liked that. I turned into the good son, the college football player. All that would look good on a resume, my dad said. Let's-all-have-a-fun-weekend-despite-the-fact-the-damn-sky-is-falling. Dad had two bottles of chilled champagne. We just sensed that at any minute something was going to blow up.

"It was late April, I think.

"Robert Kennedy was shot the next morning as I met my dad in the lobby of the Holiday Inn on Riverside Drive, where we were staying.

"It was going to be the father/son talk that we never had. And...Kennedy lay dead in a hotel basement.

"Then, this weird thing happened. My dad began talking about what a great looking girl Gina was. How proud of me to have a son on the college football team (he saw me in one game in high school and one in college. We lost both of them.)"

"'What a horrible way,' he said, 'for the school to have treated students by yanking scholarships, then abruptly shutting down the place!

"'Parents didn't have enough notice the place was in such desperate financial difficulty.'" he said.

"Then he hit the weird note I didn't expect, the real subject of his interest. It wasn't me, or Gina, or the school. It was how he had moved out on mom into an apartment in February!

"He mentioned their separation at the exact moment the Robert Kennedy assassination announcement hit the TV wire service.

"They were," Dad said, 'Working on the next step - counseling, maybe a divorce, some kind of settlement. Our marriage is disintegrating. Folks get older and "they change."'

The news about Robert Kennedy blared over the TV. I paid no attention to it. Dad was the one facing the TV screen. His confession blew me away.

He began this sappy kind of apology that pissed me off.

'You know, son,' he said, 'I have the utmost respect for your mother, but men and women sometimes discover the spark has gone out of their relationship. A marriage is like a candle whose wax is burning down. An easy wind can extinguish it.'

"For a reason unknown to me at the time, Dad suddenly blurted, 'I can't believe I'm seeing this!'

"I thought he meant my marriage, or my expression. I had no idea he was reacting to the TV announcement about Bobby Kennedy! He was changing the subject!"

As Emmett revealed this coincidence, Hughes leaned forward intently.

"You mean," Hughes exclaimed, "you were sitting in a hotel restaurant when the announcement of Bobby Kennedy's assassination came on - having a conversation about your dad's separation from your mom and your marriage? That's unbelievable!"

"Exactly how it was - a total disconnect," said Emmett. "We were talking about two different things, or focusing on two different things. Completely disconnected.

"Confused in the moment, I got mad as hell at him, and said things. 'This is bullshit. Total shit!' I said it loud. I meant the separation. He thought I meant the Kennedy thing, I guess."

"People in the restaurant stared at us. People began standing up. For a minute I thought they were standing because I was yelling at him. Maybe they thought we were going to fight.

"My back was to a TV on the wall. My dad was watching. I had no idea what he was reacting to at the time.

"'Good, God!' Dad exclaimed.

"He stood up in the booth. That interrupted my rant.

"I don't give me the 'good God' crap!' I said loudly.

"The TV was telling the world that Robert Kennedy had been shot in San Francisco. I thought Dad was mad because I was upset about mom and him."

Sarah Hughes and Robert were deeply engaged in Emmett's lengthy monologue. They both understood Emmett needed to tell it. They didn't move.

Emmett stopped his narrative.

"Hold it a minute," he exclaimed. "Where's the head? I need the bathroom after all this beer."

Robert indicated the way to the bathroom, and Emmett left them.

Sarah looked at her husband. "He's in incredible pain, don't you think?" she said. "What happened to you guys at Longstreet you haven't told me?"

Robert didn't look surprised. "What didn't happen? We had a Commandant of Cadets at Longstreet Military School, a real strict jerk, Colonel Rodman, that we all hated. Emmett had a few run-ins. We did pranks and stuff. Emmett's a tough guy."

"You never told me any of this stuff. Longstreet is in Millersville, Georgia, right?" she said, sounding disappointed.

"No real need, I guess. We were kids in a military school under the thumb of authority. It was a haven for some power-hungry faculty. Emmett wasn't having much for authority. He had fallen love with a college girl, and he played football like a real star. We can tell you some of it."

She was smiling as Emmett came back into the room.

"Now, that's better," he said. "I got room for more. I'm almost done with the story. You sure you want to hear the rest?"

"I do" said Sarah, and then I want to hear about Longstreet and that girl."

"The girl?" said Emmett. He thought he was asking about Gina.

"God, Peterson, the love of your life, Barbara Lynne what's-her-name."

"Oh, her, Barbara Lynne Jenkins. Hadn't thought of her much over the years. Don't know anything about her."

"Were you in love?" Sarah asked.

"At the time. In love with love in a high-school way, I guess," Emmett smiled and felt warm. "I got such a screwed up life-story, I didn't know which drama you wanted to hear."

"Well," said Robert, "finish with Gina and your dad. He's watching the news on Robert Kennedy, and you are thinking he is completely missing your point."

"He was," said Emmett. "We were far off base with each other. Still are."

"That's so sad," said Sarah.

Emmett continued. "Okay, actually. I got used to being off-base with Dad.

"At the time my dad looked past me. I didn't know what he was doing. One minute he was telling me about moving out on mom, and the next I was cursing.

"When he stood up in the booth, I honestly thought he was going to hit me, but his eyes were fixed on the television set over my shoulder. People were shrieking in dismay.

"'Sit down!' I ordered, 'I think this whole thing is bullshit. Sit down!' My tone was harsh. People stared at me, and at the TV, as I glared at my father."

My dad slid down in his chair at the table.

"'What else can happen? What else?' he cried.

"I just didn't get it at the time. I thought he was objecting to my language, my outrage, my marriage. I was confused, ignoring the people, and the blaring of the TV because someone turned it up louder.

"Then, it hit me.

"He was reacting to Kennedy's death, not to my situation!" Emmett paused to sip his beer. "That's it," Emmett said in a tone of resignation.

The story settled on Robert and Sarah, as Emmett sat nursing his beer.

"My God!" said Robert, softly. "I'm sorry about how that happened."

"That scene," Emmett said, looking at his beer can, "epitomizes my whole existence. You probably know that. What happens to old Emmett is not what happens in the real world. The real world seems to pass in a blur. I was so stunned by my father's announcement that he had walked out on my mom,

I was cussing and floundering. He's watching Kennedy dying, and sort of oblivious to my raving self. Absurd time."

"Well, of course," said Sarah. "It was the worst kind of miscommunication. The coincidence is uncanny."

"God knows, now more than two years later, I've seen some real shit, some bizarre stuff beyond that episode in a hotel restaurant. It all coalesced in a moment. Only difference was the assassin fired more than once, and shot Kennedy just above the heart. I just took my wife and left my parents.

"I actually felt sort of cheated. Selfish, like I was the one being shot by the one person who I'd have liked to have counted on for some consistency of purpose.

"Dad didn't know how I felt. I don't know if he saw the confusion between his remarks and the TV bulletin because ol' Emmett didn't stick around. To this day, I still don't know, because I haven't seen him since. I got one letter in thirteen months."

Emmett could see the immediate impact on Sarah and on Robert.

I really shouldn't have unloaded all this on them, especially in front of her. I don't even know her.

"You just left for the Army and didn't contact him?" Robert said.

"Yeah. He didn't bother to write me or call either until I was in Vietnam. That's the way it's been with me. Stuff comes at me, and I never know when to duck. I run, I hit, or strike. I'm not good at standing down, ducking, or getting out of the way. I lived through about twenty firefights. Guess I'm dumb lucky.

"So, now you know, Sarah, about me and Gina and my fabulous family. I haven't called because I don't have the guts just yet. I just called you guys. Some choice, huh?"

Robert was the first to speak. "I love it you came here. I saw you play ball. I watched you react to all that baloney Col. Rodman threw at us. You stood right there, and sometimes took a swing. You got guts, Peterson. Don't think otherwise. You can be strong. You are a good friend. We will find ways for you to get back into things. Believe me. It's what friends do."

They sat there in silence. Robert mulling what Emmett had shared, Sarah looking at the two of them.

Emmett had experienced more life in five years than she or Robert combined, she thought. *Do you ever really know people, even the ones you are closest to?*

Finally Sarah said, "It's late, Robert. We got to teach classes in the morning. We all need to rest. Maybe we take this up tomorrow. Emmett's had a lot going on." She even yawned.

Later, in bed with Robert, Sarah said, "I've heard you mention Emmett Peterson, how you really liked him."

"I still do," he murmured.

"His life is pretty troubled, don't you think? He hasn't much relationship with his own family. Divorce shock, to say nothing of this awful war."

"Emmett, the lone wolf. Relationships can be hard on a guy sometimes," said Robert. "He was never one to 'go gentle into that good night,' let me tell you."

She rolled onto her side, propped her head on her arm and stared at him. "I can't imagine his coming back, and on the night of his return, that woman asks for a divorce. After all he had been through. It's so cruel."

Robert laid on his back. The lights were off. "Emmett was the guy in high school who had life by the tail. And when it wagged, he wagged back. He was one tough guy on a high wire. We loved him for that. In the end, he had a tough time. It happens, but he handles it. Maybe he even invites it. It is hard. You can see it in his eyes. I kept looking for old Emmett. It's in there. He will be okay. He can still reach out to his folks, to his friends. He found us. I'm glad. Maybe a day of quiet will do wonders. He wants to talk, and it is best he does, I'm glad we are here."

"Yeah, me too," she said, "but outward toughness isn't inward toughness. Some things, like glue, just stick. Sometimes they fall apart."

"Well," Robert said, "we pray the glue finds the good stuff. He was my best friend. Probably will be again."

He gathered her in his arms, and she snuggled onto his chest. "I'm glad you didn't have to go to that war."

"Me too," Robert said. They were quiet.

> *"And you, my father, there on the sad height, /Curse, bless, me now with your fierce tears, /I pray /Do not go gentle into that good night. /Rage, rage against the dying of the light."* — Dylan Thomas

Emmett lay staring at the ceiling, sensing a kind of relief to be in a bed amidst silence. No screaming artillery, no heat oppression, just the cooling hum of the air-conditioning. He hadn't thought of Barbara Lynne Jenkins in six years.

God, she was gorgeous when we were in high school, lying on that blanket, smelling like an angel. She was flat-out a beauty. What the hell happened?

The Gina mess faded quickly.

Maybe Gina did me a favor. Who knows?

Somewhere a voice said, "Shut-up, Emmett."

He slept late.

Late the next afternoon, he and Robert went to the Mall where Emmett bought civilian clothes to replace the rumpled slacks and smelly sport shirt he had worn for three days. He stocked up on underwear and socks. He even bought some snazzy loafers, even though the guy who sold him shoes wore slick leather ankle boots and love beads with a peace symbol dangling from his neck.

"Damn, Rob, do I let my hair grow long now?" Emmett remarked when he came from the Mall.

"You might, but somehow I think you do just fine with a regular hair cut. I don't have enough hair to let mine grow long,"

"Yeah, it's the Age of Aquarius, ain't it?"

"Something like that," replied Hughes.

They met Sarah for dinner at a restaurant, and had wine. She wanted to hear about Longstreet, and this "Rodman guy you talked about."

"Geez," exclaimed Robert Hughes, "do you realize, Peterson, Longstreet was more than eight years ago?"

Emmett smiled, and his nose wrinkled in a way that delighted Robert.

"Raymond Kingsley, the Phantom, "The Ghost Who Walked." Colonel Rodman and the love of his life, Gloria. Damn, those were some days," Emmett laughed.

"Don't leave out the love of your life," said Sarah. "Tell about Barbara Lynne Whats-her-name."

"Jenkins," said the guys said at the same time.

"I'm telling you, Peterson was head-over-heels for her," said Robert.

"You mean balls over brains!" Emmett said.

Immediately, he clapped his hand over his mouth. "Damn, I got to remember I'm not in the Army. I'm sorry, Sarah. Boy talk."

She wasn't embarrassed. In fact, she liked him for saying it. "It's okay. I know plenty about 'boy-talk.' It's all you guys think about, sometimes."

"Yeah, sometimes," said Robert, and he pulled her to him.

Conversation was easy for Emmett. He felt somewhat renewed. He had slept for ten hours.

"Okay, Longstreet Military School is where I met your husband in eighth grade. Green as gourds," said Emmett. "I went out for the football team, and Robert went out for the study hall team. About the least athletic guy I've ever known, and the most loyal. No kidding."

Robert smiled. "I can hit a golf ball, remember?"

"So you said.

"We had a buddy, Raymond Kingsley, who was two years older, and a mentor to me, and a friend of Robert's. I loved him. He never studied, hated ROTC, the barracks, the marching, and all that stuff we had to do. He found everyday some thing to do to combat it. I thought he was the coolest guy in the world."

Robert took up the story. "He's the one who painted the white dome of the Baldwin County water tower. Bold in tall, black, block, letters, painted on its side:

"'The Phantom.' Beneath that in slightly smaller letters, 'The Ghost Who Walks.'"

Sarah's eyes got wide. "And, you helped him?"

"Oh, no," said Emmett. "No one helped the 'Ghost Who Walks.'"

"Okay," she said laughing, "what happened to the 'Ghost Who Walks?'"

"He disappeared," Emmett said, as if it were magic.

"Gave up his pivot shoes! He got kicked out of school," said Robert, looking at her matter-of-factly.

"I think we were freshmen when that happened," said Emmett. "It was about the coolest thing any of us had seen. It set the faculty on fire. It got him his freedom."

"But, it was on his permanent record. Expelled isn't good," she said.

"Believe me," said Robert, "it was good for Raymond Kingsley, one rebellious barracks boy."

Robert warmed to the story. "That's when Col. Rodman showed us what an asshole he was.

"Remember, Emmett? Colonel Rodman from the Administration Building steps, towering above our drill formation, announcing that Raymond Thomas Kingsley had been 'shipped,' which meant he had been kicked out of school."

"Yep, I remember that day. It pissed me off. We said at the time, The King Is Dead. We just knew it standing there in the morning chill, too afraid to look around to see if Kingsley was in his usual spot over in A Company, receiving his usual dressing down by some idiot cadet officer. Kingsley looked terrible in a military school uniform, like a duck just out of the barn yard, totally out of place. He was not there on this morning. Nowhere in sight. It was like death.

"We were dismissed and sent off to class."

"Didn't they explain anything?" Sarah wanted to know.

"Nope, they didn't have to. We saw the water tower. It was Kingsley."

"Anyway," said Robert, "we were 'fish,' which at Longstreet was like plebes. We had no status, not even a key to the flagpole. We had each other, and Rodman had strutted around and among us like a the Roman jerk that he was. We didn't like the guy at all."

"Had to figure a way to get back at Rodman. The Ghost is not dead," said Emmett.

"Not among the 'fish,' he wasn't," said Robert.

"Did you ever see this Kingsley guy again?" Sarah asked.

"Not really," said Robert.

"Oh, I did," said Emmett. "I saw him once, after I got my car up to school, the red Chevy. Instead of going home on a leave weekend, I drove to south Georgia and spent the night with him. We shot pool. And we planned a revenge. I talked to him on the phone a lot." Emmett looked at Robert Hughes. "I bet you didn't know that, did you, Rob? That the whole library thing was cooked up by Kingsley and me mostly on the phone at the corner of campus."

Sarah was hanging on every word. "This is better than television. What did you cook up?"

Emmett lit up like a young kid. "We put his car and pig in the library one night!" He beamed.

She looked aghast at them.

"You really did not! Get outta here!" she exclaimed.

"Yep, we did! A Volkswagen bug. This guy in town found us a baby pig, and we tied it in the car. Took ten guys to carry that thing up the Administration steps. Cranked and drove it right down the hall into the library."

Robert was laughing. "I helped carry it. We also told all the guys if anyone said a word, we'd kill 'em. No one squealed on us. Not even that pig. It was perfect."

"We shoulda ate that pig, Robert. We didn't think of that," said Emmett, watching Sarah's reaction.

"You wouldn't have done that," said Sarah. "A little pig who didn't know what kind of trouble you were making."

"Oh, yes, I would have, and fed it to Rodman," said Emmett, "with extreme pleasure."

"That old bastard tried to get us. We hated him," said Robert.

"Well, sure," she said, "but what did he do?"

"Okay," said Emmett. "Here is how it went. I was car nuts. I had an old Chevy. I got a guy who worked in the cafeteria to show me how to hot wire a car. He was fantastic and showed me all the tricks.

"My favorite car belonged to Colonel Rodman, a navy blue 1955 Volkswagen Beetle with white flecks of paint chipped off it. It had character, more than Rodman, and solidity, like a bullfrog."

"Colonel Rodman rarely had the car worked on," said Robert, "because he rarely left the campus. When he did sally forth, the car spewed a plume of blue exhaust. We knew when he approached, because the car gurgled and snorted. The oil plume would rise majestically behind it as it settled itself with an occasional belch or backfire."

"It was a fine piece of junk," said Emmett.

Robert took over the story. "Rodman was proud, single-minded, even arrogant, but he really didn't take pride in his car's engine, just its appearance. I don't know why Emmett loved it so much. Most often Rodman's Beetle sat in front of the Ad Building like a shining piece of blue-black coal. Each morning before ascending the steps to his office, Colonel Rodman would meticulously pluck the leaves from the space below the windshield glass. It was no wonder the car had chipped paint."

A waiter came to their table, and Emmett bought them a second bottle of wine. They ordered cheese cake and four plates to divide. "We might be here all night," he laughed.

"Take your time," the waiter said.

"I'm not watching my waist line tonight," said Sarah.

"Good thing you don't have to fit into a Volkswagen Beetle," teased Robert.

Sarah slapped his shoulder. She loved being the center of attention.

"Dang, you remember the wife of Gen. Evans, Gloria Evans?" asked Emmett.

"Who is going to forget her? Gloria Evans was the school president's wife. She drove that long, black Buick, wearing her dark cat sunglasses, white gloves, and loose blouse. She had this long shock of auburn hair that blew in the wind.

Robert looked at Emmett. "You insisted she was off to visit her lover three days a week in Macon!"

Emmett raised his eyebrows and turned to Robert. "I don't think she had to go that far actually."

Robert nodded, knowingly. "Nope, probably not."

Sarah looked at them. "You guys were over-sexed, weren't you?"

"Oh, you bet we were," said Emmett.

"Hey, it's the military. They didn't put salt-peter in our tea for nothing, wife!" said Robert.

"Shut up," she said. She poured the wine all around.

"Don't know what 'over-sexed' means," said Emmett. "I do know that Gloria Evans was at least ten years younger than her husband, and very tan and quite, vivacious!"

Ha!" injected Robert. "'Vivacious,' that's a good one for her. We thought she was a very sexy momma. We conjured great fantasies about Mrs. Evans. Most cadets preferred waxing the President's car just for a chance to glimpse

Mrs. Evans. They liked that better than other chores, or walking the bullring."

"Bullring?" asked Sarah.

"Where we had to walk when we got demerits for something we did wrong. It was a ring we marched around for punishment," said Emmett.

"I'm surprised you didn't camp out there," she said.

"Some guys did," said Robert.

"I didn't," said Emmett.

"You played football. Football players never got punishment," said Robert.

"Well, some of us are privileged."

"So what did this Col. Rodman do about the car and the pig in the library?" Sarah asked.

Robert laughed. "'When the culprit is found, you will hear from me.'" He imitated Rodman's voice perfectly.

"Colonel Rodman was out for evidence," Robert said. He searched the dust bins in our rooms, paint splatters, sniffed for kerosene, looked for grease, rope in closets, cuts on our hands. Cadets stood for hours listening to him lecture and being shaken down, while cadet officers made searches."

"They found nothing," exclaimed Emmett proudly, "because Kinglsey told me how to cover the trail."

Continuing the story, Emmett took up the imitation of Rodman. "'Gentlemen,' he said, 'there is a thief among us, a barbarian, who has come in the night, who has removed and tampered with personal property. He has dese-crated personal property. He is our enemy and will be hunted down!'"

Sarah began to laugh. "This needs to be recorded. Really, it didn't happen like this."

"I'm telling you," Robert said, "the guy was a frigging Nazi cartoon."

Emmett lowered his voice to a dramatic baritone. "Somewhere in this school is a person - a malig-nancy on the honor of The Corp! It is your duty to expose this person, so Longstreet Military can purge him from The Corp.

We are not a place where thieves may haunt the night, lurk in the shadows, or disrupt the good order of our institution, or our mission."

Like an identical twin, Robert took up the imitation. "'After thorough reconnoiter and interrogation, we have found nothing. But...the investigation will continue until this coward comes forth - and he-will -come-forth!'"

"'And you will hear from me,'" echoed Emmett.

"He sounds like a Nazi," said Sarah. "You guys could take this on stage, the one-two-dramatic brothers."

They men looked at each other and laughed. "It's what we shared," said Emmett.

"Comrades in pranks and punishment. That was Longstreet," said Robert.

"So you were never caught?" Sarah asked.

"Nope," said Emmett, looking proud as if to see if Col. Rodman was in the room.

"Never caught. Rodman might have killed us," said Robert.

"So what did Barbara Lynne think of all of this?" she asked.

"Barbara Lynne wasn't on the scene yet," said Emmett.

"What grade were you in? I thought you were high school seniors?" she exclaimed.

"God, no, we were in tenth grade."

"Tenth grade. You were devils," she said.

They finished off the cheesecake. Not many in the restaurant remained.

"So, Barbara came later?" asked Sarah.

"Not much later," said Robert.

"Let him tell it. He is the story teller," said Sarah. She thought for sure the reminiscing was great for Emmett.

"I thought we were one-two drama brothers?" he laughed.

"Yes, but she wasn't your girlfriend," Sarah said.

"Emmett's women all resided in the dramatic arts. He had a wife, Gina,

In the Tomb of the Soul 45

who he called his 'dance hall queen' and a high school sweetie who was his movie queen," said Robert. His familiarity had become bolder with the wine as he finished off bottle number two.

"We should get out of here," said Emmett. "I can tell it at home." So they left a large tip and walked home.

Later that evening at the house, Emmett told the story of Barbara Lynne, how she may have been the love of his life.

Three

Bewitched, bothered, and bewildered....
— Cole Porter

The prank blew over after two weeks.

At the local movie house the previews indicated that *Picnic*, a movie starring William Holden and Kim Novak, would begin showing the following Sunday. Holden was an 'O.K. actor,' but Kim Novak was a sensation. Some bets had been taken that she would show up naked in *Playboy*, but an equally strong contingency believed otherwise. Emmett was an admirer of what he called 'feminine pulchritude,' though he never went near girls, only viewed a collection of *Playboy* center-folds cadets had gathered for two years and passed around. It was Milledgeville in 1961.

The anticipation of the movie was great because Sunday afternoon was the best social hour of the week, when all the girls from the local women's college, the high school crowd, and the Cadet Corps descended on the movie house regardless of the feature.

Emmett said he would go. He rarely attended movie outings, preferring to work in the shade on his old Chevy. On this day he was fashionably late and had to take a seat to the right of the aisle in the back. He slipped into a vacant seat next to five college girls.

The movie began. As William Holden heated up with Kim Novak's character, discovering her in her mother's backyard, Emmett became acutely aware of the girl next to him. She had begun to breathe quickly. He listened to it. The pace of her breathing was in perfect consonance with the romance of the film. It was sort of exciting. Emmett had not dared to look at her

"Could you use a Coke?" he whispered, unable to contain himself. "I'm making a run."

"Sure," came a soft reply.

Emmett really had to pee.

He returned with two Cokes and a bag of popcorn. He had been careful to wash his hands.

Her breathing began again. In time he became more aware of her responses than the movie plot. He never looked at her. Five minutes passed, and he offered her popcorn.

She grappled with the sack. He thought he felt her fingers through the paper on his right leg. They shared popcorn for the rest of the film. He spent two dollars. It was worth it.

When the film ended, a smattering of applause, and the houselights came up dimly. Beside Emmett was Barbara Lynne Jenkins, a tall, slender, blonde girl with shoulder length hair, brushed to a high sheen. She was wearing a forest-green tam and a tan sweater.

"I'm Emmett Peterson," he grinned. Then his confidence sagged. For the first time he felt an aching awkwardness about his last name.

"Hi! I'm Barbara Lynne," she exhaled her last name, "Jenkins. Thanks for the popcorn."

"No problem," said Emmett. They stood looking at each other, Emmett grinning. Barbara merely looked into his eyes. People pushed up the aisles.

"Great movie!" he said to her. He had no idea what it was about.

"Oh, yes. The best. I love William Holden." She held his eyes with her own.

"Meet you at the Ham House, Emmett!" someone yelled as they pushed by.

"Okay!" he answered automatically, pulling himself away to let Barbara Lynne pass and he followed her up the aisle.

Outside, the afternoon had deteriorated, and a shower threatened. Emmett made his goodbyes, and he looked after Barbara Lynne, who headed up the street. Her tight skirt was unavoidable.

"God!" he thought, just as he was shoved from behind.

"What did you think of that, Peterson?" his friend Robert Hughes chortled.

"What do you mean? What do I think? She's fine, you idiot. She's fine."

"Always knew you had a peter, Son!" yodeled his friend, Herman Cord, the shortest guy in the school, who was standing at Emmett's back.

Emmett whirled around toward him, eyes flashing. "You better bite it, Cord, or I'll cut off more than your knees."

"Okay! Just an observation, man. No harm meant." Cord had a talent for bad timing. The Coach said he played football that way. Mostly the team agreed, but he was always following them.

That evening Emmett talked privately with Robert Hughes about Barbara Lynn Jenkins. He had no idea how to approach her. He spent the evening in contemplation. She had to be older. But how much older?

"What if I called her dorm?"

"Which dorm?"

"Well, hell, I could go and sit outside and wait to see her when she came out. It would work if I went at dinnertime, but I would have to risk skipping chow here. I could phone the dorm and try to talk to her...what would I say?

"Maybe you could invite her for more popcorn," teased Robert. He was a loyal pill-of-a-guy, smartest in the class. "You might could say, 'I liked sitting with you at the movies feeding you popcorn.'"

"Duh!" said Emmett. "I just wish I had left something behind. I could have stolen her cap or something. Hell, I might have stolen her purse. Then I could take it to her!"

"You are a damned thief! Peterson." Robert said. "She has done a number on you. A real number."

"Shut up! Don't make me mess you up."

Emmett was so befuddled he dithered on for a hour. Finally, he concluded that he would wait until the following Saturday night and see if she would go to

In the Tomb of the Soul 49

the evening movie, a double feature.

Later in the evening, a week later, several cadets were talking in the barracks lounge when Emmett strolled through.

No one made a move to approach him, but all watched. Emmett only nodded and went into the latrine. Cord and Hughes shot in after him.

Over the sink, looking into the mirror, Emmett saw them, as he finished washing his hands, and started in on his hair.

"Great evening, huh?" Robert Hughes had asked.

"Charming," Emmett replied, and wet his comb and repositioned his part. "Actually, I'd say, very rare." He pocketed his comb and pushed past them out the door.

That was the beginning of Barbara Lynne Jenkins' hold on Emmett Peterson. He managed to see her or phone her everyday for the next two weeks. They were lying together under the elm trees on the front campus, studying in the college library, and sitting at the drugstore over French fries and Cherry Cokes. He remarked to a friend he felt he had known her all of his life.

"If it is possible to know a person for a lifetime without having really done so, I know I know her like that."

Later, he said, "She's a descendant of Bonnie Parker, who was her grandmother's first cousin."

Herman Cord wanted to know who Bonnie Parker was. Emmett was aghast at his ignorance.

"She was Clyde Barrow's lover, man," Emmett said, incredulously. "A friggin' bank robber, dumb ass!"

"So?" replied Cord.

"Hey stupid, they killed about 50 people in bank robberies in the 1930's with machine guns. You got ta know some history, man! Major Burke not teach you nothing?"

Herman Cord was impressed with that.

Emmett had other occupations suddenly. Friends in the dorm didn't count as much. He spent time thinking of things to do for Barbara, things to buy her, little tokens of affection: one carnation, a friendship ring, until finally, he gave her his class ring, and a wallet-sized picture of himself in his football uniform kneeling on one knee in the grass. The ring was a five-ounce affair containing an aqua marine stone, pale blue, "Just like her eyes." With the offer of his ring went a gold chain.

She wore them religiously. The weight of the ring made a pleasing depression on her chest. She had this way of holding it between her forefinger and thumb when she talked to him. They had serious conversations about intimate subjects, like the names of their children: Dawn, Amber, Chris, or Jason. She would tease him with simpering glances, revealing to Emmett her fondness for him, even, as he called it, pure love.

It was 11PM after the dinner at Robert's home, when Robert said, "Emmett turned philosophical after a time. He was a regular Platonic scholar. "There is ordinary love, and there is 'pure love, which is what the gods have. That is what we have. Pure love.'"

Robert shook his head at Emmett, who sat relaxed in his living room. "My God, for weeks Emmett preached about love and their devoted times together, everything from favorite sports, music and food, to water skiing and romantic books."

"I think it's sweet, Emmett. You fell in love," Sarah said.

Emmett shrugged, "Maybe, a little. More than a dozen years ago, almost."

"Sarah, you would not believe how smitten this guy was," Robert enjoined. "We couldn't find him because he'd be with her on the front campus lawn, lolling on a Tartan blanket in the afternoon. Weekends he'd play football and go with her to listen to Nashville Late Night, and the music of Johnny Mathis. He loved Mathis's songs."

Robert did a warbling rendition.

> *Chances are*
>
> *Cause I wear a silly grin*
>
> *The moment you come into view*
>
> *Chances are that*
>
> *I'm in love with you.*

"I told him he was a moon-struck sheepdog! Whipped-down and drugged with love."

Sarah Hughes laughed at Emmett. "You better find this woman, Emmett. She might be the savior of your soul now that this war is over."

"And that bad marriage," added Robert Hughes.

"I'll think about it. You know, Rob, that wasn't all the story." Emmett looked serious. "Remember Rodman and Gloria-baby-Evans. I'm always in circumstances I didn't choose." He wasn't laughing. "The beginning of the story of my life was that day at the lake."

"I tried to forget that," said Robert.

"What happened?" said Sarah. "You have to tell."

"Simple enough," said Emmett. "Me and Barbara Lynne caught 'em."

"What do you mean? You caught 'em? At what?"

"Come on, wife," said Robert. "They caught Rodman and Gloria doing the dirty in the woods."

"You've got to be kidding?" she said.

"We did, and it broke us up." said Emmett. "Bad time."

Sarah was incredulous. She had to hear more.

"I actually never heard the whole thing," said Robert.

―――

The leaves were turning green in late March that year. It was 1964, Emmett was a senior. Barbara Lynn was a college freshman. On a Sunday afternoon, Emmett had watched Mrs. Evans drive away and heard Herman Cord chortle,

"There she goes - hornier then a cat on a HOT wood fence!"

"You mean, 'Cat on a hot tin roof! Dummy!" said Emmett.

"What ever! I bet she could make the smoke come right out of your ears - ring up the old peter-meter!"

"You'd wilt at the sight of it, Cord."

"Cord is over-sexed!" injected Robert, but Emmett continued the story.

He climbed into his own car. "Robert, get him some palm oil and tell him to shut up! See ya later!"

He was off to meet Barbara. They planned to go to the lake and look at the leaves, maybe take the blanket, and watch the sunset. He thought of her kisses, like brushed satin to his lips.

In minutes Barbara was at his side with the windows down, her blonde hair flying across her face. She brushed it away and put on sunglasses.

God, she was beautiful.

They drove into the country to the lake.

The radio played gently, as he turned into the vacant lake lot bordering the spacious property belonging to the school. For years Longstreet Military had maintained a recreational center for its faculty and students. The lot was huge, and in the middle of it, the school had constructed a pavilion with a stone grill, and a bathhouse down at the lake's edge. A long dock extended many feet into the lake, where students could bring ski boats on weekends, if they knew town cadets who owned them.

Emmett had scouted the surrounding area to discover an isolated, overgrown logging road where he could pull his car without risk of scraping the paint from the overhanging tree branches. He was certain no one knew of the spot. It was shaded and cool. Like a knight errant, he brought his maiden where he had first kissed her - felt his own heart flop at her touch. They were free to let their imaginations wander. So special had the place become that they had named it, "The Summer Place," after a movie they had seen together at her home near Macon.

This afternoon was no different than the last ten or so they had spent. They first walked to the shoreline, surveyed the trees, and the fall line of the adjacent shore. The days were growing warmer, and they recognized the shift of the wind and the approach of the changing season in the afternoon breeze.

Returning to his car, Emmett retrieved their special blanket from the trunk, and his chemistry book, and walked back to the clearing that afforded them cover, yet a view of the lake, and the setting sun. Barbara Lynne waited for him smoothing a place and tossing aside sticks.

"Shhh, Emmett! Listen," she whispered. "The wind in the trees sings,".

He stopped. It was not the song of wind, but of faint music from a car radio. Maybe he had failed to turn off the ignition in his car. He checked. It was off.

They listened again. On the breeze, the sound of music, came dancing toward them, through the tangle of brambles to the right of their bower - rising and falling on the breeze and between the rustling of leaves.

Emmett's mind switched gears. He gestured to Barbara to follow him to the shoreline, where he nimbly guided her fifty yards down and away from the sound. He slipped into the bushes, pulling her after him. Both were deadly quiet. He looked into her face, and saw the flush of excitement making patches on her throat.

"Who is that, do you think?" she whispered.

He put his finger to his lips for silence. With hand gestures only, he indicated he would search. She should wait, but she protested. She would go with him. So he relented, and they crept back, keeping low to the ground, heading toward the opening in their bower. As they entered the path, he pointed to his foot, showing her how, if she put her toe down first at every step, she could walk silently. She imitated his movement exactly.

Beside their car they crouched and waited. Clearly, the music again lifted on the wind. Around the edge of the car, he crept to study the dense growth from where the music came. A mass of foliage, tangled grape vines, bramble, cat briars, blackberry, and poison oak impeded the way. Up the path where the car had traveled was a better opening.

Emmett felt keyed-up. He wanted to hunt, to see where the music was coming from. His energy telegraphed to her.

They moved up the path to where two pine trees guarded the less dense way into the woods. They made very little noise.

His mind raced.

Who would invade their privacy? Hadn't he been careful to select a secluded, magical spot to share secrets?

The mission had its own urgency, but no purpose beyond a reconnoiter - see who was there, be undetected, and leave. They would simply find a better spot for themselves later.

He took Barbara's hand and slipped into the opening.

What happened next on the day Emmett had spoken of only one time and to his two trusted friends, Cord and Robert Hughes, and later, he had made a call to Raymond Kingsley. That conversation happened on their last night at Longstreet before graduation in 1964.

The friends knew and sensed Emmett had undergone a change, but no one could have guessed at what had happened.

Emmett and Barbara Lynne had quietly stepped into the woods to follow the thread of music. The path was dense, but not impossible. Crouching in undergrowth, Emmett forged slowly ahead, his eyes keenly on the perceived direction of the music. Barbara followed him.

A large, triple-trunked, tulip popular obscured his vision, but the sounds were distinct. Soft talk and moaning.

Stretching to peek through the split in the trees, thus edging ever so close, he stared through the opening.

On a blanket lay Colonel Rodman with Gloria Evans straddling him. Both were naked. She strained with her head thrust back. He cupped her breasts in his hands, and leaned upward to kiss them. They moaned in lovemaking. Her hips rhythmically rocked in unison with his; her breathing made an audible puffing. Light beads of perspiration stood on her forehead and her eyes were half closed.

Emmett felt a flash of fear and his legs sag. He also knew Barbara saw everything. He gasped for air. It was so gross he momentarily froze.

Rodman turned his head and opened his eyes and looked straight at Emmett.

He and Barbara fled at such a rapid pace, Emmett did not recognize the terror, just the jagged sense of recognition on Rodman's face and his fear, like a laser.

Their eyes had met. The two of them scrambled into the car, snatching up their own blanket, and slammed the door on it, leaving part of it trailing along the ground, gathering mud and nettles as he powered into reverse. They sped back to town, saying little - absorbed in their own thoughts. He dropped her at her dorm. She took the Tartan blanket.

"I'll call you," he said. She had not answered him. He went straight to his room and locked the door.

His mind raced with awful, lurid possibilities. He had called up images of betrayal, and scenes of personal desperation. He might be thrown out of school. In his heart he knew that he would hear from Colonel Rodman. So often he had imaged himself before his inquisitor, a dirty peasant before a master. The scene made a clear picture in his mind.

Sarah saw Emmett's demeanor change completely as he reached the high-point of the story. The affect on him was dramatic.

"It scared me so bad," he said, "I concealed my own terror. I put it somewhere. Imagination seized me completely. I saw the specter of Rodman raise his whip and snap it. I was his covert villain in the night, who stole his privacy. All I heard was the grunting and moaning of lovemaking in the woods. I was a mess.

"At midnight I remember that I took a shower, and tried again to sleep, but my mind shifted to Barbara Lynne. *What was she thinking? The sight of the two adults groping was sickeningly gross.* Barbara knew that. We hadn't talked about it at all.

"You know, Robert," Emmett said, "it was as if Barbara Lynne bolted from my car and out of my life.

"What no one knows is that later that night Rodman came to my room and tried to bribe me."

"I knew that guy was a son of a bitch," said Robert. "He tried to bribe you *how*?"

"Money, a lot of it. Sell my soul, I suppose. I was seventeen."

"Holy crap," said Sarah.

Robert looked at her. Not language she usually used. "He was a jerk!"

Sarah sat silently, intent on every word.

※

This was Emmett's next story.

※

A knock on the door made me bolt straight up, wet with sweat and tears. I felt sick. My clock read 0330.

The knock, authoritative, came three times. I knew who it was. I had to answer it.

I grabbed a robe and towel to dry myself and opened the door.

Colonel Rodman, fully dressed, polished and shined, waited in the hall.

In the Tomb of the Soul 57

"I hope you have not been asleep too long, Emmett. 'To sleep, perchance to dream...,'" he said sarcastically. "You and I need to have a little talk. May I come in?"

Rodman had never called me by my first name. He closed the door quietly. My heart was pounding. It was the only time that whole school year I wished I had a roommate.

Colonel Rodman seated himself and flipped on the study lamp, bent it down toward the desktop, and motioned me to sit in the other chair facing him. It was just like an interrogation room, I swear. There was no military formality to it at all.

Robert Hughes and Sarah listened.

"The bastard was gonna scare you into not saying anything," Robert observed. "I'm sort of remembering this. You told us some of the story the night before we left school, but I remember just snatches of it."

"Just wait," said Emmett. "It gets good."

"And, this really happened to you?" said Sarah, sitting forward on her seat. "This guy was a tyrant."

"'Tyrant' is mild," said Robert.

"It happened," said Emmett. "He was speaking to a civilian, not a cadet on that night. He was calm as could be."

"We must talk, Emmett," Rodman said, "about what you and your lady-friend saw this afternoon." Rodman chose his words carefully. "What you saw, what she saw, what I saw - all this could have grave consequences, you understand?"

"No shit!" exclaimed Robert Hughes. "That guy lived to menace us at Longstreet."

"Oh yeah, he did!" continued Emmett.

"'Men must confide in one another on occasion,' he said to me, in that pseudo-dramatic tone of his, 'especially when there is a delicate balance attending the mission.'" Emmett echoed Rodman's exact words. "'We have to trust one another. In battle you learn to trust your comrades, trust your brother. Did you know that I served in combat in Korea?'"

"You know," said Robert, "I think I had heard that. He served near Pusan."

"Well," Emmett said, "I didn't care if he served in China at the time. He just came on with this manly-trust thing. He told me, 'I learned about trust, manly trust - the trust of comrades-at-arms while in Korea. Do you think you and I are engaged in a situation where intimate trust is called for?'"

"I guess so," I replied.

"'I know you saw me with Mrs. Evans. I have loved her for three years. I believe she loves me. This has been a delicate situation. And it continues to be so. Wouldn't you agree we have a delicate situation here? You, me, and Mrs. Evans?'"

"He sounded like a guy in a movie, like Bogart or something as Captain Queg," said Robert. "God! You sound just like him."

"Lot of time to remember this," said Emmett.

"So, how did you respond to his 'delicate situation'?" Sarah asked.

"Yes, sir.' I said, 'I agreed. It is delicate.'"

"I was so scared I thought I'd piss in my PJs."

"'You are almost a man, Emmett,'" he said to me. "'You are beginning to understand the power involved in relationships between a man and woman. You know about intimacy, I'm sure. You have a lovely lady. Are you in love with her?'"

"'I don't know, sir, maybe.'"

"I'll tell you now," Emmett continued, "my mind was at zero. I even thought the guy might shoot me or something. But, he kept on talking."

"'I am in love with Mrs. Evans!'" he said.

Obviously, I was thinking. *You are screwing the hell out of her!*

Sarah laughed.

"'This matter between us,' Rodman continued, 'regarding what you saw, must remain top secret. Is that clear to you? Absolutely top secret.'"

"Then, he stopped. Sort of waited to see if the order settled into me. It was like he had planned this perfectly. He was fiercely good at what he was doing. I'm just there shaking in my bare feet."

"'I know we have had our differences in the past,'" he said.

"Rodman laid it on me. I can remember this like yesterday, every word he said."

"'I have challenged you regarding your behavior,' he said. 'I even suspected you of the incident with my car. That all has passed. You've distinguished yourself as an athlete and student, so I know that I can count on you to understand my meaning about *manly trust*. You're a man now. Do you follow me?'"

"How long did this go on?" Sarah asked.

"Seemed like and hour," Emmett said, "but about five minutes. You got to realize that Colonel Rodman was like a petty god among us all. We feared him."

"Sarah," said Robert, "he was a frigging Nazi!"

"You know what he did?" asked Emmett. "He reached into his jacket, pulled out an envelope. and shoved it at me. I remember thinking, 'Oh crap! He's going to shoot me.' I really thought that.

"He shoved this envelope at me and said, 'Open it, son.' His tone was almost affectionate. He was a great actor."

"Most tyrants are. What was it?" Sarah asked.

"It wasn't the keys to his Volkswagen, I can tell you," Emmett said. "It was money."

"'Lay it out. Count it!' Rodman said.

"I pulled out the money and laid fifteen one hundred dollar bills evenly on my desk."

"'That's yours in exchange for absolute silence, Mr. Peterson! It will buy that lady of yours something nice.

'Do we have an understanding here?'"

"It was a flat-out bribe, and I knew it. Here was a bribe from a man who scared me so bad I was almost sick. He was a guy I reviled because he kicked my friend out of school."

"You mean Raymond Kingsley?" asked Sarah.

"Yes, Raymond.

"I kind knew then that Rodman had ruined my relationship with Barbara Lynne, too. Here Rodman was," said Emmett, his voice tinged with regret and resentment, "buying my silence, so that he might continue seeing Gloria Evans and ruining a lot of my stuff and my relationship with my girlfriend, who I might have loved. The moment was completely obnoxious.

"Then, he laid one on me a second time.

"Rodman said, 'If you say nothing about this, when we reach the end of this little hunt, your graduation, there will another $1,500! You can walk away from this, as can I. . . . Agreed?'"

"I shoulda raised the ante on that bastard, but I didn't!"

Emmett pushed back in his chair, remembering how it was.

"That's how it was. You want to talk about compromises, moral choices. This was one," Emmett said. "Take the money and be rich, or not take it and be miserable or dead. Kicked out of school.

"I wanted to get up from the desk and walk away, the way he did to younger cadets he wanted to intimidate. The ultimate pay-back for this bastard, I thought. I had his number. He knew it, and money was his way of buying out of it so I caved, took the dough. He left."

"He really was a bastard," said Sarah.

"More like the devil," said Robert. "He literally was buying silence, and your soul. That's classic abuse."

Robert turned to Sarah. "You can't imagine how we hated this guy. I've said it twenty times tonight. Looking back on it, it was his ultimate power trip," said Robert.

Sarah, fully engaged, said, "He was also an abuser, masquerading in the Army uniform, which makes him a coward."

Emmett had never really considered the impact of Rodman, how it affected his values. He just knew, at the time, that he was scared to death.

"I actually believed that walking away meant risking my life, and certainly a chance to finish school. Rodman, probably, he would lose his job if I told someone, but he would know I told on him. He would come after me. That was a given. I just caved.

"It was my first real moral stalemate. *Save myself and keep the money. Not take it and maybe not graduate, and even die.* I didn't want to die, that's for sure. Sickening part was he had the upper hand because I was a kid.

"He was amazing, so poised, so cool? We call it brazen. Having an affair with his boss's wife, literally under his nose. Having me on the hook for $3000 and my silence. He was a real dirt bag."

"What did you do? Weren't you really pissed off?" asked Sarah.

"I was scared stiff. He paralyzed me. Barbara Lynn was mad at me. I was scared. I waited. I watched his eyes because I wanted to see him blink just once.

"He never did. He got me. I picked up the bills and the envelope and put them in my bathrobe pocket. He just walked out the door. Another conquest."

"So you got the other $1,500 after graduation?" asked Robert.

"I did. He mailed it to me at home with a note. He wrote, 'Trust is a good thing.'"

"How about bribery, intimidation, adultery, cheating! Not good things. He looked right past all that, didn't he?" exclaimed Sarah. "That's unbelievable. It's illegal to do what he did."

"Did you spend the money?" Sarah asked.

"Nope. It's at home."

They sat in silence in Robert and Sarah's living room.

Emmett had not told anyone about the money or the bribe. Now, he realized in a peculiar way that the episode with Colonel Rodman had taught him how to pick his way through some thorny moral issues. He had killed people in Vietnam because it was a war. In that one moment, when he had hand-to-hand combat, he had hesitated to stab his adversary. He didn't need to stab him. His strong blow to the face of guy had broken his neck.

The choice to walk away with the money was different, but it was a kind of salvation, secured in the heat of a moment when he was almost eighteen. Rodman had enabled Emmett to know how to react at a level not usual for many folks. Rodman had, in his perversion, even showed Emmett that human compromise is somehow justifiable even when it appears terrible, like war.

For the time being, Emmett felt comfortable. The money lay in the same envelope in a locker he had shipped home before he left for Vietnam. He had not looked at it in five years, never been tempted to deposit or spend the money. It was, to his mind, tainted.

"What happened to Barbara Lynne?" asked Sarah. "Did you tell her?"

"I didn't tell anyone. We talked a few times. She wanted to go with me to the school's authorities, either hers or mine. Longstreet seemed out of the question because Rodman was the authority. Maybe we could have told a teacher, like this guy, Major Burke, who we really liked.

"She disagreed?" asked Sarah.

"Maybe I saw her three times, and each time we disagreed. We argued. It just ended."

Robert looked at him. "God knows, you loved her back then. The son-of-a-bitch helped end a good relationship for you. Really pisses me off now."

Emmett looked at him. "Long time ago," Emmett said. "I've pushed it out of my mind. So far I'm good at that."

Sarah smiled at him. She really liked him.

He looked at his watch. "So, I've killed off two evenings telling the story of my life. Not really fair."

Sarah got up and hugged him, holding him for a minute, then looking affectionately into his tired eyes. "You are Robert's true friend, and I see why."

Emmett felt warm at her touch. It was time for him to go and begin again. He had the Gina-thing to deal with, and home. He'd get by, he thought. Robert was a good guy to come back to.

The next day he called his mother and that afternoon caught a bus home.

Four

I can't get no

Sa-tis-fac-tion,

Cause I've tried,

And I tried....

— M. Jagger & K. Richards

NATHAN KUBALLE, ALABAMA COUNTRY BOY, RAISED ON A cattle farm by his alcoholic father and doting mother, rarely went back after four years playing for The Bear. He bummed around south Alabama and the west coast of Florida.

At Cocoa Beach, he first saw Ronnie Bayer, the most beautiful young man he had ever seen, riding a short surfboard. He appeared to Nathan more athletic and sculpted than any ball player in the stable at Alabama. Nathan had slathered himself in suntan oil and sat on a beach towel and watched him. He had never felt quite as excited as he watched Bayer attack wave after wave until he finally stood up for a short ride and dived off just before being tossed.

Nathan watched for nearly an hour.

"You nearly made it up," he said exuberantly to Bayer, as he walked by. The man stopped and beamed.

"Yeah," he said. "You were watching. It ain't Hawaii."

"You surf in Hawaii?"

"It's where I live."

"Really! And you come to Cocoa Beach, Florida, to surf!" Nathan's teasing tone made Bayer smile.

"No, I'm training to fly. I'm in my eighth week of flight school driving F-105 Thunderchiefs."

"God," said Nathan, "that's cool. You made it this far."

"So far, so good. What about you? You're not sporting some honey are you?"

Nathan leaned back on his towel and continued to stare at Ronnie Bayer.

"Nope, just in town before reporting to Camp Jackson."

"Wow." Bayer's eyes locked on to Nathan. "You got the call from Uncle Sam, the man. Crazy times."

"Crazy like dead, but I don't think they can get me. I'm too quick."

Bayer was friendly, and sat down on his board with his knees pulled up. "I guess if you sit here long enough you'll score some honey. Right."

Nathan felt his throat constrict. He'd felt it before in conversations, but not with a man who looked like Ronnie Bayer.

"Look, I'm Nathan. Who are you?" He extended his hand.

"Ron Bayer. Glad to meet you, Nathan. You not taking a dip in Mother Ocean? It's a quiet day."

"Let's go," said Nathan. They ran into the surf.

Soon Nathan was trying the board and failing. Ron seemed to improve with every wave. After many tries, Bayer suggested they go have a beer.

"We can grab a beach shower and go to up to Bernard's. It's just about a block."

"Sure," said Nathan. "I know Bernard's. Let's go."

He had nothing whatever to do for four more days.

The two men spent the next four days together, and on the final night, they slept on the beach, throwing a large towel over the two of them.

Nathan knew it might have been the best night of his life. Bayer was gentle and sweet, a beautiful man in every way.

At seven the last evening, he bid Ronnie Bayer goodbye, and caught a flight from Melbourne to Atlanta. On the ride there, all he could think of was Ron Bayer, skimming on the waves of Cocoa Beach.

The flight and bus ride into town took five hours, plenty of time to think, and dream.

I'm riding the fence, he thought.

He felt a glow from the time with Ron, but he also knew that most guys would be trolling for women. He hadn't really been looking for a boyfriend, or a woman. He was just getting some sun before the onslaught of basic training. "A one-time-thing," he thought. "Just an adventure. I'll forget about it."

When he did sleep on the flight, he saw the waves rolling, green and foamy. Ron Bayer's wind blown hair licking his forehead in a pseudo part. Beside him, he felt his own somewhat clumsy self, straining to balance and falling over. Time after time, he woke himself as he fell into Ronnie's arms.

It was after all a one-time-thing.

After 16 months Nathan Kuballe was a 'greenie,' a 90 day wonder. 2nd Lieutenant Kuballe was assigned to an Army Intelligence unit and shipped out to Vietnam. His head full of numbers and procedural material, he had no time to think. Down time conversations usually involved questions about Alabama football. Did he know Namath? Did he love the Bear or hate him?

Nathan played flag football while he was in OCS, and excelled as a flanker. They called him 'Bama,' and Nathan let them. He was quick and had good hands, but he had never been comfortable at Alabama and couldn't explain why. His position coaches kept saying, "Kuballe, you got to put-out more. It ain't high school." After two years of trying to please, he just played and focused on graduation.

At Officer Candidate School he was a star, and he liked it. His training unit won the Colonel's Beer Bash, as best flag team on base. He had scored seventeen touchdowns for his battalion team, blowing by the opposition. He wasn't going to say he only played in eight games in four years for Alabama. He carried a degree in physical education.

After six months of Officers Candidate School, he earned his bar, and spent another five months training in the Intelligence Corp,

Now he carried orders for a unit forming out of Camp Holloway south of the Demilitarized Zone, called the DMZ. He later spent three months in Saigon, then was sent down to the 1st Logistical Command at Long Binh near the Delta.

Nathan sat in a ready room at Tan San Nhut, a long, sweltering hut with two struggling, cooling generators at either end. New arrivals and other enlisted waited for flights out or in. He spent hours alternately lying on a wood bench with his head on his luggage or flat on the floor. The concrete was warm, so he sat up for awhile until his backside ached. He pulled off his fatigue shirt and sat in a wet tee shirt. He estimated the temperature in the hut was eighty-five degrees.

A corporal, who snored, shared part of a bench. When the GI was not sleeping, he entertained. He was going home happy.

"I was at the Dogpatch, man, outside Da Nang," the GI said. "Choppered in and humped that shit for four weeks. Damn, I got picked for seven patrols in two weeks. Talk about some stinking crap. Sit all the damn time, slapping flies and mosquitoes. Toilet flies, I call em. Them suckers will drain your blood. Charlie rained mortars on our asses day and night. My platoon sergeant, who didn't mind seeing my ass out of there, would say, "Harrison, get off your lazy ass. We gonna send you to see the Buddha man.

"We'd hump out up and down those friggin' mountains. It wasn't no swamp in the valley, it was vines and shit and rock and snakes, damn rice paddies. Hand-to-hand crawling. What we doing in this shit, man? That's what I want to know? My prick got so wet with sweat and mud, I probably got water warts on it. They sprayed so much of that Agent Orange shit on us, we probably all will pee yellow needles."

Kuballe had no choice but to listen along with the dozen or so other guys. They all became familiar with Harrison's shrunken dick and miserable duty.

"Man, I got to hate this war, man. Working for Westmoreland, my ass! Sacrificing, I call it. Ain't no winning about it. Kill gooks, another hill, kill gooks, another firefight. No cause was ever completed out there. Find a pot to shit in and cot to sleep on, that was my cause.

"One time we went to his little ville and rounded up these gook girls. Good looking, some of them. These other dudes wanted to fuck all of them, but the old Sarge threatened their asses to get 'em to leave 'em alone. Guy had no sense of poontang. You fight a war and you get no poontang. That ain't no way. Man's got to have a sense of poontang."

"So you left 'em alone?" someone said.

Nathan felt annoyed by the constant rapping.

"Well," Harrison swelled, not wanting to let a good story die to leave himself un-manned, "There was this one little girl with a tight ass. Looked like a brown olive to me. Real fine. She hung around us all day, and that night I give her some chocolate and a cigarette. She screwed me that night. First pussy I had since Saigon. She don't say nothing, just pulled her dress up and let me do it real slow. I'm telling you, man, that was some good pussy. Sort of like hometown pussy, if I closed my eyes."

Emboldened by the laughter, Harrison turned to Nathan.

"Now the Lieutenant, here," he said, eyes twinkling, "I bet all of you, he gets plenty of Asian pussy. Right, Lieutenant?"

With hard eyes, Nathan captured him with his stare, and waited before answering.

"What's your unit, mister?" Nathan said bluntly.

He did not consider reasons why he was blunt, or why the vulgar story angered him. It just did.

The GI's eyes watered measurably. "Sir, I didn't mean nothing. Just a story. I didn't hurt her or nothing!"

"I didn't ask you if you hurt her. I asked you the name of your unit?"

"B Company. 4th Battalion, 170 Tactical Group, sir. Am I in trouble, sir?"

Nathan rolled away and stared at the wall. The Corporal pulled himself into a knot and remained sullen and silent.

Nathan wanted to tell him he was going to report him for abusing civilians, but he knew the promiscuity went on throughout the ranks. The pussy story and the question of his unit stopped Harrison from talking.

Nathan fleetingly wondered if he could have done such a thing himself. The thought made him sick. He didn't mention any of his own stuff, or think about it. He had known plenty of it.

The sight of dead VC made him sick. He had seen plenty of them. Dead women were another matter. He looked upon them just long enough to count, or note the method of their dying, then turned away. Other guys ignored the dead VC men, but were fascinated by dead women. Some were smitten with sympathy and muttered, "Would you look at that bitch! She don't deserve being chewed up like that," he heard some say. More than likely, they'd poke the dead VC and say "motherfucker" under their breath, and mean it.

Nathan knew he was vulnerable on the issue of human nature in wartime. His nature was suspect, even to himself. He didn't understand how to react, or what to think. He had been there six months. Six more to go.

Once he reported a GI who had shot a dead VC sniper then ripped open the man's chest and put his hands into the dead man's entrails.

When Nathan reprimanded him, the soldier turned a dirty face toward him. "I'm just making it easier for the maggots to get to his fucking guts!"

Nathan thought about shooting the soldier on the spot. It revolted him.

Maybe Harrison of the 170th Tactical unit was right. The fucking war warped the mind, made people do things they never dreamed of until they got to the bush or the swamps, or humped the mountains, hacking away vines in heat so oppressive one panted rather than breathed.

It was making him mean, he thought. *His secret life was gnawing on him from the inside.*

Another Marine GI, leaning against the quonset hut wall, asked if anyone heard the story of the guy up at The Rockpile, who was shot in the bush near the CO. Everyone thought he'd wondered off to take a dump. When he was found, he had his pants off and was holding his penis.

"They shot his ass while he was jacking off."

"Reckon they missed his pecker. Shot him right in the head," the soldier said. "At least he was having sweet dreams when he went," another said.

"Some wet dream!" another said.

Everyone laughed.

Nathan listened. He couldn't get the picture out of his mind of a guy lying there with his pants down, shot through the head.

When his number was called, Nathan climbed aboard at chopper for Long Binh. It was mid-November 1969. Nathan knew that Long Binh was the jailhouse for the US Army, that a stockade riot had occurred earlier in the summer. Rumors flew how black inmates full of drugs and frustration lay siege for ten days to the stockade. It had the derisive name of "LBJ's Jail."

Nathan was going there to sort through some of the mess, knowing that it was tainted with racism, drug abuse, affected by the unrest at home, the King assassination, and "Black Power" movement rumors. It became an issue of overcrowding, boredom, abuse and neglect. He'd get to delve into the particulars. It wasn't a pleasant task. Rationalization was easy. He was not in the riot, neither was he directly in harm's way. So far in his tour, Nathan had never taken fire. At Long Binh, he'd read and write reports, maybe play some ball, and let the MPs, who controlled the place, the 720th, clean up the physical mess. His job was to manage the fall-out of what had occurred. The sad fact was no one at home knew about Long Binh riots. Maybe they didn't care.

That evening he was met by MSgt. Chris Aston, who became his driver, to take him to his billet. Five bodies in bags waited to be loaded and choppered out.

Two GIs struggled to lift the last body on a gurney to be transferred. The flap on the bodybag flopped open exposing a face. He was a blonde kid, about 18 or 19 years old. Nathan starred at it. This young man looked asleep, even peaceful. His mouth curved in a contented smile. His lips were pink, accented by his blonde fuzz of a mustache.

It was haunting in a strange, beautiful way, thought Nathan. As they lifted the body, he saw the single bullet hole, a clean, pure shot over the boy's left eye. As the body was moved, the kid's head flopped to the side, and his eyes opened, pale, ice blue, lifeless, vacuously starring at Nathan. He felt a brief chill, the indelible scarring in his mind that this boy's face presaged remained with him for a long time.

"First corpse, Lieutenant?" Aston asked.

"No," Kuballe said.

"You look a little green around the gills."

"No problem, Sergeant." Nathan snapped.

"Yes, sir," said Sgt. Aston. "We are loaded and ready to ride, sir. I'll be your driver for a long time, sir." Aston's smile was warm as he snapped off a salute Nathan returned it and climbed into the front seat. Aston pulled a cigar from his pocket and offered on to Nathan. It was a gesture that bespoke respect.

Nathan thanked him and took it. He didn't smoke, but he put it in mouth anyway.

Aston was a stocky man of about twenty-five with dark hair and kind brown eyes.

"It's nice duty, Lieutenant. We do a little of everything here from supply to replacement. Don't get hit much, but when we do, the mortars miss. We can usually clean out any nest or attempts to infiltrate quickly. Got a lot of arty on base, a unit of special forces, pretty good quarters, especially for officers - even got air- conditioning. Beer at night.

"Here, I got papers for you, and the Captain at HQ wants to see you."

He handed the papers over to Nathan and drove on.

It was good duty, and Nathan slipped into an easy rhythm. Aston took care of him. They developed a friendship and some familiarity. Nathan drank a lot of beer, ate charcoal steak, and believed if he stayed in camp, he might make it home by June. It was November.

Long Binh had all kinds of gear, even beach wear, reclining chairs, any item a soldier might need from ammo to armament, large and small trucks, jeeps, loading equipment, heavy equipment, tanks, helicopters - even a sun tanning deck. Once Nathan saw a row of 5HP Craftsmen lawn mowers and cases of Venetian blinds - he also noted a unit of Army nurses. The Officers Club was good, he thought, always festive, decorated for Christmas - a place to gather, sing, get drunk, and brag. At a beach party, Nathan drank too much and passed out doing the limbo under a stick - everyone got drunk.

He became friends with his company's executive officer, and another Sgt. from San Diego, Burt McCallister. McCallister had been a professional water skier before he was drafted. The Dong Nai river and several tributaries ran near Long Binh, and there were many boats docked at piers on the "Nai." The wide channel and swift-moving current looked inviting. One could see several hundred meters up and down the channel. McCallister wondered if he could requisition a boat, or bribe a crew with food and beer to take a group out on the river to water ski. That would be a trick, but a possibility.

Daily routines occupied Nathan: report writing from field logs, interrogation reports an supply lists. He took care of business, seeing that Sgt. Aston passed his work up the chain. His main focus was on interrogation reports, which occasionally required him to chopper to surrounding firebases for the interviews with personnel regarding operations when he wasn't occupied with the fall-out from the earlier riot. He disliked these trips off base and over to the stockade, especially if the area in the field had been hot, or if it still contained remnants of firefights. Often they did. The stockade was drab and full of sullen men behind tall strands of concertina wire. Towers every one hundred yards linked the fence and were manned by bare-chested men under small thatched roofed covers, who constantly cleaned their .50 calibre machine guns.

In the field the sight of rubble and ruin to burned out villages and litter bothered Nathan, but didn't seem to phase others. McCallister would drink his beer and call the firefights "dance parties." Each flight out to the "boonies" for Nathan was like visiting the belly of the beast. He never mentioned fear or revulsion, but his memory of the kid's face in the body bag on his first day, the dead cows, and chickens, the scurrying, naked children, the sullen old women squatting in the dust, who peered at him from under the awning of thatched roof hooch or a pointed hat, all bothered him and made him hurry through his work. Young Vietnamese men especially bothered him. Distrustful and haughty, they stared with glassy eyes at him, allowing their children to run naked among the rubble. He didn't like the stories of snipers hidden in the bush at the edge of villages, waiting for a chance to pick off a stray GI. He didn't like the busy, haughty manner of the Southeast Asian troops, especially the fellow officers, who were officious, and sometimes ignorant. Suspicion hung in the air like humidity.

Nathan never admitted his fear or revulsion. He kept close company with Sgt. Aston and McCallister. Neither of them engaged in rash talk of operations or maneuvering units. Nathan liked that. They talked about sports, fascinated that Kuballe actually caught passes thrown to him by Joe Namath. They went to movies, like *Alfie*.

The day came when McCallister announced he had found a way to water ski on the Dong Nai. "Others have done it. We can do it!" he exulted. "I'll give an exhibition. Burt-O-matic on the Dong Nai!"

"Get off it, man," someone said. "It ain't safe. How you think you pull that off?"

"Shit, it is too, safe!" argued McCallister, "Safe as heaven. I know a guy who rides one of them PBRs, Riverines."

A PBR, or Riverine, was an armored, low-water fast patrol boat, used for patrols, searches, operational insertions, and river traffic control. PBR 119 operated out of Long Binh. It often had mounted .50 cannons or machine guns.

"This Riverine dude might can get 'em to tow me for a price," McCallister said, "A Riverine rat boat will make more than 25 RPMs, perfect to ski behind. We all chip in and go! What'da ya say?"

McCallister made a huge deal out of it, getting guys to buy in with cash, beer, food, tapes of music, even a FM radio that would pick up Radio Vietnam. Hey, it's the Stones, man," he sang out. "Can't Get No Sat-is-fact-shun!" He created a hometown atmosphere, riverboat party. "A blast! Fucking Callaway Gardens," he preached to anyone who would listen.

Especially, he wanted Kuballe to go along. "You need the change, Lieutenant. I'll show you how it's done. Stud like you can become expert in ten minutes with me teaching you."

After badgering Kuballe for a day, Nathan agreed to go. McCallister had charm he liked. He sought out his Riverine friend, and the pilots bought-in on the trip for cash, beer and food - just to see McCallister "do this thing."

"You ain't skiing naked behind my boat, son," the boatswain said.

For the days leading up to the "Bash," McCallister told tales of his prowess on skis, jumping, crack-backs in the wake, whirlies, dropping a ski, going slalom, skiing backward, even trying it barefooted.

"Shit, you in the Nam, man," some said. "You gotta ski backward. Charlie might be watching. You got to watch all sides, or he might shoot your white ass!"

"Charlie ain't shooting," bragged McCallister, "He's gonna be so amazed he'll clap." His enthusiasm infected everyone who would sit and listen to him.

When water skis showed up lying on McCallister's bunk, the gang knew the Bash was on.

"If we had some catfish, we could charcoal 'em. It would be the Fry on the Nai!" someone suggested.

The day was closing in, and the weather turned blisteringly hot. Nathan accompanied McCallister to the dock, and they were off before 7AM, when the river steamed from the heat, and the sun glowed in the mist. It was strangely beautiful. The water was smooth and muddy brown. No one paid attention to the debris of limbs and leafy branches floating by.

The two boat handlers and the Crew Chief were in high spirits, and beer flowed within minutes of the departure. They would go down stream a mile and ski back to the pier. They bribed the Channel Officer with a case of beer.

McCallister, excited, posed on the rear deck, his feet in the skis, and he imitated his run as the boat plowed into the middle of the muddy river.

"Don't worry," he yelled. "I'll be dodging them limbs like the Lone Ranger."

No one heard him.

Several hundred yards from the pier, the boat slowed. McCallister hit the water and was up behind the boat surging along as the RPMs whined, using an orange rope with part of a softball bat for a ski rope handle.

Nathan watched him cut across the wake, venturing parallel to the boat's side, allowing the rope to go slack, then cracking back against the wake, creating torque and speed. Flying high, clearing five to six feet of air, then he slapped the water with his hand as he landed on the opposite side. The river debris was washed away by the wake of the Riverine.

The boat pilot cut the boat sharply, whipping McCallister into the wake. He lay flat against the water, the skis cutting deeply, kicking up a 'rooster tail.'

"He's just like goddamn Callaway Gardens," some one yelled over the whine of the engine.

Nathan was focused on the show. The other men debated their own prowess on water skis as McCallister, dropped to one ski, zigzagged back and forth, tucked the rope under one leg and cut out over the wake with no hands.

No one noticed the first shots, not even Nathan because of the engine's roar. The pilot was focused on guiding the boat away from the shoals and aiming it down the channel. To Nathan the shots were only ripples on the water from a wet ski rope. When the rope snapped, the boat left McCallister dying in the wake.

At that moment Nathan knew there was a problem. McCallister was over 100 meters behind them before the pilot noticed the rope slapping the water like a wild tongue.

Everyone discovered the shooting at the same moment, as the boat took hits down the side. Bullets bit into the deck and sent splinters ripping and exploding over those leeward of the gunnels. Nathan was bare-legged in a bathing suit. He saw one of the deck's shards pierce the leg of a guy nearby. Nathan hit the deck of the boat hard and slid into the side, trying to clutch something on the flat deck floor. Water and blood sloshed about. The engine whine was combined with the rattle of the .50 cal. machine gun mounted on the roof of the pilot's house. The gunner was working the shoreline mercilessly, as the return fire and smoke grew thick.

Nathan heard the screams of several fellows. He heard himself praying, "Oh, God! Oh, God!"

As the boat reached McCallister in the water, the firing from shore seemed to let up. One of the crewmen dove over the side. Nathan stayed low, pulling a towel over his body. The sweet smell of Cordite hung in the air.

It became eerily quiet as the scream of the engine subsided. The .50 cal. let loose a long volley.

McCallister clambered over the side, landing on Nathan. He muttered something about "Lipsky took lead." Lipsky was the crew man who dived over the side to help him.

The Crew Chief gunned the boat again, and it leaped forward and raced toward the pier about a mile back up river.

Nathan felt his hair dancing; he pulled the towel around his head and covered his ears.

They had not found Lipsky at first until he was pulled over the gunnel, chewed up by machine gun fire.

"Oh, shit. I'm hit, I'm hit," another kid was yelling. He was the one with the deck shard stuck in his leg.

The boat raced back up the channel. Medics were summoned to meet them.

Blood and water washed over the deck, along with spilled hot dogs and runny baked beans, where cans burst from the shell fire. Rolling around their feet were hundreds of shell casings from the .50 cal.

The wounded man kept moaning.

Nathan was shaking. He didn't remember leaving the boat, or the stream of cursing coming from the Crew Chief.

McCallister wasn't around.

Toward the evening, Nathan became ill. At dusk he was completely sick, nauseated, aching and weak in every limb. In a restless sleep, he dreamed of home, his mom standing in the kitchen, his dad seated over a crossword puzzle. Cicadas sang in the trees. He lay naked in the bunk sick, like falling forever through a crack in the barn loft, stumbling closer and closer to the sound of firing, and the constant crack and rattle of the machine gun.

He tossed on the bunk, then fled to the door of the bunker, and had dry heaves until his knees buckled.

Chris Aston found him crouched against the stockade door in a cold sweat; he helped him up.

"You must have drunk some river water, Lieutenant," he said.

Aston carried Kuballe, like he would a brother, to his own bunk and laid him down. Nathan was shaking with fever. Tenderly, he got a wet rag and wiped his forehead.

Vaguely, Nathan knew Aston was there beside him. He was in a cotton-filled, woozy dream. Through his fever, he saw Aston sitting, then squatting beside his bed, but he also saw hawks and doves fly up. A distant memory of a guy at Cocoa Beach flooded into his mind, and a lingering sense of fear and disappointment came over him.

Aston held Nathan's head over a steel pot, as Nathan tried to puke all the atrocities of war and memory.

In the same dream, he felt himself lifted by a blonde, American GI, a boy with soft pink lips, a quaint smile, who stroked his shoulder tenderly. In the dream the boy had a red hole in his cheek, so Nathan kissed the pink lips and felt warm.

Later, a medic wiped his forehead, took his pulse, and pushed on his stomach. Aston stood off to the side muttering.

"I think he gulped a bunch of river water," Aston said. "I tried to get him quiet."

Nathan just wanted to be held again, like home. His life was empty; he had a hole in his brain, and he was hot.

The medic left. The fever came back. Nathan felt hands on his upper body that bathed him, stroked him gently, always moving with pleasant gentleness.

When the fever broke, he awoke to the face of Chris Aston, who smiled at him and said, "Oh, Nathan, I...."

They were quiet. It was dark. Aston slipped his hand beneath the sheet covering Nathan.

Five

...like young heirs and alchemists misled
To waste their wealth and days.
For searching thus to be forever rich
They only find medicine for the itch.
— *William Cartwright*

In 1969 Nathan Kuballe flew home from Saigon. He went immediately to his family's farm in north Alabama, determined to focus on changing every aspect of his outlook. He shook off the war, his relationships, and his old ways. He wasn't going to wander around. He would do something he loved. He knew football and numbers. The games he played from college through his training, through his tour in SE Asia remained the things he loved most. Weights and running were in his blood. He would coach.

In the fall of 1970, Kuballe returned to the University of Alabama for a year, used the GI Bill to get a teaching certificate, and applied for jobs. Veterans weren't popular, so he didn't mention he served in Vietnam. Newspapers were not part of his routine. He did school, resumes, and physical workouts. He tried to date.

In appearance Kuballe wasn't bad. He had an athletic physique, blonde hair, and a tan. Women noticed, Evelyn Macklin in particular. She was a legal secretary, who went to the gym in Tuscaloosa, where Nathan worked out. They became friends, if not lovers.

In the spring of 1971, they were married and honeymooned in Georgia at Callaway Gardens and on to Florida. He forced himself to watch the ski show at Callaway and never mentioned the episode on the Dong Nai River with McCallister.

Evelyn was the most observant person he had ever known. She saw the nervous perspiration break out on him while they watched the water show.

Later, she asked him if he had enjoyed it.

"Sort of a dumb way to show-off," he remarked.

"What would you have liked? A nightclub?" remarked Evelyn. "Nathan, you are such a weirdo. We can go to a club. But, no strip joint, now."

He laughed.

They went to a nightclub. He even danced. The next day they drove to Orlando, through the orange groves to West Palm to catch the Yankees in spring training. Evelyn loved it. Mickey Mantle had retired in 1967, but she knew the Yankees because everyone did. Nathan was pleased.

There Mantle was in uniform as an observer, still looking tan.

When they got back to Tuscaloosa, Nathan received a job interview and offer at the Hilliard School for Boys in east Texas as an assistant football coach. Kuballe felt his life shifting and changing. He liked everything about the school, especially the pudgy coach, Hal Rivers. They took to each other immediately. He took the job to assist Coach Rivers, who was about 11 years older and overweight. Nathan thought of him as pudgy.

In the summer he and Evelyn moved to Texas. For the next several years he coached with Hal Rivers, and their football reputation grew as a powerful tandem. The team won significant football games in a private school league.

Evelyn easily got a job in a law office. Life seemed very good for Nathan, who was distracted by Hal Rivers' down-home, folksy manner. He adopted Nathan as a younger brother, or a son. His ease of manner absorbed Nathan completely. They spent extra time together, fished, and talked "foo'ball." Hal Rivers loved the fact his assistant coach had played ball at Alabama. It did not matter at all that Nathan was not a star. He was around The Bear, and that in itself was grounds for some worshipful talk.

Evelyn, at first, loved the country-day-school life, the parental involvement, but as the years flowed by, she began to feel Nathan slipping away from her. She couldn't explain it. When she questioned him, he excused himself to "go out to the school to meet Hal. Coaching duties," he would say.

"What's so special about school and Hal Rivers?" she would ask.

He would laugh at her, "It's a coaching thing. Lots of details to make a team click. Takes planning."

"Okay, as long as you aren't planning with a couple of bimbo women in the locker room."

"God, no, Evelyn! No girls allowed."

Off he'd go in the summer to camps with the boys, and on weekends in the off-season to watch film. It was, he said, a time-consuming life. She should understand that.

She saw less and less of him and did her job, did the housework, and talked with girl friends. She was independent enough, but she wanted Nathan, wanted to feel his closeness, his masculinity, feel his strong body next to her. Her needs, she thought, deserved to be met.

The Friday night out always included Nathan's friends, not her friends. Saturdays, he went to the school gym, either to work out, or do whatever football coaches liked to do.

Grass grew in the yard, paint peeled around the gutters of the house. Things, she felt, piled up at home. He was gone.

"Hal and I are going to the lake to fish tomorrow. I'll be in Sunday afternoon."

"Be careful. Don't drink too much. Hal likes his beer."

"Don't worry, Hal floats" He laughed.

"You know the grass out back and out-front is getting really long. Neighbors talk."

"I'll do it Sunday evening."

"And the porch screen is tearing off. Bugs are coming in. I'm going to have to move the zapper into the house."

"I'll get it," said Nathan, and hurried away.

He never gets around to anything, she thought. Certainly not to her.

It was the sex that began to concern her. In the first year or two of their marriage, each time she touched him, he seemed ready to consume her. He'd come home in the early evening. Before they could eat, he'd have her on the couch, the floor, and sometimes in their bed. On the weekends they'd lie together panting from their love making.

Gradually, the newness, the eagerness began to wane, not a lot, but some. Evelyn was an eager lover. She began to notice she was more the initiator than he. She'd give him long, sensuous massages. She'd nibble at his ears or piddle in his neck. He'd become aroused.

A time or two, however, he'd say, "Easy does it, woman, a man needs his rest." She would leave him alone. When he said, "Evelyn, I think we should stop. I'm really tired," she got annoyed.

The relationship took on a perfunctory air.

Their social life became Hilliard faculty gatherings: Dan Jeter, the Headmaster; his wife, Maggie, the perky social secretary for all things Jeter and Hilliard; old Sam Burke, the school's Master Teacher, who had come from a military school in Georgia; Harry Parsons and his fat wife, Britches, who seemed altogether out of the circle of educators, but very much loved by everyone and longtime friends of the Jeters'; of course. Hal and Edna Rivers were in the group, and various other coaches and teachers. After-football-game-parties were regular gatherings. The men gathered around beer coolers, and women chatted in the living rooms, gabbing about children, tennis matches, and food.

Evelyn was expected to work with wives of other coaches to see that the party table was bountiful at some one's house every Friday night from mid-August to early December for home games. Evelyn tried to be dutiful. Beer flowed, stories abounded, and people laughed. Nathan seemed comfortable, especially when the team won, especially when he and Hal were lauded for game plans. When they lost, she knew she could lose him for the week prior to the next game. When the season ended, the party spirit lessened, but at least once a month someone had everyone over. Texas was barbecue and tossed salad, with the beer and wine. It was hot outside. Pools were everywhere, even hot tubs. It seemed nice, but it was repetitive.

Saturdays were late-sleep-love-making mornings. These intimate times, too, seemed to change.

Evelyn Kuballe's breathing grew heavy. Nathan felt her tongue search his tongue as she lifted herself up on him, loving his strong muscled chest and tight stomach.

He held her loosely. "She can do the work," he thought to himself, as she eased down, and he entered her. He had made sure she had an abundant supply of birth control. "I got enough kids to worry about without one at home," he had said. It had hurt her feelings. He apologized.

Now, her efforts were eager, his involvement was slow. He even thought of other things, not that she didn't please him; she was good, and she was vigorous, all right.

Her hips began to pump. He kissed her shoulder. She didn't feel it. She was focused on her own pleasure, and she moaned. Today, she would fulfill herself. If she could make him have an orgasm, it would thrill her. It wasn't her goal; she was there for herself and made the most of it.

Nathan had gone over in his mind the ordeals of sex with Evelyn. He tasted her mouth upon his, listened to her breathing, her moaning with pleasure. He tried to stay erect for as long as he could, but sometimes he'd wilt, and she'd complain.

"You maybe need to see a doctor, Nathan," she said more than once. "You seem to have difficulty, don't you?"

"Not really," he said. The remark hurt him, however.

"Maybe we could go together. Sharing with a professional could enhance our marriage and our sexual relationship."

"Is something wrong with it?" he snapped.

His tone might have threatened her.

"I'm okay. When I have things on my mind, I might be slow. That's it. It's got nothing to do with you, with us. I'm just a slow lover sometimes. I can compensate in other ways." He smiled.

He didn't like remembering his past, but he knew, deep inside, his lovemaking with Evelyn wasn't as good or as fulfilling as at other times long ago, in other places, with other partners.

When she lay her head on his chest, resting from her vigor, he smiled a long, deep smile. She saw it. It made her happy.

He quickly grew soft.

When she tried to mount him again, he pushed her off. "That's enough," he said. "I got to get to work at the school." He felt her grow rigid. He knew he should hold her, so he did. The acrid taste of her kisses was in his mouth. Perspiration glistened on his chest and stomach as she rolled off of him.

It was over. She was breathing heavily and pulled her knees to her chest.

"Maybe you are getting better," she said, then paused. "Nathan, do you love me?"

He didn't answer right away. He had been thinking about something Hal Rivers had said about hiring a third coach.

"Of course," he answered. "Why would you ask me that?"

She hesitated. "You just seem detached sometimes, sort of distant. So, you think things are working okay for you?"

It annoyed him when she got like this. She persisted: "I mean is our marriage working for you? Are you really, really sure?"

He pushed himself up on the side of the bed and reached for his underwear, knowing he should reach for her. He sighed, long and heavily. "Honestly, Evelyn, do we have to discuss it again? Of course, I love you. There's nothing wrong with our marriage." He slid the sheets over his legs and stood up. There's nothing wrong with me or with you. You like it, don't you?"

"Oh, I love it," she said, "but do you love it? Do I make you happy?"

"Yeah," he responded, but he knew his voice was flat.

She acted as though she didn't hear it. She tried to remember how it had felt, to summon up an image of Nathan as an enthusiastic lover, so eager for her he could barely contain himself. This wasn't the case. She stretched upon the bed as he went into the shower.

She heard the water splash against the walls. He had left the door slightly open. Maybe a secret invitation.

Should I go into the shower with him? Warm water, suds - I could soap him up. He'd find himself in there. I believe he would.

She slipped out of bed and stole into the bathroom, shedding her gown. He had left the end of the shower curtain inside the tub slightly open. She stepped over the edge and came up behind him.

"What is this?" he exclaimed. She wound her arms around him, pinning his arms and the ability to use his wash cloth. Soap slipped from his hand. She pressed her breasts against his back.

"Get that soap, I'm giving you a foamy. If it were whipped cream, I'd lick it off of every inch of you."

"Sure," he said. "You better get a towel and dry off. I have to get to the school and look at some blocking assignments we want to put in this spring."

His tone dashed her enthusiasm.

"Damn it, Nathan," she snapped at him. The shower burst up her as he stooped to retrieve the soap from the floor.

"Damn it!" she said again.

Soaking, she stepped out of the shower, and didn't stop for a towel, but flung herself into the bedroom, slinging water everywhere. She jerked the towel robe from the closet and wrapped herself in it.

Nathan finished, dried himself and came out. He had seen her like this before. What was he to do?

She walked out of the bedroom and slammed the door. He really didn't care.

She didn't understand much football, how much work it took, or appreciate how much he enjoyed the talk and management of the team. It was the work with Hal Rivers. He loved that. *She doesn't get it.*

He whipped the towel over his back.

Down stairs in the kitchen, he found Evelyn slumped at the table with cup of coffee before her. Her hair was wringing wet, and it dripped onto the kitchen table.

The coffee pot bubbled.

"You are a mess. Did you make enough coffee for me?" he asked.

She didn't answer. The chasm widened as he poured himself a cup. He opened the refrigerator door.

"Hey, we got no cream."

"Use creamer," she answered.

"What's wrong, Evelyn? You have a headache?"

"No, I don't have a headache."

"Well, you are holding your head like you have one."

She emitted a long sigh. She was weeping.

"Are you okay?" he said quietly.

"Not really." Her voice was cold.

"What is it?"

"I don't know. If I knew, I'd do something about it."

"You feel sick," he said.

"I feel…like a fool, actually." Her eyes filled; her voice broke.

"That's not good. You're no fool. Why do you feel like one?" His voice had an edge, which he didn't intend, but could not help. He felt imminently superior to her.

"You make me feel like such a fool!" she blurted.

"Me? What have I done to make you feel like that?" He had been leaning on the counter beside the sink. Now, he stood his ground and looked squarely at her.

"You don't have an idea, do you? Not a clue in the world. It is all about the god-damned football team."

"I just made love to you, and you act like this? I might be the fool."

"That's it, you don't know. We make love, and you don't know."

"Know what? What is it? I know we make love. How does that make you feel foolish?" He stepped toward the table to sit. If they were going to fight, he'd win. He didn't have to stand.

"Look," she began to sob. "I was there. I was the one who wanted...you... wanted...." Her voice trailed away. "I so much want you, and you just tossed me out."

"I don't disagree with your wanting me. You made it obvious. It's the way you are. I just don't understand why you are so upset. I really don't. I'd like to, but I gotta get going. It is Saturday. We wake up, we make love. It is what a lot of couples do. And, that makes you feel like a fool and it's my fault? Geez!"

Evelyn was in a silk gown. The purple of her robe reminded him of grape juice. She was a tall woman, with dark hair, and athletic legs, full figured. Her interest in his sports' mind had brought them together. She reminded everyone that she had conquered the Alabama 'jock.' She did it so often that it embarrassed him.

"I wish you'd stop reminding people that I played ball for Bear Bryant. It sounds like bragging," he would say later. "Not that big of a deal. I rode the bench." She'd call him 'lamb.' She'd poke him and tease him. He would laugh.

Now, she was looking at him with tears rolling down her face, pain in her swollen eyes.

"I love you so much...," she murmured. "I try to give you pleasure, hoping you'll like it, but you don't ever...." Her voice trailed off.

"I don't *what?*" Nathan felt himself growing hot. She really hadn't said anything that should make him angry, but he was growing angry. "I don't *what?*" he asked a second time.

She didn't answer.

"What *is it* I don't do?" He pulled back the chair and sat down. "Tell me? Maybe I'll do better."

"You *don't respond to me!* To my needs. You don't respond."

"Honestly, Evelyn, what are you talking about. *I don't respond to your needs.* That is such crap! I try. Look around, it is your house, your neighborhood, your kitchen, all your stuff. *I don't respond to you.* Damn, that's a good one."

"See, you're mad when I bring it up," she said. Her face was red with frustration and pain. "You don't know how your actions affect others. It's not right, especially, when we make love. Please, can't we see someone? Can't we?"

He was hot now, on the verge of serious anger. She had pricked something deep inside.

"Look," he said, "we don't need a doctor. I got stuff on my mind. You got to understand the kind of work I do. It takes time to be successful. It's what I am. Sometimes it stresses me and Hal out. Jesus Christ, I don't need a doctor for that. I don't need you to point it out."

She sat in her chair, more in control now. "I'm not pushing. I'm scared for us. It is affecting us." Her voice began to break. "I try and try to...." She sat unable to speak.

He sat barely able to look at her red, tear stained face. He studied the floor. Light streamed in the window, making bright, dappled swirls on the linoleum. He got up and poured another cup of coffee.

"I know you try, Evelyn." His words came out softly, and even, but his tone was flat.

"You don't *know*," she shot back.

"Okay, I don't know. But, I don't know what it is that I don't know!"

She didn't answer.

He leaned against the sink and peered out the kitchen window into the light, so bright he couldn't see into his own backyard.

He waited for her reply. When she wanted to be upset, he could wait. He never left her in this state, so he watched the breeze move the leaves.

"You just make me feel…" she sobbed, "like such a fool…like a…."

He slowly turned. He could see teardrops, limp pools on the table top. Her nose was runny. She rubbed her face. He tore off a piece of a paper towel and laid it beside her.

"You aren't a fool," he said as gently as he could muster. "None of this makes any sense to me at all."

"No, you wouldn't understand. That's the problem," she blurted. "You don't try to understand anything. My feelings! You don't understand them. God damn it, Nathan!" She stood up. "You make me feel like a whore! A slut. Here I crawl all over you. For *what?* Slam, bam, thank you ma'am! You lie there like I don't exist. You give me a small sense of caring. You either roll over, or walk away."

Nathan stood there. Every defense mechanism he possessed was triggered. *She didn't understand him at all, not even close.* A thousand times he had told her he loved her. A thousand times he'd let her have her pleasure. A thousand times he had lain there while she nibbled his neck, or blown in his ears.

She looked at him with disdainful eyes.

"You treat me just like a whore! I'll bet at those clinics you and Hal go to, you fuck five or six sluts. You might even do it to spite me. *You are useless, Nathan! Useless!*"

Rage shook him. He stepped toward her, threatening.

She dared him with her eyes flashing.

He thought he might hit her.

Instead, he slammed the coffee cup into the sink, shattering it to a hundred pieces. The loop of the handle dangled in his hand. He let it slide off and clatter on the tile floor.

"I don't have to listen to this!" He stormed out the room.

"Impotent bastard!" she muttered, and buried her face in her hands.

Upstairs, he tore off his sweat pants, kicking them into a corner, yanked a pair of jeans from the bureau, scattering socks and underwear, slipped on tennis shoes, grabbed his wallet and his car keys, and dashed down the steps, two at a time.

Only a few minutes passed, before he was in his car roaring down the driveway.

In the cottonwood trees the *damn* grackles were squawking. Giving no real thought to where he would go, he slammed his Camaro into second gear, and roared toward the school, trying to steady his breathing.

Get Hal Rivers, run a few miles, make myself sweat. Get the bitch out of my mind. She had no right to say that stuff. No right at all!

Hal hated weights, hated running, but he'd indulge Nathan Kuballe. It was their ritual, their special time. He thought of Hal sitting on the weight bench, his stomach hanging under a navy blue tee shirt. He never touched a weight.

He was there to spot Kuballe and give encouragement.

"You animal," he'd say. "You fucking tiger. If you were younger, you'd be my linebacker, and we'd win state."

Hal seemed to love him unconditionally. Nathan was warmed by Hal's adoration, and teased him often. It was the stuff of their relationship.

"Rivers, I'm in your line now. I'm carrying your football team. I got to stay in shape to pick up the pieces when your back aches, and your old knees creak. You piss all the time, Coach, so I got to be there for you.

"Get on the floor. I'll give you a massage. You're my fat rabbit." Hal seemed to love the banter.

Nathan sat on the man's flabby butt and worked his shoulders, leaning into the massage. "You got more hair on your back than Jane Russell had on her best hair day," he'd exclaim.

It gave him pleasure to feel the old man's flabby muscles. He sat and worked them in long strokes, pushing his fingers deep, making the Coach grunt and groan. Sometimes these massages would last half an hour or more, until Hal would be limp, and even nod off to sleep letting loose bubbly farts, and breathing heavily.

Nathan would cover him with a towel like a sleeping child and leave him. He'd go up to the gymnasium and shoot baskets until Hal showed up.

Hal would say, "I guess I fell asleep."

"You think so?" Kuballe would say and grin.

Hal would grab a basketball an hit set shots time after time. They'd watch film of a game.

"Why can't a tight end set the edge," one would say. "Shit, got to deal with that this summer!"

They'd laugh, then go for coffee at Wares Cafe, discussing their boys, drawing up plays, and chatting with folks from town who saw them there.

"Been watching film," Hal Rivers would say; "Preparing for fall ball."

Kuballe would nod and be the assistant coach.

Hal would tease, "I got to do a lot of work to get the Alabama squirt to understand my system like me to get them boys ready."

Everyone knew Kuballe played at Alabama. Not many brought it up. It was Texas and sacrilegious to talk about Bama football. Nevertheless, Kuballe loved it.

Hal made the days grand, and on this one, when Evelyn had been so cruel, he delivered.

Nathan told him that Evelyn was never satisfied with anything.

"I don't help around the house, repair the screen doors, mow the damn grass. Hell, the woman thinks I'm handy-dandy. I tell her I'm a football coach, not a damn hired man."

"She'll get over it," said Hal in his most sanctimonious tone. "Women have to be in charge, or think they are. Jus' buy her some flowers. She'll come around. Women is always big on flowers."

Kuballe knew that was not the way with Evelyn. He knew the truth. Down deep he knew the truth. Maybe she was on to his ambivalence. Still, her words were like hot irons laid to his heart.

If she really knew him, she would know how close she was to the secret places in his heart, to the private tomb in his soul.

"Know what you can do?" said Hal. "Take her to that steak place out by the Park. Feed her some nice red beef. Good blooded girl like Evelyn would like that. Little red wine. Things'll heal real quick. Especially if you just spring it on her. Just spring it on her tonight, knock her off her feet. You win the war."

Life to Hal was easy. Flowers, steak and red wine. Or a good linebacker or two, a quick running back, maybe a tight end, or a large nose-tackle, those things made Hal happy.

He wore no masks, asked for no favors, only a back rub on Saturday and good company. He liked to be quiet at times. Almost reverently quiet.

"What you thinking, Hal?" Kuballe would ask.

"I ain't thinking nothing. I'm listening."

"To what?"

"To my own soul spinning inside. Like to do that. Feel my blood running, my gut working. Just listening to the sun shining. Know what I like, Kuballe, besides massage?"

"No, what? Laying farts."

"I like the shouting of the game, the pads slapping, the zip of the ball, and the smell of all that grass rising up into the wind. That's what I like! So I'm listening for passing of time till we can do it again and make some scratch with the team."

"You're a poet, Hal. Know that? A football kind of poet."

"Naw!" said Hal. "I'm sort of content. Got a good school, good coaching staff, some players. I got you as a friend, stud from Alabama - and I ain't going to give away no secrets about the pine bench Bear Byrant made special for you."

Hal made Nathan Kuballe laugh and feel better. Hal grinned. "I give you my offense any day, any day!"

There would be silence, and he'd would mutter, "Just get her some flowers and take her out for steak. She will forget it all."

Nathan was just the opposite from Hal. His mind was cluttered, especially when personal relationships were on the surface, like now. All he saw in his mind was her nudity, her straining effort, her tits bouncing above him.

God, if there were flatter places, plains of simplicity, softness of grassy fields, and cool meadows. Maybe cows standing silent, munching. Maybe a kid with ball trying to make it spiral when he kicked it, make it hiss with a spin. He liked the shouts, too, just like Hal Rivers. He liked the pop, sting and pain of the hard hit, man on man, slick bodies clashing. He liked that. He even liked Hal's farts in the weight room.

Nathan liked the time of completion, of being utterly spent from competition, aching in a good way, smelling personal energy given up. The wetness of the jersey, the tight game pants. It was an aching pleasure.

It wasn't like sex with Evelyn, her panting, her moaning. That completion was to him empty, unfulfilling.

The time with Hal working out was different and stimulating. It was the pushing and pulling of massage. The straining of moving the barbell, of repetitions, not the second go at another orgasm with Evelyn, but the grunt of Hal Rivers, contented like a cow with a cud.

Hal was a large, lovable child, for whom he cared deeply.

After a long morning with Hal Rivers doing the old routines, Nathan felt better. Maybe he'd follow Hal's advice. He'd show her he wasn't a useless 'bastard.'

In the Tomb of the Soul

Six

I have a handkerchief bundle of memories....
— *Carl Sandburg*

Samuel Ellis Burke spent many good years at Longstreet Military while his wife, Loreen, was alive. He lost her to cancer five years after he began his career at Longstreet. Even the slog through Germany at the end of WWII wasn't as difficult as nursing Loreen through a year of misery, fighting the beast.

Sam had entered World War II at 19, a recruit from Boston. He had been raised by his Aunt and Uncle, both rigid Catholic, blue-collar folks, who took their brother's boy into their home when Sam was 14 because his father had been killed at sea, and his mother had died from grief. He attended a convent school, was shaped by the rigid rules imposed by the nuns, and he learned to love books and study. He went off to war carrying his rosary, a pocket Bible, and a head full of Latin, history, and poetry. His finest moment in the war was taking Holy Communion at Notre Dame the day after the Allies liberated Paris from the Nazis. He came home in 1946 and entered Boston College, majoring in English, and went on to Yale to read history and study Latin. Teaching was in his blood, as was the Latin Mass. No one was more grieved than Sam Burke when the Latin Mass was replaced by English.

"The church went from high and beautiful formality, to homespun and pedestrian," he would say. He went to mass at six AM every day no matter where he was. When a Latin Mass was available, he went there.

When his students at Longstreet would ask about his wartime experience, he would answer, "Ah, Mr. Peterson, World War II, the great camping trip. Hiking and camping." That was the extent of it.

After Loreen's death, he lived alone among his books and his music, burying himself in the life of the school, the classwork, and sports. He was a jazz expert, spinning LPs endlessly, and having in his school office an extensive collection of books on jazz history, all the old, great players. He loved Glenn Miller, Benny Goodman, Lionel Hampton, and Harry James. When his students would mention rock and roll, he would not turn up his nose. He'd say, "Music was meant to played on wind instruments. Guitars are nice, but instrumentality is where the mind loves to go." Then, he would ask some obscure question of the students regarding musicians like, Bill Bixby or Martha Tilton. They would look at him with blank faces and think he was out-of-date or peculiar. He would tease young faculty by saying, "Sir, I'm old enough to remember Doris Day before she became a virgin!" Colleagues who knew of the actress would roar. Some wondered who Doris Day was. He would nod.

What arrested his students was his tendency to speak Latin he never translated. He would leave them baffled. This habit also intrigued his colleagues, whom he rarely addressed by their first names. It was always Mr. ... or Mrs....

He could frame an argument succinctly. He held opinions strongly stated.

"The boy is an unmade bed. Let's not ruffle his sheets more than he already has," or, "Please, Mr. Peterson, your unfettered use of the superlative in your own expression of accomplishment diminishes the achievement. Humility is oftentimes good as a pie slowly eaten;" or, "I take umbrage with that remark, burnt umbrage!"

Suffice it to say, Samuel Burke became an iconic teacher at the military school. Three yearbooks were dedicated to him by senior classes. He attended all the games, especially the football games. He was famous at those games for his piercing shout, that rang out in the stadium, "Let 'em play, ref!" which he would vent more than once at nearly every home game when a close penalty was flagged.

"Major" Burke was especially fond of alumni. Each Christmas he would write long letters, reviewing everything from school food to new additions to the campus, the buildings, even to the landscaping. The letters came to be legendary and highly prized by those fortunate enough to receive one each year. They were not thrown away, but stuffed in file boxes and kept, to be pulled out and compared over the years.

He opened one of his letters with memories that begin with the individual and soared to grand philosophy, and ended with an announcement:

As I was leaving church after Mass the Sunday before Thanksgiving, I was hailed - Isn't that what happens to a chief? - and turned to see if I could make out who it was. He introduced himself as Emmett Peterson, whom I remembered as my student in American history, a football extraordinaire. He had returned from Vietnam, looked hearty enough, and said he had just returned from visiting an old mutual friend. We had about ten minutes of reminiscence, and, yes, I remembered his best buddies, Raymond Kingsley of water tower painting fame, and Robert Hughes, himself a teacher in Atlanta.

The meeting set me on a chain of thinking that, for me, everything at Longstreet has passed from future to present to past, and this year has seemed to stress former times, the good old days, the years of yore, and those dear ones I've lost. I have re-acquainted myself with graduates from years gone by...And I wondered if... 'Now sleeps the pride of former days,/ And glory's thrill is o'er,/ And hearts that once beat high for praise/ Now feel that pulse no more." It's a lamentation in the Moore poem.

The Longstreet days are coming to a close for me. I must seek some new ground, but I won't seek it without looking back at the joys and sorrows I've know. I'm like the statue of Longstreet. Not staring at the Texaco Station down the hill, which is now a Seven Eleven Convenience Store, but to the west.

I'll be leaving Longstreet for a small school in the Hill Country of east Texas and Latin masses.

Merry Christmas. Christmas should not have us by the throat, as P.G. Wodehouse has observed; it should have us by the heart, and soul.

A joy-filled Christmas and a Happy New Year to you all."

Mr. Burke left Longstreet for The Hilliard School in east Texas. He took with him a file box of names of former students, an old Remington typewriter, and his penchant for letter writing. He understood the sacrifices, the wisdom, the hard time-consuming work it took to put a school together, especially a new one. He knew that traditions were not in place, or rituals or habits. They had to be taught and re-taught until they became part of the fabric. The new headmaster seemed dedicated to building, or weaving that fabric. People shape a school. Mr. Dan Jeter, the Headmaster, seemed to know that.

It became clear to Sam Burke that he could help shape the school in wisdom and honor, help instill a sense of purpose, and of pursuit with excellence. Jeter had gathered a faculty of strength and vision. He wanted some venerable teachers with credentials of experience and knowledge to help add to the culture of The Hilliard School. He spent a day and a half with Samuel Burke, re-reading his vitae, and talking school business. A collective understanding and respect quickly grew, as Dan Jeter saw in Sam Burke a Master Teacher and colleague who could enrich the school.

Burke possessed a sharp intellectual insight imbued with quick wit, and disarming opinions. His vocabulary was large.

As one letter in the file remarked: "Samuel Burke has eyes everywhere on and in our school. With wit and humor he can disarm, alarm, and charm students and adults alike. He once told me that I had 'a propensity for peeling bananas with a broad sword that is going to cause us someday to do the split! Some of us are too old for that!'"

On another occasion, he had made a correction in the behavior of a particularly loose-mouthed cadet. "Sir," he said, 'you should take this advice and inculcate it in your affective domain.'"

The cadet had looked at him perplexed, and had said, "Yes, sir."

Jeter loved Burke's ability to criticize and humor colleagues and students. Burke told Jeter in the interview that he made it a point to re-read *The Great Gatsby* every year. "I find it to be a good way to clear my head and shed some of the cheapness of the world we live in today, where sheer vulgarity seems to be winning out. It's a book of taste and charm and wonder and wit, full of grace and dignity. It ought to be required reading for any new teacher at this school or any other."

Sam Burke had buried his beloved Loreen at the edge of the Longstreet campus and moved to The Hilliard School in east Texas. He took a large house in a green neighborhood in Lofton, Texas, and walked the three blocks to the school's campus. Quickly, he resumed the same patterns he had followed at Longstreet, without the title of "Major Burke." He was simply 'Mr. Burke,' or 'Mr. Sam,' to his colleagues.

Immediately, he pushed for quality, collectively earned and disseminated, not with accolades, but with Latin and wise-cracks. A good job often earned a question: "You know what was good about that?" or "You know what was wrong with that?" His teaching life was about students' efforts, their failures, their oversights, their shortcomings, and their successes, tempered by cajoling and teasing. "Your spelling, sir, can give ulcers. Of course, I don't get ulcers, mister, I give 'em. I'm a carrier of 'em!"

Mr. Sam became the Master Teacher, an example that Dan Jeter needed. They became comfortable, collegial friends. When storm clouds gathered over The Hilliard School, Jeter was glad Sam Burke was there for support and wisdom.

SEVEN

...the slings and arrows of outrageous fortune...
— Shakespeare (Hamlet)

THE HILLIARD SCHOOL, SET IN A PINE FOREST IN LOFTON, Texas, was an east Texas gem. As a day school, it attracted students from Shreveport to Longview.

On the day Coach Hal Rivers died, Dan Jeter, the Headmaster, stretched his legs under his desk, shoved his reading glasses back on his forehead and massaged his eyes. It was 4:10. He had to get away from his desk. Staring out the huge window that opened onto a shaded courtyard, he watched boys straggling from the gym, dragging their book-bags, and punching each other. Jeter had been Headmaster at The Hilliard School for twelve years, and he liked his job. The school was strong and stable.

He buzzed his secretary. "Miss Lillian, I'm going for a swim. Hold my calls, please, and could you get Maggie on the phone."

Unfolding his 6'8" frame, he stretched again and shoved the budget papers from himself. *Fundraising is a pain in my aspirations!* he thought, smiling at his own joke. His phone rang.

"Dan, it's me," sang his wife.

"Maggie! Great! I'll be at the gym for a while, swimming, then I'll come back and finish some phone calls. I'll be home about 6:30 or 7. Middle school baseball's today. I need to go by the game. Okay?"

"I guess so," she replied, "but I thought we were going to the Reader's Club tonight. I may go by myself."

"Ah, I'd forgotten."

"I know," she said.

He heard her disappointment.

"Can you beg off for me? It's Willa Cather, isn't it? Do me a favor and tell

Emily that I'll be at the next one. Promise."

"You owe me, Dan Jeter. You know how much you owe me?"

"I'll pay you when I get home, count on it." He smiled to himself.

The line clicked, which made him look at the receiver.

"Oh well," he thought. "I got too much going. Willa Cather! God-almighty."

Straightening papers on his desk and thinking of the cold plunge into the pool that would invigorate him, he went out across the yard and up the hill toward the gym.

A dozen middle-school boys in dirty brown shorts scrambled after a plastic football. The mob moved in a cluster with shouts and grappling; outstretched arms shoved and reached for each ball. One always timed his jump too soon and fell among the rangy knees of the others, tumbling the group into rubbery piles. Every year the school gardeners planted new grass in the yard, seeding it thoroughly along the plots by the sidewalks. Every year it was worn from boys' games.

Jeter paused to watch the melee.

"Mr. J! Mr. J!" called a plump kid. The boy skipped on one foot and sailed a miniature football over the heads of the others. Dan back-pedaled a few steps and caught the ball with one hand. Skipping twice, he threw it above the trees. A couple of the boys paused to watch. The opposite gang of kids, like frantic ants, went scrambling and shouting after it as it fell.

Dan laughed and turned toward the gymnasium. Inside, the swimming pool steamed behind a wall of glass. He pushed open the door to the Faculty Locker Room and felt a rush of humid air.

Harry Parsons, Superintendent of the Locker-Room, sat on a metal folding chair. Fresh towels, cologne and deodorants lay on towel laid out on a card table beside him. Harry was one of the school's characters, a veteran who had been wounded on Iwo Jima. He had a wooden leg. Dan Jeter had known him for years. The old man had won a Bronze Star and a medical pension after the Second World War. As the campus character, Harry was happy to give four or five hours each afternoon to staff the athletic facilities, wash game uniforms, and towels. He liked to entertain. Each afternoon Harry turned things over to the coaches and held court, sprawling on a metal chair, telling them stories and teasing. He was allowed one cigar each day, a campus privilege just for him. A novel lay upside down on a towel. A clean ashtray held a smoldering Hav-a-Tampa cigar. He liked to roll the cigar between his fingers and say, "I never had it so mild." He made coaches laugh.

"Afternoon, Capt'n," Harry said. Harry gave everyone a rank or title.

"What you reading, Harry?" Jeter asked, noticing the book resting on his knee.

"Trash novel! Butts and boobs! Called *Southern Whiskers*. Dirty book - very dirty book! Got it from Nathan Kuballe. Readin' a little steam - see if things has been moved around. Folks still do it like they always did. This *is* a dirty book. Surprised Kuballe'd give it to me, but then nothing the man does surprises me. It ought to be banned. I had to take a look at it to just tell him how bad it really is. He don't read what he gives away."

"Now, what's on your mind, Captain? Taking a swim?" Harry asked.

"A swim is right. I'm gonna test my armor."

"Well, don't let it rust." said Harry. "Water temperature has dropped two degrees since this morning. Maybe the heating system is about to go again. Better wear long johns if you're going in that pool." Harry shifted and his girth filled the folds in his khaki pants. "It would take a whole heap of folks to drag me into any kind of water sixty-eight degrees. Cold water gives a man the short arm!"

"Cold water, Mr. Harry, circulates the blood. Makes you move. You ought to unstrap that old leg and come in with me. We could use it for a float." Dan loved to trade barbs with Harry Parsons. To Harry, everything was on a physical level. If it did not provide creature comfort, it wasn't worth the time.

"Capt'n, if I was to get in that water, I'd sink to the bottom. You'd have to call a crane."

"You'd float like a cork, Harry!" Dan laughed.

"I crawled in a lot in nasty water. I don't never sit in the water. It makes me pee."

"Then I don't want you in my pool!" Dan grinned and slipped his trunks over his long legs.

"No, sir, I'll stay right here, smoke my stogy, and think about you wallowing up and down. I'll be just fine. I'll get the heater people out here in the morning."

"You do that, Harry. And look, if I'm not back in here in thirty minutes, get the pole and fish me off the bottom."

Dan often swam alone, plunging into the emerald pool and hearing the water slap off the tiles. The clean dive, bubbles surging by his streamlined body, long strokes, easy rhythm of his kicking – breathing on both sides, ducking, somersault, pushing off, back and forth. His body conformed to the rhythm.

Ten minutes slipped by. As he turned, he heard Harry shout, "Capt'n, you got a phone call from Miss Lillian. She says it can't wait."

"Shit!" Jeter exclaimed, and came dripping from the pool. Harry flung him a towel and limped away. Dripping, Dan picked up the telephone.

"You should get out to the track, Dan; there has been an accident with Coach Rivers. Serious. He's been struck with a discus." Miss Lillian was all business.

Minutes later, watching dust from the approaching ambulance, Dan Jeter stood on the field near where his football coach lay, surrounded by a group of frantic boys and a few adults.

The accident had happened quickly. Coach Rivers had walked out of the woods into the path of a discus that struck him like an iron pancake.

Jeter's tennis shoes stuck to his feet. The laces had whipped his ankles as he had run, vaulting an iron rail around the sidewalk, and dashing out to the middle of the field.

A crowd of athletes surrounded the fallen coach, as Nathan Kuballe worked over his friend, giving him mouth-to-mouth respiration. Rivers lay limp and pale, bleeding from both ears. He had a quarter-sized dent above his left eye. The purple wound on his forehead was barely bleeding.

The ambulance siren howled against the mounting wind and turned out onto the field.

"Back up. Let 'em through!" someone shouted.

Nathan Kuballe pounded on the man's chest. The medics went to work.

"I got him breathing again. He just walked out and it hit him. Keep him breathing."

"We got this, Coach," a medic said.

Kuballe entered the ambulance with his friend, while the other coaches herded the boys toward the gym. The air grew crisp. Banks of gray, turnip-like clouds gathered, and the sun cast jagged shadows through the bleachers. Wind swirled dust at the empty pines and licked at Jeter's damp legs as the ambulance, lights and sirens going, raced off the field and headed toward the hospital.

Alan McConnell's final throw of the afternoon had struck Coach Rivers' head. In Dan's mind, he saw the wobbling discus, dropping from the clouds, and heard the thud; he imagined Hal Rivers' knees buckling, and blood spilling from his ears. He heard the boys shriek. "It hit Coach! It hit Coach!"

Letting Nathan Kuballe handle the issues at the hospital, Dan remained at school, deciding to go later. Nathan and Rivers were like brothers.

Inside the gym, Dan telephoned his secretary, then Alan's parents. He had comforted the boy as they waited.

Sam Burke sat beside Alan. He watched him and dabbed his own face with a towel. Alan was pale and sickly looking.

He kept saying, "I just threw it, and there he was. Honest. He was just there, and it hit him."

Alan's parents arrived, held an agitated conversation with Dan, and left with their son. Alan had a towel draped over his head, and his mother's crooked arm wrapped around him. Police would, no doubt, want to talk to him later.

In the athletic conference room, Jeter, having twisted his long frame into a desk chair, sat in mournful contemplation with Sam Burke. Mr. Sam loved sports and went to many practices, helping where he could.

Outside the wind clattered in the tree branches.

"I told Alan that sometimes bad things happen, that we'd get through this. Doesn't look good," Sam murmured.

"Yeah," sighed Dan.

"Why was Hal in the woods? I can't figure that. Of all people. No one ever goes in there. I'll have to ask him," said Sam.

Dan remained silent.

"He probably had to take a leak and didn't want to walk up the steps. That's Rivers." Sam said, staring at the worn carpet. "It really doesn't figure."

Over in the locker-room, meanwhile, Harry Parsons sat reading. He knew that something was wrong when Miss Lillian called him to get the Capt'n from the pool. Then, he heard sirens. Long ago Harry had learned that if trouble came, he could wait on it. So, he continued to read.

Harry knew all about The Hilliard School, all the boys, faculty, and Headmaster. He had known Dan Jeter since his youth when his own father knew the Jeter family. Mr. Jeter, Sr. had been a newspaper publisher.

Sirens got no business on a school ground. Some kid done broke something.

He thought the book was okay. Lots of sex. He would wait until somebody came to tell him what was going on with the sirens.

In the silence, his mind wandered, and the dripping showers reminded him of old times, Guadalcanal, when he was only nineteen.

Came there with the last Marine units after things was secure; took two weeks mopping up. God-almighty, it rained, he thought. Under a poncho at night, he had listened to dripping sounds just like the showers. He saw the dancing light of fireflies and remembered loneliness of night duty.

The siren in the distance whined again like a mosquito, then disappeared.

Earlier in the afternoon, Coach Kuballe had given Harry nine sour towels.

The son of a bitch is too lazy to drop the damn towels into the hamper after he has used them. Just crammed them into his locker and let 'em stink! he thought.

Harry considered Kuballe and Rivers with a mixture of contempt and humor.

That pair will sit for hours talking sports, laughing, and making up wild-assed plays. Crap no kids could run. Rivers wants Kuballe to install a kick-back play.

Harry thought it was ridiculous. "Probably got a rule against it," he said.

Part of my genius, Coach Rivers had said. *When the other team kicks off to us, we send our guys down, see. Not setting up return blocking. We'll have the kid catch it on purpose and punt it back down field. Our guys would be waiting. It'd be a free ball. We'd recover on their five or six. Not have to worry about no run-back.*

Nathan Kuballe had stared at him, eyes twinkling. *You're are a genius, Hal. It's against the rules, but it is ingenious. Ball's dead when we catch it.*

I never read a thing about it being against the rules to punt it immediately, Rivers had insisted. *And, it don't matter a damn bit, Coach. We should try her. All they do is call a delay penalty.*

What if they give 'em the ball where our guy got tackled bringing it back?

Then, it is your fault for letting me put it in the offense! Kuballe said triumphantly.

The Bear never ran no kick-back plays as I recall.

Rivers had laughed at his own joke.

Hey, Kuballe? Hal had asked one time as they were changing in the locker room. *When you an that pretty wife gonna give me a running back? Give her something to do while we are here winning football games.*

We aren't trying to have babies just yet, Kuballe answered. *And how do you know we will get a running back anyway? Might be a girl, a cheerleader. How'd that be, Coach. Your assistant from Alabama has a little blonde girl cheerleader! All full of pigtails,* Kuballe replied.

Aw, come on, Coach, big stud like you can ought to control that sort of thing. You gotta get after it!

The banter and mock arguments had lasted for days.

Hot-damn! Harry thought, Kuballe will harass him. Call him a lard ass. Them two lingers like bad farts.

Harry, never considering the injury was a faculty member, smiled at the comparison, took a draw on the stogy, and returned to his novel, *Southern Whiskers*, and read how Cal led Loraine into the barn where the stallion waited.

The wind outside grew fierce.

Eighteen hours later Hal Rivers was pronounced dead. The school went into mourning for its football coach.

Mr. Sam Burke arrived very early for Coach Rivers' Memorial Service. He sat in the school chapel, thinking about Rivers and Kuballe. Hal's death had numbed the school. Kuballe was especially shattered.

Schools are not places for the dead. Quite the opposite, they are living entities. Nothing is more lively than a school campus. The buildings sleep like people do, and awaken at the first screech of tires in the parking lot, or the clatter of metal cans emptied by the morning crew. Classrooms and hallways contain the ultimate human struggle, the quest for knowledge, joy, understanding, as well as the means to peace and contentment.

Burke sat in the quiet, remembering the win over Pinewood School two years earlier, a glorious victory known as the "The Dub/Armstrong Win."

That win had to be Hal's finest hour. Coach and Nathan had celebrated it ever since. They sat in the teacher's lounge drinking coffee, rehashing every moment, or watching the film on Saturday mornings for a year.

The papers had been full of the exploits of Randy Gibson, the Pinewood Hawk, who had gained 2,200 yards the season before, and 175 against the Hilliard Eagles! This season was different. Hilliard had led the division and would meet Pinewood for the East Texas Private School Championship, a chance to move on to the Southwestern Prep Title against Houston Prep. Their concern was how to stop Pinewood's Gibson. Kuballe convinced Coach Rivers that if Pinewood won the toss, Andy Armstrong, Hilliard's best hitter, would "tune" Gibson as he bucked the line.

"If Andy can stick him, put his helmet under his chin, we can send the message."

When the game began, all went as planned. Gibson came through the middle, the Pinewood tackle missed his block, and Armstrong stood Gibson up, driving him into the ground. The Hilliard team rejoiced, because they had rehearsed that moment like a scene from *Macbeth*. The "Armstrong hit and Dub's kick" within 10 seconds of the kickoff had set the tone. Victory of 10-7 was sweet.

Hal had folded his hands on his stomach, closed his eyes, and the two relived the game time after time.

Burke smiled inside as he remembered, while the sun worked its silent way over the chapel altar and down the aisle. The room filled, and the service began.

Schools do not need funerals. They should paint glorious history of the boys who attend there, who go on to great achievements, not have to memorialize beloved faculty. Hal Rivers had lost a son in Vietnam almost five years to the day that he himself was killed in this freak accident. Kuballe seems to have been that son who passed away. At least Hal enjoyed several years of time with Nathan. Requiescat in pace.

Mr. Sam listened to the Headmaster's eulogy.

"Perhaps, the flaw of mankind," Jeter said, "is that we do not let the difficulty in our lives penetrate our hearts. Hal Rivers was such a good man, and good father. He sent a son away to war and found some peace coaching and teaching here at The Hilliard School. Through his work, we were made sharper, a bit faster, and we reached farther, then one fine day the silver cord snapped.

"From the words of *Ecclesiastes*: 'Remember him before the silver cord is snapped and the golden bowl is broken, before the pitcher is shattered at the spring and the wheel broken at the well, before the dust returns to the earth as it began and the spirit returns to God who gave it. Remember him, fear God, and obey his commands; there is no more to man that this. For God brings everything we do to judgment, and every secret, whether good or bad.'

"Harold Osborne Rivers, born June 1, 1927; died March 3, 1976; teacher, coach, husband, father, dear friend."

Dan Jeter paused, looked over the assembly of faculty and students. He folded his notebook and sat down. Reverend McLain gave a closing prayer.

Sam watched Maggie Jeter lay her hand on Dan's knee when he slipped into his seat beside her. Sam would go to the McConnell home. He saw the McConnell family sitting off to the side. Alan sat beside his father, who kept his arm around the boy who had tossed the fatal discus. His mother wept quietly.

When the service ended, Sam watched the McConnell's approach Hal Rivers' widow. Each embraced her. Alan seemed to hold her longer trying hard to tell her through his touch that he was the innocent victim in this tragedy. Alan's face was pale.

Mr. Sam needed to go to them and then drop by to see Nathan and Evelyn. Kuballe was shattered, and Evelyn clung to his arm like she would a life raft being pulled by a strong current.

Mildred Rivers, understandably devastated, held no animosity toward Alan McConnell and held onto Nathan Kuballe, who sat with her and Evelyn during the service.

There they were, each weeping openly, the three people Hal Rivers cared for most outside his family: his wife, Lillian; Alan McConnell, his player; and his dearest friend, Coach Nathan Kuballe.

The reason for the folly of Rivers' stroll that afternoon remained hidden and unspoken in the wind that blew the trees at the graveside.

"Leave the axe of memory dull on that score," Burke thought. He quoted Tennyson to himself:

> *Dear as remembered kisses after death...*
> *Deep as first love, and wild with all regret,*
> *O Death in Life, the days that are no more.*
> *– A. Lord Tennyson*

After the service at the graveside, a few members of the faculty spoke to Dan. Nathan Kuballe with Evelyn lingered, as the cemetery people began their grim work over the open grave. Sam Burke had slipped away.

Dan and Maggie moved to Nathan and Evelyn. Maggie hugged him. "I loved Hal, you know, more than a brother," said Nathan.

"I know you did. And he loved you too," said Maggie.

"You did all you could, Coach," said Dan. "We have to move on, for the school's sake, the sake of the boys, for the sake of Coach Rivers, and especially for Alan."

"I know. I went by the McConnell's house last night. I thought the roof might crumble on me, but I went. It may have done him some good. I don't know about me."

"Sure. Sure It'll take time, Nathan." Dan looked into his hollow eyes and felt the pressure of his hand.

That evening at home Dan Jeter and Maggie ate a late dinner. She opened a bottle of Chardonnay they had gotten for Christmas. They rarely drank, but after this day, wine seemed right.

"Long week," she said, settling on the sofa, patting the cushion for him.

He sighed, feeling emotionally drained. Extending his legs over the marble-topped coffee table, he moved under her waiting arm. On this night, his wife looked particularly attractive. They sipped wine together.

"You did a lovely job today," she said. "Where did you find those lines so quickly?" She was looking down at him; his eyes were closed.

"I got a Bible Concordance. *Ecclesiastes*. Hal Rivers made the sort of death that bothers me the most. No explanation for it. Accidental. Senseless. My Aunt Maude once told me when life got complicated, a person should read *Ecclesiastes*.

"It's the most mortal book in the Old Testament," he said. "That's what I did. I will never understand why Hal was in those woods, or walked out when he did."

There was silence - only the ticking of the antique clock.

"All is emptiness," Dan murmured. "The Lord doesn't need to explain to any of us why the Coach was in the woods or came out when he did. That struck me as I was reading and thinking about the memorial. There's some great stuff in that book, particularly Chapter Seven:

> *I am resolved to be wise, but wisdom is beyond my grasp -*
> *whatever has happened lies beyond our grasp, deep down,*
> *deeper than man can fathom.*

Dan uncrossed his legs and shuffled them. His words trailed off. She stroked his hair and gazed at him.

When he had finished his wine, he put the glass at the far end of the sofa. He rolled up to her shoulder and softly kissed her neck, nibbling the lobe of her ear with his tongue.

"You're tired, aren't you?" she whispered.

"Not tired so much as in need of a little comfort." He felt her turn to him. "Can I be the one?" she whispered.

His tongue in her mouth was his answer. He could hear the change in her breathing. Their kisses clicked softly. The night lay undisturbed save for the quickening of their breathing and the ticking clock. He slipped his hand beneath her sweater, found the snap of her bra, undid it. Feeling her nipple grow firm, he caressed her breast with his fingers. Her leg pressed against him, and she slid it over his, kissing him deeply. He felt her turn against his thigh, the gentle movement in her hips, a growing pain at his knees as they pressed into the marble's edge.

"We should go to bed," he whispered, pulling himself upright.

"I think so," she said, slipping quickly away.

He watched her instinctively fix her blouse as she headed down the hallway. Picking up the glasses, he returned them to the kitchen sink, checked the front door, and clicked off the living room light. In the dim light of the bedroom, the covers were laid back, and she was waiting.

Experienced in their pleasure, he allowed her to shift beneath him, as he moved upon her, then they rolled together. She was on top of him, finding her own rhythm, an old ritual, warm and alive.

Eight

For all the history of grief, an empty doorway, and a maple leaf.
— A. MacLeish

Three weeks after the memorial for Coach Hal Rivers, Dan Jeter strolled the half-block across campus to his office. The morning was all cottonwood. The trees shed their white velvet in the Texas breeze, settling on the lawn, corresponding exactly to his mood. The sad days had passed to a degree, replaced by early spring with jonquils in bloom. Several lingering evenings with Maggie over good dinners and wine had restored his confidence, his sense that the school could survive the tragedy.

Hell, he felt a sense of consummation, a clearer vision, the certainty of being loved, and some sense of contentment. So he marveled at the beauty of the campus, dappled in the fresh sunshine and felt eager to begin anew. Much had to be done to conclude the school year. The paramount issues were the restoration of the boys' sense of life's tough turns, his faculty's morale, his football program, a new coach.

Should it be Kuballe, or should he consider someone else?

It was a tough call.

Having arrived at seven AM, he unlocked his office and turned on the coffee pot. Ms. Lillian always had coffee ready to percolate. He treasured the early morning time when there was no traffic to his door or phone calls to take.

The room was sun-drenched. He had a habit of running his hand down the coarse hair on the back of the stuffed coyote perched on a black pedestal beside the window. Its paw was lifted, and its nose dipped slightly as if it were scenting the wind.

This unusual gift had been from his Executive Committee on the occasion of his seventh year at Hilliard School, that had been five years ago, an inside joke about his sniffing out monetary needs that vexed their planning schedule and challenged them to seek ways to fund new programs at the independent school. They had called him "the School's Monetary Predator."

"A god-damned coyote who scarfed up every extra bit of treasury the school's Annual Fund collected," someone had joked. They gave him this trophy, a coyote killed off a west Texas ranch, embalmed and restored by a renowned taxidermist.

"At least this poor animal had not been hung on some fence," Maggie had said. She called it 'grotesque,' but Dan could hardly not display it.

"The son-of-a-bitch deserves some dignity in this life, though it be *Anno Domini*."

Dan had laughed. In a prominent place, it sat. On a few occasions he had used it to defuse tension. That had worked. *A good, working coyote is always a stuffed one*, he thought, chuckling.

Dan had not been ten minutes reviewing a backlog of paperwork, re-reading the memo from ten days earlier about the request of transfer of library funds to the school's weight room project. It riled him every time he looked at it.

"A damn *coup-de-grâce* in the making" he muttered. *Priming for a frontal assault on a board member was better handled in the freshness of the morning anyway, the old, moneybags-son-of-a-bitch.*

A tap on his door interrupted his ruminations.

Mr. Sam stood waiting.

"You're up early, Mr. Burke. I thought I was the only one who haunted the hallowed halls before a decent hour," said Jeter, ushering him into the room.

Mr. Sam flung his shoulder bag on the sofa, and paused only a second before Dan gestured him to the further end of the couch. Sam Burke wore his corduroy jacket with the soft leather sleeves as standard attire.

Once he had smoked an old pipe, but the school had insisted he stop. The lobby against tobacco products always hit a strong note with Dan Jeter. For years Sam had carried his pipe in his jacket, but a recent bout with angina had curbed the smoking habit. Image had been only a pretense anyway since he had shed his khaki Longstreet military uniform for the tweed of a new private day-school.

Mr. Sam was very trim and rosy-cheeked with flecks of gray brushing his large ears and swooping into a gentle flip over his neck. He looked every bit of sixty, but reflected, as well, a soft gentility, and wise demeanor, belying his thirty five years in the independent school business.

"I wanted to catch you before the day grew long, and we got side-tracked into other routines. Early morning suited my notion best to talk about Hal's passing. Been nearly a month now." Sam began, mincing no words. "I also know enough about these difficult moments in the business of school operation to offer an opinion. Recognizing how this tragic loss has caused us all some concern and anxiety about the future. It isn't easy, replacing a football coach in March. No simple matter, but in this circumstance, a greater challenge.

"While I had a thought, I just came by. You'll be hunting for a replacement for Hal River's, tough as that is. Hal can never be *replaced*, of course."

Dan nodded. He was always challenged by Sam's directness, and his articulate manner. He respected and, even coveted, his wisdom. Sam Burke was the only man he knew who spoke in paragraphs.

"It's my judgment that the school, for a lot of reasons, doesn't need to put a current faculty member in charge of the football team this fall. That's a tough call, but, experience tells me new faces and new ideas carry far better after a sudden loss than familiar ones, particularly when familiarity governed much of Coach River's way of doing things."

Dan Jeter loved how Sam could cut right to the point to reflect a depth of understanding perceptively and mildly critical, at the same time.

"Death never comes conveniently. Does it, Dan?"

"No question," said Dan. *Sometimes timing impedes progress, he thought. Burke's an old hand, a pro, never political. He takes the high road first.*

The old bastard has not wrung his hands. Appropriate grieving, then on with his work, the school, the programs, conveyed without the hassles, only sensitivity.

Of course, Dan had thought about the ordeal of hiring a coach; he had his contacts, some opinions about the position of the program in the school, its focus.

Kuballe covets the job. He has been Hal's assistant for six year.. Always there are parents to think of, dads, who have vicarious lives to lead on Friday nights through their sons, or through their own arm-chair quarterbacking. 'If my kid don't play, it's the coach's blind-fault!' That was high school and that was sports.

Jeter had often thought a football season's success projected the direction for the rest of a school year. Everyone's tone was more upbeat when the team won. Once after a situation with some parents about playing time on the basketball team, Dan had blurted out to Maggie he thought every school would be better if the kids were locked in the gym for ninety minutes and told to play their game.

"The rest of us would stay out! It's a god-damned mess, this sports' craze," he had said to her, and spilled his coffee.

That had happened after the Hilliard team had lost a play-off game to St. Paul's Christian, a team that was to have been a doormat.

Maggie had laughed at him, gotten a rag, and made him wipe up the spill.

"So, what's on your mind, Mr. Sam?"

Dan's legs went up on the marble top coffee table in front of his conference sofa.

Burke settled back and wondered to himself if the school would ever hire a headmaster who did not drink coffee? He had not touched the stuff since his Army days, but he did now, a pleasant indulgence. He put his penetrating eyes on Dan Jeter.

"I happened to get a call a couple of nights ago from an old student of mine from Longstreet days, a young football flash named Emmett Peterson. Every once in a while a student sticks with you, This Peterson boy is one. He took my

American history class as a freshman, very unusual, and he became engrossed in the subject. We talked a lot. He was a helluva linebacker as freshman and went on to be a real defensive star at Longstreet Military. Went to play in college.

"I left after his last year in '64 and came here, but Emmett always remembered my classes and sent me clippings and postcards. He even phoned me once or twice over the years asking about his college major, or just to catch up.

"There was an ordeal involving a mess at Longstreet with an administrator that Emmett was on the tail-end of. A matter of being in a place at the wrong time, I suppose. That situation and how it was handled made it easier for me to leave and come here. Emmett graduated on to new things.

"This was a great young man. Went on to college out west and played some ball, then served in Vietnam. I didn't heard from him for several years, but he contacted me after his return, and I helped him with finishing college. Then, the other night he called me again to catch up, pure coincidence. He had just gotten his Masters degree.

"I knew he had gone up to Springfield College in Massachusetts on the GI Bill after the service, finished up as an undergrad in history and took a Masters in physical education. He's teaching history and coaching JV football back in Atlanta at a big public high school. He had been at it for a while.

"What occasioned his call was pure reminiscence. He isn't fishing for a job. He had seen another old Longstreet boy, Robert Hughes, who I taught. They were close.

"Emmett wanted to know what I was doing, and if I remembered the name of a General, who fought in the battle of Shiloh, who was from central Georgia. I had no idea who he meant, but we had a great conversation. I had no notion Emmett would choose education as a profession.

"After that call, it occurred to me that a young fellow - about 28 or 29, unmarried, full of energy, who has played a lot of football, and has teaching experience, might be the ticket for us. This youngster is worth a look. He'd be unproven as a head coach, but if I know him, he'd do the job. He's been in some tight places and knows himself. I think he won a couple of medals in Vietnam for bravery. Never mentions it. I got his number if you want to call, also got his address."

He fished a card out of his jacket pocket and slipped it over the table to Dan Jeter. "I don't need to be involved any more than this recommendation. I do know a winner when I see one. This is a winner. A fine young man, and bright. Do what you need to do. And, I hope you don't think I am disrespecting the memory of Hal Rivers, or trying to slight Nathan Kuballe, by coming in here. We do have some big fish to fry before we can play in September. You know the kind of fish fry we'll have to put on, and, *sir*, it ain't going to be a banquet.

"Think about it. If it's not a match, no harm done. What I do know is that the life of any school is in its students, and their comings and their goings. Students don't really have historians to chart that, or their lives while they are with us, except through old goats like me. Alumni associations might think they do it, but they really don't. Yearbooks and such aren't enough. What you and I know, Mr. Dan, is that a school has a Life and Lives; they are organic. We must always keep that in mind every minute, even when we face a tragedy like this one.

"Great person, Emmett Peterson. He is alive and well."

Burke did not wait to read Dan's eyes, or even note his response. He had delivered his message, put the school first, and deferred to his boss.

"Thanks for the coffee, Dan."

He took up his bag and walked out of the room, leaving Dan Jeter sprawled on his sofa. The whole meeting took about ten minutes.

Dan didn't even thank him. He knew Sam had wanted Hal Rivers to live very much, but Dan also knew Sam was no sentimentalist, no softy in matters of education, or the school's position relative to its programs and students.

Funny, I thought Nathan would come by: he may, he may. That could be ticklish. Kuballe would be a possibility, but Sam may be right about going outside. Maybe Nathan is too close to the situation to be even-handed. He's an emotional guy.

Dan lingered with his feet up on the table, turning in his mind, remembering moments with Burke on the night of the accident. Sam had wondered why Hal had been in those pine woods and remarked that they would have to ask him when he got well. The comment had haunted the moment. Dan had thought of it more than once as he did now.

So... how to proceed? The question is of inside or outside help with football?

Football is important, but in the wrong hands, it could be a disaster in several directions. Wrong messages get sent, he thought. *Nathan Kuballe could be so overcome with grief his effectiveness here at Hilliard could be compromised.*

Dan Jeter recalled the episode at Farley Granger School where the team got tacit approval from an assistant coach to hurt a kid from another school. They created a 'tackle fund' to pay off the player who put the boy out of the game. They had done it, giving the player a serious leg injury. A lawsuit ripped the school like a lightning bolt, coaches, parents, players, and school officials. It had been a topic for three or four years at the Headmasters' meetings for independent schools. Farley Granger had lost enrollment and nearly collapsed.

If this Peterson kid was any good, he would have to teach, show through his discipline, and his leadership. I'd have to trust him implicitly. Coach boys and deal with a distraught Nathan Kuballe. A tall order.

Dan also wondered what some of his faculty perceived the program to be, how it tilted in their minds, too much emphasis, too little, its effect on other sports, on the arts, and on the general culture.

Hal Rivers was a good person, a fair coach. Hilliard wasn't feared as a powerhouse. Needing to win more had never been an option, never even discussed.

Among parents, a different story.

Rivers wasn't the sort to produce great players. He wasn't a salesman, wasn't flashy, Just a character in his own right.

Where does the damn program need to stand for more to be both affective and educationally sound? Got to be across the board winners from debaters to fullbacks to actors and musicians. We need a bass drummer who is a defensive end!

Maybe we take all this too seriously. Maybe we need a young fireball coach who plays by the rules . . . maybe I need an enema!

Dan rose from the sofa when he heard the outer office door open. It was Miss Lil. The day had officially begun.

Maybe Sam Burke is right. We need a kick in the butt here, a young son-of-a-gun to put us up a notch or two. Worth looking into.

An hour later, Dan scribbled a note to Miss Lil. "Let's contact Emmett Peterson at this address. Letter first, then phone follow-up from me." He handed her the note and the address card.

He flipped on his Dictaphone and began:

"Dear Mr. Peterson: In a recent conversation with your friend, Mr. Samuel Burke, I learned that you were coaching football and teaching history in Atlanta. He spoke very highly of you. I doubt, however, that Mr. Burke mentioned to you that we have an opening here at The Hilliard School. . . ."

The letter went into the mail that afternoon.

In ten days he had Emmett Peterson's resume. It told him a lot about the man: education (major in History and minor in Physical Education, then a new Masters Degree), divorced after serving in Vietnam (a Silver Star and Bronze Star for Gallantry), college credentials (excellent), his football experience (Best Defensive Player for four years in high school and two years in college, and named Little All-American his freshman year). His current employer extolled him, as Mr. Sam had said.

He called in Sam Burke for a second consultation and showed him Emmett's material.

"Tell me a bit more about Peterson," said Dan.

Mr. Sam just smiled.

"I knew him best as a scattered cadet at Longstreet. He was a leader from the time he stepped on the campus. He was not always an angel. In fact, he was bit of a heller, in that he tested the codes, like youngsters do, especially in a military school where restrictions are tight and standards are high.

Jeter smiled, "Military school is tough."

"It was tough.

"The football field was his main attraction, though he was a good student, and in the upper fourth of his class. I'd also say he cut quite a swath through the dorms among the younger cadets.'

"How do you mean?" Jeter was curious.

"I can't say for sure, but there was prank that was so clever and thorough no one was ever caught or even questioned. The work of an engineering genius. One night a small car was placed in the library, a feat so clever that it took four maintenance fellows and five hours of pulleys and tracks to get it out and down the steps of the building. Had a squealing pig in the cab, tied to the steering wheel.

"Cadets intensely disliked the high school Commandant, sort of like the Dean of Students. It was his car. I know they loved the torment they put him through. Kids' stuff.

"That's pretty good," laughed Jeter.

"Emmett wasn't implicated. No one was ever caught. I'd bet a month's salary he was behind ever bit of it. Organizing genius. The code of silence never wavered, never cracked. Drove this Colonel Rodman nuts for several weeks. He marched those boys, inspected them, and harangued them. Not a single crack in the Corp."

Dan sat staring out the window. "Is that all?" he asked. "Sounds like a wild stallion."

"There was an incident in the late spring before Peterson graduated that came to light the following school year right after he had finished and gone to college to play ball."

"And?"

"Word had it that Emmett was serious about a college girl, who was about a year or two older. I think her name was Barbara Lynne. Can't be sure.

"They went to a secluded spot at the lake near the city and parked their car to do what teenagers like to do. The story was they discovered the Commandant and the President of Longstreet's wife in full sexual splendor.

"The situation came up about a year after it happened. After Emmett graduated, Rodman confessed to the affair and was fired. The President filed for divorce. Pretty ugly. Rodman later told folks that Peterson and his girlfriend had seen them. It was also the year I resigned to come here."

"You said the girl's name was Barbara Lynne?" Dan asked.

"I think so. It's been a long time," said Mr. Sam. "What is relevant in all this is Peterson was a typical young man. He made himself into something after the war. He hasn't mentioned the war in the notes or conversations. Two medals reflect a lot. You can send for his service record, I suppose. We never discussed the demise of Colonel J.W. Rodman. I'd stake a lot on this young man being of quality."

Dan smiled. "Two things occur to me. I'm somewhat relieved that we must only deal with replacing a coach, and not a sexual escapade of one our faculty! Second, it is curious his girlfriend had the same name as Maggie's niece, who is from Macon. Just a coincidence. I'll let you know about Emmett's visit to campus. I want to meet him."

"That's good," said Mr. Burke. "Also, just for the record, Nathan Kuballe's heard some rumors you are looking outside the school for a replacement. He came to see me. I told him nothing about recommending Peterson, but I did say I supported your position if that were the case. I did my usual 'school first' speech. I could tell he was not happy, which is somewhat understandable. Maybe you should introduce those two if they are to work together. I didn't sense Kuballe's eagerness to leave. He's just full of grief. It's a tough situation."

Nine

...into the breach....

— *W. Shakespeare (Henry V)*

Several days later, Dan Jeter summoned Nathan Kuballe to his office for one of the more difficult conversations of his career as Headmaster at The Hilliard School.

When Nathan entered, Dan could still see his sleep-deprived eyes. When he mentioned Hal Rivers, he saw the water mount and the struggle Nathan had discussing his friend. They sat on the long sofa and faced each other.

"I appreciate how close you and Coach Rivers were," said Dan. "It's been almost forty days since the Memorial, and I've got to move the school along. I wanted to thank-you for running the spring football practice and holding everything together."

Nathan was quiet. "Thanks," he said.

"I also," continued Dan, "wanted you to know what I'm thinking about the head coaching position."

"Yes, sir," said Kuballe.

"Based on the magnitude of our tragedy, I have decided to interview some folks outside the school."

He saw Nathan visibly shift, maybe flinch. Nathan said nothing.

"I've invited a candidate here in two weeks to talk with us all."

"Oh," said Nathan.

Of course, he's hurt, thought Dan.

"I want to share with you my thinking. The school's pulse is attached to its football program, a growing tradition that you and Coach Rivers have built. Everyone appreciates that.

"However, Hal's presence was, and remains, so vivid in everyone's mind I feel like the school might stand still for a year or more if we aren't careful. The cloud of grief might remain, which is understandable for some, but not really a good thing for a place like Hilliard that fosters all-around young men.

"While we can never replace Coach Hal's spirit, a new face, with some new ideas, might be good to help the whole place recover and move forward.

"I promise you that you can have a part in that if you wish. And, I also recognize how much you might covet taking Hal's job. I am, however, as the Headmaster, going to think beyond the emotion of the moment, and talk with this other candidate. I wanted you to know."

Nathan sat in silence. He wasn't stunned particularly, but he felt sadness and loss. He cleared his throat.

How was Hal's memory going to be sustained?

For a moment Dan thought Nathan was going to say nothing and walk from his office.

He looked at Dan for a long moment.

"I was hoping," he said, "to carry on Hal's memory with our boys,"

"I know that," said Dan nodding. "I also know that losing him is such a blow to everyone we might not get through the loss if we stay with staff who worked for Coach Rivers for so long. It might sound tough and cruel, but I'm trying to be objective for the whole school. I feel it's a duty I have, Coach."

Nathan looked away.

Dan waited, expecting the argument to come. It didn't come.

"It would not surprise me if you wanted to leave Hilliard. I'd help you find another position, maybe even a head coaching position. However, if you stay, I'm going to raise your salary by $5,000 commencing in the fall. I'd count on your knowledge and experience to help any new hire adjust. I feel confident about that.

"However, I feel equally confident that a change in direction for the team would be good for our school. Maybe, even good for you. I've got the backing of the Board of Trustees on this."

"When is the other guy coming out? What's his background?" Nathan asked.

"He's a graduate of Springfield College, has a Masters in P.E., and played several years of ball for them. He will be on campus in a week or so." Dan looked straight at Nathan, who stared back at him, his eyes red-rimmed.

"Okay, if he's got experience, but Springfield's not a big football program."

"No, it is not," said Dan, "but it supplies some big-time people to the sports world. This guy graduated with honors five years ago. He's single, brings a lot of other experience to us."

"What's that?" asked Nathan.

Dan thought he detected just a touch of resentment in Nathan's tone.

"He won Bronze and a Silver Stars in Vietnam," said Dan.

"Oh, yeah! Combat in 'Nam. I don't know if that's a qualifier. I spent my year there." Kuballe paused before continuing. "I just hope he learned some football along the way."

"He did. He was All-American at Springfield. We will talk to him. You should talk to him, too. If you stay with us at Hilliard, I want you to be his assistant, give him all the support. Share your knowledge as you and Hal accumulated it. It was good. Maybe introduce him to the team when he comes in. Also, make sure he meets Alan McConnell, who should be integral to the team in the fall."

Nathan sighed heavily, then spoke slowly, "I want you to know, Mr. Jeter, I love the school, but I cared for Hal like a ... brother. He was eleven years older than me, treated me like a son, or a brother. We were just damn close.

"I also feel like the school owes him a visible sign of its appreciation in time. I could do that by making our football team a constant winner. I tried to get Hal to open up the offense. Can't say I was successful completely, but we were gaining on it. He was old school. But, he had good habits. He tried. Damn, he tried hard." Nathan's eyes filled.

"Yes, he did," said Dan. "Think about your position in the critical middle of this, Nathan. We will talk again. I'll have Ms. Lillian let you know when the new man is on campus."

Nathan shook Dan's hand and left the office As his mind tumbled with thoughts, each was a mixture of sadness, pain, and now resentment, boring into him. He headed to his own office and closed the door, locking it behind him.

Hal was really gone now, and some one else will come in to coach.

There was only Evelyn now, a woman whose single-minded demands haunted him, unlike the simple, easy-going surrender of Hal River's.

Nathan stared at the red brick facade of the library wall rising toward a grey sky.

Losing Hal has made my life a shambles.

He remembered the panic on the day Hal died, the pallor that came into Hal's ruddy cheeks after he was hit. The hideous dent in the bone above his left eye, the taste of Hal's mouth as he tried to blow life into him. Hal's lips were purple like fat grapes, tainted with blood.

I tried to save him.

"Damn it to hell," he said and sobbed quietly.

Evelyn doesn't understand any of this. Jeter doesn't get it, waxing on about the future of the school, the culture, the atmosphere. Hell, he doesn't sense that Hal was more than coach. He deserves so much more. He was a best friend, loved by every one, not just me. No raise in pay will help heal what I feel. Sort of cheap of him. Jeter's being a pompous bastard. I should go tell him and just walk out. Take your fucking money!

Doesn't he know that I could bring some respect to Hal's memory? School doesn't get that. Money doesn't make Hal's loss less of anything.

This new guy won't understand either. Never knew Hal. Never knew what we were building together. We'll be living in a world where ignorance is bliss, and Hal...will be some guy lying dead in the grass and forgotten. It's not right.

Nathan sat there considering the sacredness of Hal's memory and formulating what it meant. *Maybe it was a barrier for what was to come, a new coach, new face.* He would not allow Hal's memory to die. He would not find another who was so easy, so blessed with simplicity as Hal.

You could really talk to Hal. He knew how to listen, say stuff to set you straight, calm your mind: 'Jus' buy her some yellow flowers. She'll like 'em, especially if they are yellow. Women are like that.'

Hal could think of stuff. 'You guess we ought to get a bus an take the team to Lake 'o the Pines. Let the young butts have a day. Take the whole staff, leave the wives at home - make it jus' the boys and us. What'd ya say?'

Nathan watched the window blur with his own weeping. He gave no thought to anyone knocking. He could sit and remember, and weep. *Gawd, it is pitiful, but I need to do it. I can't help it.*

I just can't be quiet like Hal could. He'd say, 'I like to smell the grass, Cubes, the sweet earth done be chewed up by cleats and watered with boys' sweat. Best smelling grass ever. Sweet grass smell is better than a soapy shower. I just like to hear them kids grunting and shouting. And you like it too. Young fellows playing a man's game in the sweet grass.'

Nathan spoke out loud to Hal. "Remember the fishing Hal, that trip we took after last season?"

'Sure I remember that, Lake Rabun. Got the shit sunburned out of my fat stomach.'

Nathan smiled. They had rented a boat, just the two of them, and sped away to a remote area of the lake. They set their poles, let the boat drift, pulled the beer cooler out, and spent the day.

Hal loved beer better than anything else. He drank five or six and peed over the side of the boat. Then, he belched tremendously. 'Hear that? It echoed.' He nestled down, belching and giggling. 'Do it get any better? Cubes. Do it get any better?'

Then, he answered himself, 'Hell no, it don't!'

Nathan remembered how he'd taken off his own shirt and posed for a moment on the bow of the boat, a half-drunk pose.

'You look like one of them ancient Greek guys.'

He had inhaled so deeply that he made himself dizzy, as though he was sucking in the entire lake with Hal, then he exhaled slowly, and turned to see Hal embraced by the sun, a floating, jolly boy draped over the end of the boat.

He had felt like kissing him.

They had done no fishing, but floated all day, lying up in a cove, barely speaking. They didn't need to. They were one.

Nathan sat looking at nothing. He waited until he got control of himself, and left his office.

Ten

Now I was young and easy under the apple boughs....
— Dylan Thomas

The first person Emmett called when he got the invitation to visit Hilliard School was Robert Hughes. He was lit with excitement.

"Might be a stepping stone. I could become a college phenom!" he said. He would fly out in several days and spend a long weekend. "You got any advice for me, pal?"

Robert was a regular oracle. "Take a sports jacket. Visit the nooks and crannies of the school. Talk to the staff. Go to the gym and check that. You wouldn't want go to a place with lousy facilities. I can tell you, Peterson, staff people are your best asset in any school. They see behind facades. Did you ask why the last coach left?"

"He died," said Emmett.

"Died! Did they say what got him? Coaches don't die, unless they are old and have heart failure."

"I didn't ask how the guy died. Didn't seem right. I was pretty excited."

"Well, check out the faculty, visit some classes, and ask some hard questions. I didn't do much of this at my school. Of course, they didn't come after me. I went after them because I knew the reputation from grad school. I got pretty lucky, I guess. But, you, check it out. Eight hundred miles is a long way to move to make a mistake."

With his mind full of questions, probabilities and excitement, he accepted the invitation to visit Hilliard School in East Texas. He phoned Raymond Kingsley.

"Hey, I got a job interview in Texas," he declared.

"Texas! Are there schools out there? I thought there was Indians and cows.

You don't want to get scalped, Peterson. If you do, don't call me, because I sell bail bonds and don't do scalping head-wound stuff."

Emmett laughed. Kingsley had no serious bones in his body. He and Emmett had stayed in touch over the last few years since Emmett returned to Atlanta to coach.

"You lookin' at coachin'? You'd be a good one," said Kingsley. "Remember a game at Longstreet where you scored a touchdown by just yanking the ball away from the quarterback and running to the end zone. Teach them Texas boys how to do that one. My favorite play of all time."

"Only TD I ever scored."

"Come on, Peterson, you probably scored in other ways."

"Shut up, Kingsley," laughed Emmett. "How's the family? I swear to God, I'm coming to see you after I get back from Texas. If I take the job, I'll consult you for advice."

"Only advice I got for you, Peterson," said Kinglsey, "is don't step in no cow shit. Them patties be like mine-fields out there. They do play some good football on the plains. I seen 'em on TV. They got that Earl Campbell guy, big stud. He is gonna go high in the pros," Raymond exclaimed.

"Maybe," said Emmett. "I asked how was the family?"

"Oh, that. Right-er than rain. Growin' and orderin' me around. Three girls means I got to be moppin' up estrogen everywhere. Wife's in charge. I just bring home a paycheck. I'd be dead if I was single."

Emmett loved Kingsley's home-spun vernacular and how he had changed from the edgy rebel he knew at Longstreet into the faithful home-body-husband, conquered by love. Military school was not the place for Raymond Kingsley. He didn't do books, marching, drilling, or inspections. He said so, and acted it out. He was, however, loyal and true. Emmett recognized it.

Raymond was the only guy he confessed to about his involvement in the library/pig prank.

"I got even with Rodman for you," said Emmett. "Turns out he got fired because he was a sly pig after-all. You know I signed the note around the pig's neck, 'Remember The Ghost Who Walks.'"

"Appreciate that, Peterson, even after fifteen years. I might have been the first 'Ghost Who Walks', but you was the last. You graduated from that hellhole. I just painted the water tower."

"It was a good job," said Emmett, laughing. "So, I'm going to Texas to see what's there."

"Like I said watch them Cowboys play ball. Kind of like them cheerleaders too, but the wife don't let me look at them too much. Lots of long-legged women in Texas. Be careful one of them girls don't snag you, make you a 'goldern' calf roper. Your legs ain't bowed. Good luck to you. I look forward to hearing what happens."

Emmett went to The Hilliard School in Lofton, Texas. He had a reunion with his old teacher-friend, Mr. Sam Burke, visited his class and thought it resembled the same material he recalled from his days at Longstreet. He spent fifteen minutes with Dan Jeter, who sent him off with instructions to see the school and meet the coaches for lunch. Coach Kuballe would meet him and show him around.

"I'll set you up to meet me at 4:30," Mr Jeter said, "and we can discuss some things. Tomorrow, I'll spend some time with you as well. You and Mr. Sam have some catching up to do. You should wander around some without guides showing you the way. Maybe meet some students."

Dan Jeter was both kind and formal. He said, "By the way, Coach, just call me 'Dan.' We reserve the formal stuff for meetings."

Emmett's morning was a whirlwind. He couldn't recall having met so many people from Mr. Sam's class to the history department offices, to the gym for a walk through, and into the lockers for coaches and players.

Harry Parsons was folding and stacking towels when Emmett walked into the locker room. He introduced himself and looked around.

"So, you're the new guy interviewing for the coaching job?" said Harry, never looking up.

"I am. From Atlanta."

Harry gave him an awkward handshake. "Name's Harry Parsons. Don't many come in here, less they asking for something. Uniform, towel, cleat wrench. I can't keep cleat wrenches. I don't have a stock pile."

Emmett smiled at Harry's lilting emphatic tone. "I was just getting the lay-of-the-land," he said.

"Oh, yeah, this was Rivers and Coach Kuballe's domain. Them two could smoke up more bullshit than I got in a stogy. Sad about Coach Hal."

Emmett did not respond immediately. "I gather he died on campus."

"Yep," said Harry, plopping down on a folding chair. "Just walked himself slap into a discus. Right into the path of it. Caught him right above his left eye. He didn't last long. Really weird. Don't nobody talk about it much. Tore up Kuballe. I saw you met him."

"I did, just for a minute. We're gonna talk later when he's finished class," said Emmett. "He seems pretty quiet."

"Well, that's his grief sucking on him. Him and Hal Rivers was a pair. Inseparable pair, goofing like a couple of young dogs, ribbing each other, planning football plays like they was at Dallas or Houston. Produced a couple of good teams, too. Over here all the time, even on weekends."

"Good rapport," said Emmett. "Planning makes for a good team, I know that. You say Coach Rivers was hit by a discus. Was it thrown by someone?"

"Yep, kid was practicing. They say he just walked outta them woods out there straight into it. No other reason given. Weird. Them two coaches done alright together. They sure did in a crazy way. Rivers always yukking it up, and Kuballe being the deep one. Gotten deeper since the day Hal Rivers died, too. I can't say, or shouldn't say too much.

"If you can't say something good about a guy, just keep your mouth shut. Anyways try to do that. He's from Alabama, and I ain't a big fan of Bear Bryant."

"Oh, yeah," said Emmett.

"Yep, that Bama coach is arrogant, wearing a wool hat in the summer. Never liked a guy to wear wool hats. Full of himself."

"He made some tough guys tougher."

"That he did, but give me the folksier kind any day. Don't have to drive a player into the dirt to make him a player, in my opinion."

Harry went to the dryer that had ceased spinning and pulled out an armful of hot towels.

"Shit! Hot! Got to check the thermostat on this thing." He noticed Emmett staring at his wooden leg.

"I was gonna ask you what's your story, but I see you done noticed I have one. A bit more obvious than most fellows."

Harry stuck his leg out and whacked it on the metal leg of a folding table. "This here is my medal from Iwo Jima. You know Iwo, don't ya, Coach?"

"Sure," said Emmett. "I know Iwo Jima. Lose it there?"

"Yep, nearly bought the farm that day, but was dragged out by a buddy. Now, I'm folding towels in a locker room full of football athletes. Might seem funny to some, but it is similar. One kind a war deserves another kind. You from Atlanta or just working there?" Harry asked.

"I'm a coach at the big public school there for the last few years. I know Mr. Burke. He was my teacher," said Emmett.

"You dodge the draft teaching?" asked Harry matter-of-factly.

"Hardly," said Emmett. "Drafted and served."

"Vietnam?" asked Harry. He raised one eye-brow. "What were you?

"Infantry, Special Ops. Around Bien Hoi, a lot."

"Nasty stuff. I was a Marine in the Pacific. Kinda similar, maybe."

"Yeah, maybe." Emmett felt a kinship growing.

"Tell me some more about the coaching situation here, Mr. Parsons?"

"Wait a minute. Don't nobody call me 'Mr. Parsons.' It's got to be 'Harry.' And, don't never call me 'Sarge!' I left that behind 30 years ago."

"Good enough, Harry. What about Coach Kuballe? I got to meet the guy in an hour. How come he isn't a candidate for the job? Seems like he'd be a natural to take over from the other guy?"

Harry felt the same kinship that Emmett noted. He looked off toward the exit to the swimming pool, thinking how to he could answer a pointed question. Emmett followed him.

"Probably entered his mind more than once to ask for it. He loved Hal Rivers, like I said. You'd think he'd be considered, but I been knowing Dan Jeter since he was knee high to a jack rabbit. He thinks in larger ways. I don't know. Looks like Jeter knows how to stand back and make a judgment. He don't rush things ever. He has thought this thing over. Been about six weeks since the Coach died.

"Kuballe come in here all sad, and tried to sweet talk me into thinking he was fine. He weren't no finer than a piece of rust on that water spigot. He wants the job, but his pride won't let him strike for it. He's a tough fellow. Quiet most of the time now since Rivers ain't here to badger him. Likes to be called a stud, likes to lift weights with the boys, shoot baskets, and be a jock-type. Got a real pretty wife. I don't know when he spends time with her. He's okay, just don't talk much at all.

"One other thing. He did a tour in Vietnam, too. Never told me, but Rivers mentioned it. Kuballe don't talk about the war, I reckon.

"That's okay. There's some that does and some that doesn't. Then, there is those who dream about it sometimes. Makes me sweat. I never go near that pool because it's humid as hell in there, and it gives me the willies. I did a little time at The Canal, as in Guadalcanal. Don't have much to do with water, except to take a shower. And I sure as hell don't take no bath."

Emmett liked Harry Parsons. "I appreciate your time, Harry, and more than that, I appreciate your service. Thanks for talking." He looked at his watch. "I'll come in again before I go. I know about humidity. That shower dripping could get to me too. We'll talk."

Emmett had managed for a long time to leave the Vietnam War out of his thoughts. Meeting Harry made a difference. They were brothers-at-arms in a way.

Harry thought to himself as Emmett left. *That's a solid man. Dan knows how to pick 'em. And, I don't know a damn thing about him, more'n I knew when he walked in. He is just solid.*

Eleven

I have let things slip, a thirty year old cargo boat
Stubbornly hanging on to my name....
— Sylvia Plath

Nathan Kuballe eyed Emmett walking toward him across the campus. He decided to be cautious and see how this coach reacted to him. He waited until Emmett caught up. He was carrying a white notebook, and shook Emmett's hand firmly, as they exchanged pleasantries.

"We can go to my office," said Nathan.

"Fine."

Emmett waited, then opened a conversation. Nathan didn't look at him.

"So, you've been here quite awhile, I suppose?"

It was a question on the edge of truth.

"Seven years," said Nathan, his stride quickening.

"Wow," said Emmett. "That's long enough to know the place pretty well."

"Pretty well," said Nathan.

It was clear that Nathan was nervous.

Emmett tried only pleasantries. "I've been in Atlanta five seasons."

"I heard," said Nathan.

"So, Mr. Jeter talked to you?"

"He did."

"Well, I guess this is harder than I thought." Emmett tried to smile. It was tough. He felt himself being awkward. "Sort of like on ice skates for us, I guess."

The lightness of the remark made Nathan smile slightly. *At least the guy is honest.*

"You might say that," said Nathan as they approached his office on the back side of the gymnasium.

It was an ample space, decorated with pictures of teams, a University of Alabama letter in a tan frame hung behind the desk. On top of a file cabinet open half-way down sat a plastic framed picture of a woman. On the desk, among the litter of papers and yellow pads, scribbled with football plays, was a photo of Nathan with a large, older man, who carried a big stomach. On another wall was a picture of Bear Bryant, looking stoic and proud, another of Kuballe and Kenny Stabler. There was an orange, plastic-covered sofa with silver arms and legs shoved along one wall. It was littered with towels and a few Hilliard tee shirts and a pair of sweat pants. The room smelled like a locker room of minty ointment for sore muscles and sour towels.

"Sorry about the mess," said Nathan. "I'm not a housekeeper."

"Know what you mean," said Emmett, studying the array of memorabilia. "I'm no maid myself. I don't even have much of an office; just space with two other guys."

"Hum," said Kuballe. He flung the note book on the desk.

A chalk board was on the other wall with scribbling on it. In one corner in blue chalk was a message: "Meet you at the weight room 9AM tomorrow. Hal." The message had a circle around it and a date above the circle, '2/18/77.'"

Emmett noticed it as he studied the room.

"We ran the Veer," Nathan said. He gestured at the notebook. "Hal loved it. I was down at Houston to a clinic and met Bill Yoeman and learned it there. I'm the coordinator."

"I'm familiar with that," said Emmett. "Yoeman was there in 1965. We called it the 'split-back veer' when I played. I'm a defensive guy myself. I'm glad to know you got familiarity. I know the offense because I ran from the 5-2 defense in college."

Nathan smiled for the first time. "We tried to kill the 5-2 a lot here. Beat the defensive end. If he ain't quick, it will drive a coordinator nuts."

"Have a lot of good running backs?" asked Emmett, warming to the discussion.

"Had a few. We could run the 'dive' or the 'outside veer.' Hal was good at that stuff, but he let me fiddle with it a lot. He ran defenses. Fiddled with that, too." Kuballe smiled again. "He fiddled a lot, poor guy."

Emmett look directly into Nathan's eyes. "Hey, Nathan, Harry Parsons down in the locker room told me about Coach Rivers and how he died. That is so rough, man. I'm sorry for you and the whole school."

Nathan stood tall. "It is rough. He was a great friend."

Emmett thought he saw emotion rising in Nathan's eyes, so he swiftly changed the subject.

"Tell me about the team coming up. What you got?"

Nathan shuffled behind the desk and sat down. He flipped open the white notebook, a playbook, to a page with several pages of complicated plays. "We got two big lineman and two skinny, but some quick backs. We got a guy who can throw off the run a little bit. He needs more speed, but he will do. I'm hoping in four months we can fine tune him to play quarterback."

"What kind of defense did Coach Rivers run?" asked Emmett.

"We tried to teach a 4-2-5. Liked to do that because it uses only one defender to tackle the dive/veer guy. High school kids struggle with too much assignment football."

"You got that right," said Emmett. "You want to play fast, just execute techniques."

"Yep, if you can get 'em to learn techniques. Drives us nuts. Plenty of times it breaks down if they set the gaps too wide."

Emmett knew that Kuballe knew his stuff. He liked they were on the same page.

"If I were to come here, Nathan, I'm hoping you'll stick around. I need a smart guy, who has played big time football, who can teach, and bring confidence to the kids. Obviously, you can do that. I'd be fine having you run offense. I wouldn't interfere. You grooved it with Coach Rivers, and that's fine with me." Emmett thought his remark was fair.

Nathan didn't respond at all to the gesture. He looked at the playbook. Emmett thought it was a way of avoiding looking at him.

Finally, Nathan said, "Hal always complained we never had good tight ends. This year we might have them. He just will miss...."

"Look, Nathan, I heard. I can't express how terrible that must be. I hope you'd tell me if my coming in with you will make it hard for you. I don't think I'm the kind of guy who is going to pass a lot of orders. We just do our jobs, teach the kids, build a team. I can't be Coach Rivers."

Nathan sighed, and looked at the chalk board, then down at his desk. "I'm a quiet guy, Coach, except I ain't quiet on the field. I let it all out. Boys seem not to mind, but I'm a yeller and a motivator. Me and Hal, we loved those kids."

"Sure," said Emmett. *Maybe I've won the moment.*

He did not add anything to the conversation.

"Maybe we should call it a day and hit the field," Kuballe said. "You can see what spring practice looks like. Maybe get a look at a few boys."

Emmett noticed the sweat stains on Nathan's shirt. It was easily 72 degrees in the room.

This whole thing was going to be hard.

Emmett watched the practice for an hour, but chose not do more than stand to the side.

The boys called Nathan, "Coach Q."

Nathan had a whole collection of terms for the players from "Slick to Knucklehead" or "Alice or Lucy" to "Stud Muffin to Candy-Butt." "Hey, don't get your feet caught in your skirts, son!" It was fast, spirited, and dusty.

What attracted Emmett's attention was the yellow ribboned wreath on a tripod at the far end of the field. He could barely see what it was, and it kept

146

haunting him. He walked around the huddle of boys and stared at it. Ribbons flapped in the constant wind. He looked back at the huddle of players and the dust whirled up. A low jet made a loud roar overhead made Emmett duck. It was eerie. He looked back toward the wreath.

No doubt it had been hung with yellow ribbons and some brown, dead flowers dangled from the firmer edges of it.

He felt uneasy. Something in him stirred as the plane's roar subsided, but the dust lingered.

What was this?

The boys ran long wind-sprints to end the practice, then huddled at the middle of the field. Emmett didn't pay much attention to the remarks or the cheers coming from the huddle. It was motivational. He focused on something deep in his imagination.

The boys began a rhythmic clap.

"Get tough, get mean! Hit 'em low.! Get get down! Underneath, move your feet!"

Their chant grew louder merging with their claps.

What was it that was inside his head?

It took him back to a place he had not been in a long time.

Emmett hated the rubbery feeling in his legs, like he had been running.

Had he actually run with the kids?

He rubbed his eyes and watched them lope once around the field, then peel off in pairs and jogging to the wreath with Coach Kuballe and four other coaches bringing up the rear of the pack. They made an arc two and three deep around the wreath and stood silently for a long moment, then broke and sprinted to the gym.

A ritual for the dead

Kuballe and the other coaches walked slowly after them, leaving Emmett watching.

For a split second, he was sitting in a chopper after he settled onto the tarmac, as men unloaded two body bags. He remembered that deep in the bush country they had left others. Six were never brought out.

No wreaths for them.

When he had gotten back to base camp, one of the troopers had yelled, "Hey, Peterson, you're a Stud-Muffin, man!"

Emmett hurried after the other coaches.

That afternoon Dan Jeter was scheduled to meet with Jack Rollins, the Board of Trustees member, who wanted to ear-mark library-fund money he had originally given for weight room renovation.

Jeter received a call that Mr. Rollins had been rushed to Memorial Hospital, where he died in the ER from a massive heart attack. The man had been a hard-driving member of the Executive Committee of the Board of Trustees, a big donor to the school, and a horse's ass. His sudden death meant Dan would miss the arrival the next day of his niece visiting from Macon, and he'd miss his meeting in at 4:30 with Emmett Peterson.

Dan was quick to decide to have Peterson come up to his lake house on Saturday with his wife, Maggie, and they could walk down by the lake and talk. He was, despite the concern about Mr. Rollins, curious to know if his niece was the same person Emmett Peterson knew when he was at Longstreet. Ms. Lillian called Maggie Jeter and made arrangements to pick up Emmett and drive him and their niece to the lake house. It could be a bit awkward, but Emmett was thinking issues at Hilliard were unusual, so why not. It was part of the game plan. Nothing could be more peculiar than interviewing for a job created by a dead Coach with that person's best friend being the chief interviewer. Now he had to look forward to meeting a visiting relative. At least that was sort of home-grown. After all it was a private school.

Later, at a dinner, arranged by Mr. Sam Burke with faculty, wives and coaches, he sat next to Nathan Kuballe. Over drinks he tried to tease Kuballe about Alabama. That didn't go well at all, so he stopped. Conversation turned to personal college experiences and children. Emmett's single status made him the odd man, and they poked fun at him because Emmett could easily laugh.

"I got hog-tied one time. That was enough." He made light of his having been married "to a dance hall queen" and his divorce after he got out of the Army.

No one quizzed him on either matter. He watched Kuballe, and knew that Nathan was doing the same. It did not matter. Nathan had not brought his wife.

"I don't know if Mr. Burke told you people, but he taught me for two years at Longstreet Military School?" Emmett said. "We called him 'Major Burke' at the time."

Emmett smiled at Kuballe, trying to affect an informality.

"Major Burke!" Kuballe exclaimed, "God, I hope you out-ranked him!"

"Not hardly," responded Emmett. "Mr. Burke was famous for taking cadets through a pretty rigorous course in American history. He worked us." He saw Mr. Sam, grinning broadly.

"Good that Mr. Peterson can bring everyone up to date on our acquaintance. He did tell you I was forced by the Dean to bring Emmett into my class or else he would have been swinging from the light cords. At that time, he believed life belonged only on the field and study belonged in the broom closet with all the mops and buckets. Emmett, you had to learn to get handy with the books. I'm glad some of you met today. Emmett was Captain of a football team that never won."

"Never won?" exclaimed Emmett. "We won. Five times!"

"Only five times in four years?"

Kuballe appeared surprised.

"Maybe it was six times, or even seven. It wasn't many times," teased Mr. Sam.

"I thought military schools fielded tough teams," said Nathan.

In the Tomb of the Soul 149

"Not Longstreet. We had two wining seasons in all my four years there," said Emmett, "the last one. Lots of turnover in players every year. Kids didn't like military schools. We did have some great players, just not a one time."

Emmett watched Nathan, sensing a game of points.

"You obviously liked it! You stayed," said Nathan, "and Burke left! Why did you leave, Sam?"

"Family in Houston. My sister. She was widowed with a youngster. My wife died. Felt I needed to be closer to her if she needed me. Change is good, sometimes." Burke didn't flinch.

"I had heard that. We'll, let that pass," said Kuballe. "What about you, Coach Peterson? You stayed. He left?"

"I had to stay," said Emmett. "My daddy wouldn't let me come home. Anyway, I'd have been ineligible to play ball elsewhere, so I stuck it out. I graduated before Mr. Burke left the school. It was interesting there. I made a lot of friends, and it helped me afterwards, I guess."

"We will see, won't we?" remarked Nathan. He tried to smile. He ordered a steak and a glass of red wine. "I hope you plan on coming out to the field again tomorrow. Coach Royston and I are putting in plays. Gonna scrimmage."

Several others had gathered at the table and introductions were all around. Patricia Royston was a medical trainer and math teacher. Coach Royston, taught English, and sat opposite Emmett. The last to arrive was Sissie Waters, who was a math teacher. She nudged Coach Royston to move and give her room.

Sam Burke made the introductions, including some of Emmett's credentials.

Coach Royston, lit up at the mention of Springfield College. "I know some folks at Springfield."

"Be careful, Emmett," said Patricia, his wife, "or he'll tell the story of how we met, and I shall faint from sheer boredom."

Nathan snorted with laughter. "You know that Patricia has been known to faint in public a lot around her husband. I think that's how she avoids him. Notice she came late, and she faints in public places so she doesn't have to worry about what Coach Royston might say."

"And, I noticed," Patricia said, "once again Evelyn is at home. Nathan, the Cube, tends to socialize without her." She gave him a strong look.

"Had to work tonight," Nathan said. "She makes more money than me."

Everyone laughed.

The meal came.

Sam Burke insisted they order two bottles of wine. Emmett drank a bit of red wine, but monitored his consumption. He wanted to be ready for questions. As the meal passed Kuballe relaxed. He had also teased Sissie Waters, coming close to suggesting that she had a boyfriend, but stopped before his remarks got too bold.

Emmett sensed tension that he couldn't grasp.

As people were finishing up, Emmett was grilled about football at Newborne College and Springfield, his playing days at Longstreet, and his work with the junior varsity players at the public school in Atlanta.

Sissie Waters blurted out, "Did y'all read that article in today's paper about the coach over in Commerce, Texas, and the wrestling tournament? I could not believe that!" Her eyes grew large.

"I saw that!" exclaimed Patricia, "His daughter, how he put her on the wrestling team!"

"What?" exclaimed Royston. "A coach put his daughter on his wrestling team? That's nuts!"

"He absolutely did! And she won a match! Outpointed a guy! It was in tonight's paper." Sissie appeared proud of herself for having upstaged the knowledgeable coaches, but Nathan Kuballe was not outdone.

"Coach Bill Brooks over in Commerce, Texas, is the best wrestling coach in the state," chortled Kuballe. He shoved himself higher up in his chair, his eyes dancing from his third glass of red wine. "I saw the article. The man's a genius, a winner. Brooks figured this team could finish in the top three if he did not forfeit his 103 lb. weight class, so he gets his daughter, this little girl, his own kid."

"Well, I'm for women's right in athletics, but I think it's awful! It is wrestling, for heavens sakes. It's rough and physical," said Sissie Waters. "It's exploitation!"

"What do you mean, exploitation?" exclaimed Nathan. "It's good coaching. He has this mean girl who is about 5' tall and weighs 100 lbs. He figured that he would let her lock up with her opponent, some kid from Temple, a wiry little guy, named Casey McGinnis, who could crush her in a minute. She is feisty little woman. Coach thought, 'let 'em lock up, then forfeit the match.' The state rule deducts eight points for the forfeit of a weight class, and six points for a loss in a singles match! Didn't know what she could do. So she showed everyone. She did it for the team! Got a point for 'em reversing the guy. They finished second in the state of Texas! Now that's brilliant!

"That trumps the women's rights thing, Sissie."

"I don't care," she said. "The State Athletic Board should ban that sort of thing! Some line should be drawn between exploitation of the sexes and coaching responsibilities," exclaimed Sissie in a spirited way. "If I was her mother, I'd kill my husband!" She was looking at Emmett in an animated, fiery fashion.

"Well," Kuballe said, ignoring her alarm, "I imagine the state will raise some hell, but they won't block the move. That would be discrimination. It's just no one had thought that girls might be on a men's wrestling team, nevertheless score a point for 'em. It just never happened. Brook's a cagey old bastard. Won that meet outright because five of his men won by pins. Eked out the win by about one or two points."

Ed Royston, not to let Kuballe have the stage to himself, told a story about the time he and his assistant had a group of eighth grade players in a hotel with five other middle school teams at a football roundup in Ft. Worth. They thought they would put the boys to bed and get together with some of the other coaches from other schools for a bull session, so they called on the phone and arranged a rendezvous in their room, inviting a particular rival coach whose reputation for practical jokes was well known.

"My room happened to be beside the elevator. The plan was for my buddy Bill Boykin, to wait in the hall and jump out in front of this unsuspecting coach when he arrived as the elevator doors opened. It would scare the hell out of him. Boykin had this huge voice. We'd all have a great laugh."

Royston could hardly tell the story for laughing at himself.

Sissy Waters kept saying, "Shut up, Ed, and tell the story!"

Ed gasped for air. "They neither one expected Dan Jeter to be coming down the elevator at that hour. Jeter jumped in fright so high that he upset that plastic grate over the neon light fixture in the elevator's ceiling, and assumed a kung-foo position ready to fight!"

"He really didn't hit his head, Ed?" Sissy exclaimed.

"Swear to God, he hit his head. Ceiling came down all over the place. We were laughing so much that he jumped so high, he hit his head. Nobody could speak. He stood there posing like Bruce Lee, the Chinese kung-fu fighter. Jeter got tickled when he saw who it was. All of us standing there.

"If he were here right now, he'd show you exactly how he knocked that plastic grate cock-eyed and got into that fighting stance. Boykin will tell you. Hal Rivers would tell you."

Ed caught himself momentarily, and the wind went out of the story. He shifted the point.

"Yeah, Hal was there. He was howling and wheezing like the rest of us.

"Anyway, for a minute, nobody knew whether to laugh or cry. All of us were standing there with Jeter. Then, this other Coach arrived, running down the steps. By this time Jeter was laughing too and making these feinting swipes at Boykin and the rest of us. Some other coach from another school walked by and couldn't figure out what was so funny. None of us could speak to explain, so he kept going. Next morning at breakfast, he saw several of us at breakfast, and said, 'You guys are nuts.' He brushed by us and got us started laughing again.

"We have some fun, Coach Peterson. We really do," said Royston.

Emmett laughed along with the others. He told them that he had met only briefly with Mr. Jeter. The big meeting was coming up in the morning.

Kuballe smirked at Ed Royston. "I'm surprised Jeter was at the roundup actually. I thought he was tied to his office, busy looking out for the direction and culture of the school." His tone was snide. "I don't think he is the biggest football supporter, I've known. I guess he is trying to get us money for a new weight room.

"How about it Coach Burke? You got an ear to his door." He aimed this remark at Burke, but looked at Emmett. Not shying from his slight of Jeter, he continued. "I can tell you, Coach Peterson, some of the boys need a lot of work in the weight room. Every year at the Final Assembly, when we parade all the scholars across the stage, I swear to God, most of them have butts wider than their shoulders! Their cans rolling across the stage like hogs rolling in gunny sacks." He paused for a moment, waiting for effect.

"You got a plan for getting your players into the weight room?" The question was directed at Emmett.

"Not off-hand," answered Emmett. "Didn't the previous coach require it?"

Nathan's eyes turned from blue flashes to slate gray. They seemed to harden like concrete. Others turned to Kuballe to see his reaction.

"Hal...," he said, "always had a plan. He was a tiger about it... the weight program. That's why Dan is determined to refurbish the place." Nathan's eyes batted rapidly.

Emmett instinctively knew his quick response had rattled Kuballe.

The table grew silent.

"Well," said Mr. Burke, breaking the moment. "For you younger folks, the night may be young. For this older man, I have classes to teach and a lot of steak to digest. I must call it a night. Emmett, glad to see you, today. I'll meet you in the morning, bright and early; say 7:30 in the hotel lobby?" He pushed away from the table and stood, reaching for Emmett's hand, as others stood.

"I appreciate you all giving me the chance to be here," Emmett said.

"I'll take the check," said Burke. "The rest of the night you are on your own." His departure was the cue for others to leave.

Kuballe looked at Emmett. His eyes were somewhat cloudy; the wine sparkle gone out of them. "Guess I'll see you on the field tomorrow, Coach. You can see how Royston's backs handle the Kuballe Iron Curtain! Think about the weight room."

He smiled, and Emmett felt relieved.

"I'll see you. Nice to meet you. I'll see you tomorrow," replied Emmett, extending his hand and felt Nathan's firm grip.

Kuballe walked away.

Sissy Waters lingered and watched him leave. "I know he is still really shook up about Coach River's death. He worked so hard to save him. He's struggling. Emmett, you mustn't let that bother you. They were best friends and been together for a long time. It's hard. We just can't believe it happened, especially the way it happened."

They stood momentarily looking at the space that Nathan Kuballe had vacated. "You know, Coach Q is the sort of guy to carry that to his grave. He gets angry and sad, really on edge. We've all been watching him with the boys each day. He's doing okay, but sometimes . . . . When you are married to the school, it makes it tougher. I thought he'd bring his wife tonight. We don't see her much. They don't have children.

"You know why he was late tonight? He was at the cemetery. Visits Hal's grave almost daily. "

The memory of the wreath at the edge of the field and the ritual the boys performed before the end of the afternoon practice floated through Emmett's mind.

"I think the summer vacation will do him good," said Sissie. "I hope Evelyn has a trip planned, or something to get them out of town. She works hard as an office manager for Benton & Rhodes, a big law firm."

She excused herself, pledging to see Emmett at the school and wishing him luck.

As he left, he encountered Ed Royston and his wife, Patricia, standing at the doorway of the hotel bar They seemed to be waiting for him.

"Let's have a nightcap. What do you say?" suggested Ed.

The three of them walked into an almost empty bar and found a booth. Emmett had enjoyed the evening. The others seemed to enjoy him, especially these two. Patricia wanted to hear more about Emmett's interest in teaching history and what he liked, and how he enjoyed his work with the junior varsity players. Did he coach at a school where there was a minority population, was Atlanta a fun place to live, had he been to Stone Mountain, was he a Braves' fan?

"The girl has curiosity," observed Ed. She smirked at him.

Together they had taken a booth in the lounge. It was 8:45 PM.

While Emmett was intrigued about Nathan Kuballe, asking too many questions seemed awkward. Nevertheless, he could possibly be working with the man. He waited until there was a lull in the small talk, then asked about Coach Rivers.

"I heard about Coach Rivers' death, but I'd like to hear more."

The request didn't bother Ed Royston, but it was clear Patricia deferred to him. She had slipped into the seat beside her husband, while Emmett sat facing the two of them. The piano music in the lounge had shifted to soft jazz.

"Oh, I don't mind talking about it."

Patricia said she was there. "I was over by the track on the opposite side. I heard the commotion and went running over because I saw Nathan running toward someone lying on the ground. I had no idea it was Hal Rivers. He apparently just walked out of the woods at about the time Alan McConnell made his discus throw. The kid would never have thrown in the direction of anybody."

Ed Royston took up the story. "Everyone was so shocked. You have to admit a fellow who has worked at a place knows where the dangerous areas are, especially during a track practice, like the shot-put and discus area. The accident really got to everyone!" said Ed.

Emmett tried to imagine the panic and the pain that rippled through boys and adults at such a time. He had seen enough war to understand the dynamics of reaction when serious wounds occur. He had seen people die, even held them. If Kuballe were the one to administer aid to his friend, he could understand.

The afternoon flashback sped across his mind.

The air in the bar seemed suddenly cooler to him.

"God, I guess Coach Kuballe was pretty shaken," he said quietly, feeling less disquietude about Kuballe.

"Kuballe is not likely to be over it soon," said Ed, who glanced at his wife and shrugged. "Nathan really loved the guy, you know. They did all kinds of things together, fished, socialized, took trips, worked out - it was like they were brothers or something. Nathan worshipped him, almost like a father, though Hal wasn't old enough to be his father. It's kind of the way he acted around him. Like close, you know, even childlike. Hal liked the attention. He worshipped Nathan, not just because he played at Alabama. It was different. We saw it. It wasn't ugly. It was just closeness of two guys. Helped him after having lost his own son in the war."

"I saw it," said Patricia. "I never dwelled on their closeness until Hal died. Nathan just went to pieces."

A waitress brought them a pitcher of beer with three chilled glasses.

Emmett leaned back into the plush cushion of the seat and quickly reconstructed the evening: the story of the wrestling coach, the tease about Longstreet and being a prisoner of his father's insistence, and remembering how Nathan's eyes shifted and seemed to change color when Hal's name came up.

Ed put his beer glass down and pushed it away slightly. "Nathan always liked to play the big jock at everything. He had Hal convinced that he was all-world in college. He wasn't really, though he did play a few times. If you checked, and several guys did, he wasn't much at Bama. Just too much talent there. Nathan loves to talk. He's immensely popular with the boys, does stuff with them, camps, water skis, fishes, hikes. He takes trips in the summer with four or five. They've gone great places. He even took four kids to South America on a canoe trip up the Amazon year before last. Word is that he makes a lot of money doing that."

"He's married?" Emmett said again, curiously.

"Sure. To Evelyn. A nice, sparkling woman," said Patricia. "We all love her. They don't have kids. I heard Nathan say that he had six hundred of them! She comes to some faculty parties and stuff. She is sort of private, but fun. Ed thinks she's great looking."

"Well she is. She's terrific looking," injected Ed Royston. "She'd have to be with Nate around. The man is expert on everything."

Patricia had her opinions. She shared them. "He's nice and all that, but you wonder how Evelyn puts up with it! All that bravado, his insistent personality, the edge in his tease. He lives for football and school. Sam called it 'ebullient spirit.'"

Emmett really hadn't liked Nathan at all until this conversation. *Maybe he'd give the man a chance, especially after learning how he'd tried to save his friend and failed.* He knew what that it was like, how it felt, and the room felt cooler again.

"Why isn't he applying for the football job?" Emmett asked.

"That's a good question," said Patricia, looking at her husband.

"You might also wonder if I'm interested," said Royston, "and I can tell you nope with conviction. I'm an assistant coach, who likes to teach English classes. No idea about Kuballe. He has got to have thought about the job. I'm not."

Emmett laughed. "Well, I'm glad of that. I did have to wonder if I was surrounded by all this competition." He had, after all, mentioned this to Nathan earlier in the afternoon. Obviously, Kuballe hadn't shared this thoughts with anyone. That could be good.

Ed Royston didn't hesitate at Emmett's question. "I'm sure its on Nathan's mind. He hasn't mentioned it, but I suspect he's gone to Jeter about it. He and Hal had set a tone for the team. To be expected."

The waitress brought fresh glasses.

Patricia was warming to the conversation, "You know how people can establish a relationship that follows the strengths of the other? Kuballe is all brawn, he's physical."

"Oh yes," enjoined Ed. "Hal would plan the games, draw plays, and Kuballe would fine tune them and put 'em in. He found players too. He also actively recruited kids to his sports. He'd see an athlete on the cross country team who was lean and tall, and be on that guy to play football. Once he really pissed off another coach when he mentioned a 6'4" center on the basketball team, wanting him to focus more on getting bigger to play tight end in the fall by skipping out on basketball preseason. They had words about it, and Nathan quickly apologized."

"That's the way he is," said Patricia, "He says things sometimes he doesn't mean, like that bull about kids with butts wider than their shoulders. If you call him on it, he gets all apologetic. Sometimes guys, even the women, have to tone down Kuballe. When you do, he seems a lot easier to get along with."

"She's right," said Royston. "He can really be up front sometimes, but if you let him know what you think, that you've got feelings, opinions, he backs off. Pretty soon you think he is your best friend."

Emmett felt more and more confident regarding what he was hearing.

"I thought tonight when I said that stuff about the former coach not getting kids to lift weights, he was going to go off, but he didn't. I sort of stepped into that one."

Ed snorted. "That was nothing."

"You know what I think?" said Patricia. "He's a lot different around men than around women. I think he is basically shy. His wife likes him. You can tell, but she is so quiet about stuff." She looked at Ed.

"I won't say he's shy, but he is more comfortable in the locker room than in the lounge. Just saying. Don't think we're being critical. He is unusual, but he is also a loyal guy and a helluva coach. You'd want Kuballe on your side. At least I would. I've worked with him for six years. He stands up for what he thinks. When Rivers put his foot down, and he did at times, Nathan listened, and got with the program.

"The death of Hal Rivers just plowed into his soul. You know, he was the first one to him. Incredible the will he exerted to keep the guy alive until the medics arrived. He was going strong over Hal when medics got to the scene."

"You were good too," Patricia said, putting her hand on Ed's. "You were right there counting the breaths. Geez, it was such bad day!"

From the droop of her head, it was clear to Emmett the subject should end.

He decided to finish off his evening by offering to pay for their drinks, but Royston was insistent. Emmett liked them both and thanked them. They promised to see each other the next day. He wasn't sure of his schedule, but he would be on the field. He had been ordered there by Coach Kuballe. He watched them leave going out of the lobby to wait for their car to be brought around. Emmett saw Ed take Patricia's hand, and she distinctly stepped over to nudge his side.

It was 9:45PM. Emmett would be ready for tomorrow. He turned for the elevator, remembering Royston's story of the Jeter in the elevator. 6'8' - he glanced at the plastic grate over the lights in the ceiling as the elevator lifted.

Twelve

Pranks and Coyotes

Emmett was up at seven. The day looked promising with sun being suffused through the shuttered window shade as he pulled a cord to open the heavy poly-fiber curtains in his hotel room.

He had his weekend breakfast and coffee in the hotel restaurant at 7:25, bacon and eggs. As he was looking over the earliest springtime Grapefruit League standings, he noticed Sam Burke headed toward his table.

"Good-morning!" he said. "You owe me a cup of coffee. Let me have a small pot," he said to the waitress, who was on his trail the moment he appeared at the restaurant door.

"Hope you slept well after a big day? By the way," he said to the waitress as she sat water at his place, "You can write my coffee off on this ticket! The Hilliard School owes me the favor of coffee."

He turned to Emmett, "I'm always charging Daniel Jeter with having no coffee pot in his office. He is a man of the desert! I am sure we'll have that experience soon enough." He winked at Emmett.

Clearly, old Sam Burke was enjoying his role as squire to Mr. Peterson.

The city of Lofton in the morning sun of a Friday looked fairly prosperous, tree lined streets with a stable, well-kept antique appearance to it. Emmett judged the place to be about twenty-five thousand persons, the shaded Main Street faded into a kind of staid prosperity of elegant old homes set back from broad sidewalks on both sides. Burke maneuvered his old Mercury down Picket Street into a quiet, elegant neighborhood beneath canopies of oaks, through gates and beneath a wrought iron archway that read 'The Hilliard School - founded 1952.'

The driveway wound beneath a planting of pecan and water oak trees toward a clump of speckled brick buildings. Small bands of boys in gray slacks and white short sleeves were loitering about, some laughing and pointing, some ready to resume the standard game of chase the plastic football.

Emmett felt his stomach churn with excitement.

Several boys watched as Mr. Burke aimed his car into a parking slot beside several other cars. Two teachers had shouted at a group of youngsters to get to their classes.

As they walked to an academic building, Mr. Sam said, "I often think of that fellow, Raymond Kingsley. You really liked that cadet. What in the world happened to him after we cut him loose, and what was that nickname you guys called him, 'The ghost'?

"You mean 'The Ghost Who Walks."

"That's it, Santayana! History's doomed to repeat itself!"

"Not exactly," said Emmett. "I think it was that comic book character, The Phantom."

"Whatever happened to him? Do you know?"

"He moved back home and became a bail bondsman and sells insurance. Has three daughters. Doing well," said Emmett, surprised that Mr. Burke could remember.

"I remember that paint job on the county water tower that he did. Impressive. Colonel Rodman and General Evans didn't seem to think so.

"Come on, we'll check the lay-of-the-land! We can go on from the teachers' lounge to my office. You have a class visitation schedule."

Being at a private boys' school gave Emmett a peculiar sense of excitement that flooded his mind with memories of Longstreet, the peculiar bond of school friends and the fine line between regulations and one's own sense of freedom. It made his throat flutter.

Walking into the library, they saw evidence of smoking at midnight on campus and mischief. Several magazine racks had been disturbed, with periodicals strewn about the floor. In some places the common library fare had been replaced with different magazines - muscle car sports, body building, girlie magazines, a copy of *Das Kapital* with the back cover missing, and three Playboy center folds, each open and spread in full glory.

Emmett began to remember his own high school escapade.

A motley sign hung across the check-out desk that read, "Seniors '74 - Sophomores Sux, Wig-Out, Fuck the Coyote!" and other less attractive comments on poster board. The furniture had been rearranged in jumbles, easy chairs up on sofas, several study desks balanced upside down four tall in odd cubist designs. A large ceramic chandelier hung from an arched ceiling with ribs of toilet paper hung over the ceiling beams flowing away from the apex. Dangling from several lights hanging from the ceiling beams were what appeared to be wet bags, leaving the message if one disturbed any bag, the contents would spill something gross. What was inside was a mystery.

"Damn, this is a war zone!" exclaimed Mr. Burke.

"Not hardly!" Emmett responded. "It's a mess! Big difference. Reminds me of home at Longstreet."

"Let's get out of here," exclaimed Burke. "I know we could be tied up with this for the weekend. A long time ago I learned to be scarce at certain times. What was your word for it back then? Evaporate. Now's the time to evaporate. God damn, I never wanted this to be in your visit to Hilliard School, home or no home."

Emmett had never heard Mr. Burke use strong language, but he could imagine that the old man could sling it pretty well if he wished.

Through the glass doors behind the check out desk, Emmett saw a woman with stiff iron hair speaking with great animation into the telephone.

"That is Sarah Franks, the librarian. She's letting the world know that her domain has been desecrated. She'll take it personally and be mad at every one for two weeks. She owns the place and lets boys have it if they are out of line. A totalitarian bibliophile!"

"It isn't personal, sweetheart...." Sam tossed his words toward her as she sat on the phone in her glass encased office, unable to hear him.

The boys pushed through the glass library doors, bounding with high excitement.

His forceful voice inspired their departure. Several of the boys looked at him with stony faces, as one muttered, "Yes, sir!"

Emmett curiously enjoyed the whole affair. He knew exactly what was going on - it was instinct. In a flash he saw himself among these furtive, lurking fellows - he, the one who adored Raymond Kingsley, the unforgiven sorehead, the disciple, baptized of the devil, a holder of grudges, who lived out in the dark to come alive and dare to get even for Kingsley's dismissal. He had been one among many, long ago. Now, on the other side of misplaced merriment, he watched the gazers, their appalling rush of near discovery, and the attraction of moving about with daredevil infamy among peers. It had been an exquisite plan, and now the rush of wild accomplishment. He was attracted to the exhilaration of surprise - the magnetism of danger. It penetrated every fiber of his being as he stood contemplating the prank.

A long day awaited. Visits to classes and a loud lunch. All seniors had been herded to the performance hall and harangued about their prank. Later, Harry Parsons loaned Emmett some sweat pants and a teeshirt, so he could go to the practice to observe for a second time.

Emmett spent thirty minutes with Sam Burke before making his way to the field. Sam referred to his office in the academic building as The Eagle's Nest. It was cluttered with books, a long double-high bookshelf and a wall hung with pictures of former students, ball teams, and even one of the General Longstreet statue that stood on the front campus of the old school. He had a picture of an old ballplayer, autographed, "To friend, Sam. Enos Slaughter."

"You may not have realized it at Longstreet, or even later, but good schools foster students who sometimes tweak the nose of the authorities. That library sign is a tweak. The message is subtle, but sent, nevertheless.

"'Fuck' isn't a subtle word!" said Emmett.

"Not that word! That is an ignorant word with little meaning. The library sign, the brown coyote! You saw that, didn't you. Mr. Jeter's mascot, I call it. You will find, today, our glorious leader in a state of, what shall I call it? Unrest! He has to sort out the sheep's clothing, maintain the decorum despite the antics, and deal with a funeral. He will either rise or fall, dress himself in calm urbanity, or be cursed by them all. Kids are hoping for the curse. He'll give the discipline to the Dean, poor guy, hoping some sense can be learned from this.

"These kids have been struck down by the death of their friend, the coach. Now they want a display, prankish distraction, one of vigor and mystery. It is a reassurance that there is life here among us school relics, the authorities, whose lives have no basis save that which young minds observe on campus and challenge.

"You know, Emmett, I had a teacher, when I was young, who said in great schools students made them great places to learn and challenging places to teach. Good advice."

He smiled. "Jeter is good. Great pedigree. Daniel Jarvis Jeter, Yale graduate, swimmer, firm, sometimes dogged, but consistent leader, many years on the job here. He knows about good school atmosphere. A man of no secrets, a good listener, yet he will be challenged to show the youngsters he is alive, and the school well.

"You'll like him, but don't be deceived by the outward displays of good humor. He's a thinker, he plays chess, and these games of boys have meaning. Nose to the ground most of time, stalking. They call him 'predator.' Apt name. So he dares to display a coyote in his office. Sometimes, he will show himself to the boys. He knows far more about young men than Colonel Rodman ever hoped to know."

Emmett was awed by this speech. "How do you do that? You

characterize things so well. You could do that in class when I was a kid. It's a talent to be admired."

"Oh, please. Sir!" Burke replied strongly. "I said that I'm a relic. I've seen it for years and years. I know the adolescent mind. Rebellious, quizzical, devious, and marvelously open. Young men have very quick sentiments, and fleeting opinions. You should be learning that yourself. Once it was you on the rambunctious end of the challenge you laid down."

Emmett smiled at the admonition. "I teach at a public high school. I fought in the war. You pluck me out of the blue and thrust me into Hilliard School, a place full of issues: from football coach to this prank, these people. It is a bit overwhelming. I can manage football. It is organized chaos with periods and halftimes. I've been in combat, which has its own organized chaos that plays for keeps. Seeing all this… experiencing all this…never been into anything like this where I get to watch, listen and decide which chaos I want to help manage or change. I'm just a coach. Here, you teach, advise, coach and you manage the place. Public school management is so indifferent. It's almost 'close your door and do what you can with the kids you are assigned.'"

Mr. Burke laughed at him in a soft breathy way. "You know what you are, Emmett?"

"I'd love to hear."

"You are a humble man, blatantly honest, and you are congenial. These are endearing traits that make others want to be led by you. People come to you, seek you out, Emmett, and they listen. The beauty is you don't dwell on it, or realize it at all. You are without the grand ego.

"Just remember graciousness, affability and humility are the best wrappers I know of for a person to possess. Those traits hold off the crap of the world, which falls on us all. It helps to possess strengths of character, to be quick in the mind, and to stand up tall. Colonel Rodman, that bastard of our shared past, wanted to rain his crap on the world around him. He tried you, Emmett.

You tried him, you endured with the help of loyal friends, who you earned. You won. You learned."

Sam gazed at his books, the decor in his office, and looked seriously at Emmett.

"This place, Mr. Jeter, Nathan Kuballe, the Roystons, Sissie Waters, people you met last night are very good folks. I know that. I told Jeter to bring you here because you know how to lead naturally and to win with people. I also told him you've been tested."

He swallowed the last of his cup of lukewarm coffee. "You went to Vietnam, a soldier."

The question snatched Emmett away from the fountain of philosophy he was pondering.

"Vietnam? We were talking about my character and the school's needs?"

"We were. Now, we are talking about Vietnam. War was chaos so rampant it will suck a person in and grind him, or maim him. I saw it in Europe a long time ago. Chaos, however, wears many masks, the bloody kind, conniving and wicked, the inexplicable kind, and the subtle kind, even the mental kind; nevertheless, it is chaos. I know you endured that and survived. Hilliard is small potatoes comparatively.

"Where did you serve in Viet Nam?"

"In the Central Highlands mostly, and in the southwest over near the border between Laos and Cambodia. An Loc. Dak To. Up north."

"Chaos?" Burke asked.

"Worse! Hell." Emmett glanced at his watch. He didn't like discussing the war. It wasn't the same as a school prank.

Burke said nothing, and several seconds lapsed.

"My war experience is a loathsome subject," Emmett said and ran his fingers through his hair. "I saw chaos, specialized, and, indifferent shit, Mr. Burke. Vietnam to me is not a nice subject for remembrance or discussion. At times it slaps me in the face to remember what I did, and what I saw. People aren't ever ready for that kind of chaos. This is different, a lot different. It isn't Vietnam."

"I know," said Burke. "It's the mask. The world isn't ready yet for the truth about Vietnam. Such experiences you had are unfortunate keepsakes, and not yet the fountainheads for discussion or life lessons on the grander scale. Yours may never be. But, it was life, wasn't it? Raw and horrible. You survived it for reasons you must discover. Some ways, they might make you stronger if you have the will to be tested in a less frantic environment where you have time to listen and watch."

Mr. Burke narrowed his eyes with a look of both wisdom and apology. "Respect for the naked truth exists in silence of the mind and memory until it has to come out. That is also honorable."

He picked up his briefcase and turned to the door.

"You and I better head out. I've got some notes on my desk, and you've got an appointment to keep. It's great to be with you again, Emmett!" He extended his hand and gave Emmett a warm shake. "Good luck decision making."

"Thanks," said Emmett, who pitched his paper cup into the trash can. "What was that you said back then, when we were getting ready to tackle a tough subject, 'Once more unto the breach....'"

"Henry V!" said Burke. "Read it. Story of your life, perhaps."

"Maybe, I got another," said Emmett, "A poem that I remember bits from all the time, and I can't recall the title. It said something about going to "prepare a face to meet the faces that you meet...."

"Ha!" said Burke. "T.S. Eliot. What? Are you 'Prufrock'?"

"I am today preparing the face."

Sam smiled.

Thirteen

Because I could not stop for death...
— Dickinson

After a morning of class visitation, Emmett received a note to come by Dan Jeter's office. He thought that was odd, but the day had been full of surprises, especially with the antics of the Senior Class prank. He was met in the reception area by a pleasant office manager, Miss Lillian Kowlowicki. She introduced herself as Miss Lillian, and told Emmett that Mr. Jeter's schedule had been shifted considerably because of his need to deal with school discipline, and the sudden death of a member of the Board of Trustees.

Mr. Jeter wanted to know if Emmett would feel comfortable about staying the weekend for a visit with him, his wife and members of his family at their lake home retreat just north of town? They could arrange for an evening flight back to Atlanta on Sunday if he could agree. She apologized, saying that one never knew when things around the school would break loose. "It has been a challenging time."

They chatted for several minutes, as she demonstrated the similar cordiality he had found among others. She had been hired by Mr. Jeter immediately after his appointment as a Headmaster. Her admiration for the faculty, for "dear Hal Rivers," was tremendous. Emmett relayed his background and mentioned his having been a student of Mr. Burke's. She liked that. "Mr. Sam is a favorite around here, so knowledgeable and wise. He sets such a good example for the boys," she said.

He knew of the change of plans. Now it was solid that he would go to the lake house. Before that he would attend a bit of the spring football practice, then meet Maggie Jeter, to pick up her niece, and head out. She would meet him at the Headmaster's office. Dan would come in the morning.

"Mr. Jeter is hoping this works out and apologizes for this change in plans and his not being able to spend 'school time' with you. It just can't be helped," she added.

Emmett said he understood.

On the field that afternoon, Emmett again stood transfixed by the fluttering wreath at the end of the track, when he noticed the boys begin a slow jog around the track. They kept in a tight group as they loped along, each player carrying his helmet in his left hand. He followed their movement thinking that Nathan Kuballe had orchestrated their warmup that included this jog. Most coaches knew that jogging was best done after some stretching. Nevertheless, the boys, whose ranks swelled upwards to forty or more, were moving now toward the south end of the field, making their way toward the pine trees and the evergreen wreath with the fluttering ribbon.

There, the group paused in a kind of semi-circle, then as if on command, they knelt in unison. Nathan Kuballe stood out above them with his back to the field, facing the trees. There was silence, and the yellow ribbons fluttered brightly. On a signal that Emmett didn't hear the boys were off to form up for a warm-up.

"Coach Kuballe makes them do that twice at every practice," said Coach Royston. "Says it makes the boys a better unit. Shows respect."

To come in and remake this program would make it hard for anyone - unless it was Nathan Kuballe, Emmett thought.

Stan Robinson, a coach Emmett had not met, produced a clipboard with a practice schedule on it. "Coach, let me fill you in on what we plan today." He reviewed in some detail the practice for the afternoon, showing him the defensive sets, and several of the offensive schemes planned for the coming year. He described a few of the players on the line and in the offensive backfield. Robinson was enthusiastic about a rising senior quarterback and a fullback.

"We have the opportunity to run some option out of the Veer," Robinson said. "Watch us work on some sets. I'm going to take the backs for the next thirty minutes. Kuballe has the defensive line, and Coach Royston handles the defensive backs. Blackmon has the wide outs. We'll do some work with the offensive line at the end of the practice and put things together for about twenty minutes as it gets on toward 5:30. Chime in any time."

"I haven't met Coach Blackmon," said Emmett.

"Ah, I didn't realize that. I thought Nathan introduced you to all the coaches. Blackmon is over there. Played at West Texas State. He's an easy guy to know."

Emmett felt comfortable. Obviously, Kuballe had instructed Coach Robinson to be the liaison. He had an easy manner. Emmett watched him corral his boys, trot them over to him and introduce each of them one by one, telling them, "Coach Peterson is looking at The Hilliard School to help us next season. He wants to see you do your stuff. So let's get after it."

It was good, Emmett felt, to get to the field, the place he loved to be. He turned his back on the fluttering ribbons.

The last boy to shake Emmett's hand was stocky, bold, and handsome fellow.

"Coach, this is Alan McConnell. He'll probably be our quarterback this fall."

Emmett felt the boy's firm handshake. His eyes met Emmett's.

"Coach Peterson, it's nice to meet you," he said.

In his eyes Emmett saw a blend of curiosity and respect, maybe a small flicker of apprehension.

"Good to meet all of you," said Emmett. "Time to get after it!" he said.

"Yes, sir!" they responded in unison.

Old familiarity, old excitement, and new turf.

Tight spirals winged from Alan, the quarterback, to some fleet young backs. Emmett took it all in - the energy, the thud of pads, grunting efforts, the hand slaps to the helmet, shouts of encouragement, and loud instructions from coaches - the minutes flew past.

Four groups were hard at work. Emmett stood closest to the backs watching, assessing their abilities. The pungent odor of sweat and toil mingled with the atmosphere of the afternoon. After a brisk forty minutes, the backs were given a water break, and Coach Robinson came over to Emmett.

"You can see, Coach, there are a few horses in this group." He showed his pride, for all eight of the players had abilities, and he knew it.

"The McConnell kid is a stud!' said Emmett."Fairly good footwork and strong arm, sort of exceptional."

"Oh, the kid can play. His temperament is great. Very coachable. You only have to tell him once. You saw the zip he puts on the ball, but you should see him run in the open field. First day out I got him at 4.5 in the 40. Five days later, he ran a 4.4."

"Wow!" exclaimed Emmett, "that's moving. I was watching his take-away from the center," said Emmett. "He needs to control his steps. With the speed of the other backs, he needs to distinguish the routes that are shallow from those that are deep. Seems like he takes a three step drop on a long route and a five on a short."

"You want to mention that to him in this next set?" said Robinson.

"No, no. It's okay. I'm only a visitor," said Emmett.

"Hell, yes, say it. It'll let the other kids know you were really watching.

Emmett held his ground. "You can say it and mention I noticed. Keep me off the hot seat."

The practice resumed, and Emmett was keen. Alan was alternating with a freshmen quarterback who looked as though his knee pads were on his shins. Three times Emmett watched Alan vary his steps, falling into the habit of dropping back without awareness of his steps. Each time, however, the ball was tight and flat to the receiver. Several of the long balls, however, arrived before the receiver or sailed high.

When there was break in the action, Coach Robinson walked over to Alan and spoke to him. Alan jogged over to Emmett.

"Thanks for the tip. You mean I should use 5 step drops on the long ball?"

"Sure, give the receiver time to make his route and his cuts. Short steps on short throws. Defender can't reach 'em, especially when they're back shoulder throws." Emmett smiled at him. "I'm glad the baseball coach didn't recruit you. You got a good arm."

"Thanks!" Alan showed little outward pleasure.

Alan returned to his throwing. Emmett let him throw five or six balls, then stepped over to him when there was a pause.

"You get the ball out fast. Speed is everything. On those short routes, those flairs, you can handle easily in three steps because you get the ball off quickly. Speed makes things happen."

The ball never varied in height but went tight and straight into the easy reach of the receiver. Alan shot a quick glance at Emmett and went to a new set. Each time his delivery improved. Emmett watched for a few minutes, then turned his attention elsewhere on the field.

Kuballe, who had not acknowledged Emmett's presence, had his linemen gathered around him and was in high and animated conversation with them. He ordered six linemen to circle up in a bulldog drill.

"Alright, Ballard I want you to be in the middle. React to a charging lineman, block him, hold him off before another charges from a different direction.

"You got to stay low and pivot. Keep your eyes moving."

On Kuballe's whistle a player fired out. Ballard stumbled and was knocked to into the middle of the ring"

"Get up, get up!"

A second lineman charged knocking Ballard backwards. Another spun the boy around, and he fell on his side. His opponent caved in on top of him.

"Ballard!" barked Kuballe, "How many times have I told you to get low, son. This is war out here. You get low, and you get leverage. Now, do it, and you won't get knocked on your ass. Get low! Get low!"

Tension mounted among the other players, who chanted their encouragement to the charging lineman selected; the smaller Ballard braced himself and squared off again.

"Get low!" Kuballe hollered. "Get low!"

Again they smacked each other, and Ballard caved with his opponent on top.

"If you fire out, you can come up under him and control him long enough. He is stuffing you, son; beating your butt. Get out of there! Come on, get out of there! I need people who want to play this game."

"Cox, get your ass in there. Show us how to do it. Get your tail down in time, come under him. A little fart like you can stall a bigger man long enough to let a back get by. You've got to anticipate, son."

The whistle blew. Cox executed the drill, and held off the bigger lineman.

"See that, Ballard. See that!"

Emmett felt chills rising on his neck as he watched. He knew the feeling from before, but this was a killing field.

Low banked clouds hid the sun. The smack of leather. He crouched, hands on knees, listening to the echoes of Kuballe's exhortations - "Get low. Drive with your feet. Lift! Drive! Damn it, you people are gonna get crushed. Get up under your man. Fire out. Fire! Now, drive! That's it. Now turn 'em! It's war, men!"

Emmett was on his knees, watching, heard the grunts, the slap of leather ricocheting. He remembered the impact, sense of having driven into a man. How he crumbled on top of him. *Air whistling, then exploding, scrambling, clawing at the earth, the thud. The stunning thud of collision.*

He struggled with his own breath, watching the bulldog drill, *tangles of vines and legs.*

Ballard fell next to him hard from a blow. The boy writhed to recover his breath.

The lineman, who stood over Ballard, reminded Emmett of himself, how he had stood once in moment from long ago.

"Are you hurt, Ballard?" demanded Kuballe. "He knocked the wind out of you, son. Breathe easy. In and out. I've told you repeatedly to stay low. You need to get in the gym."

The boy was straining. Emmett watched seven others, huddle in a knot looking down. He heard a voice say, "Don't hit him with your forearm. You'll kill him!"

Who was really saying this? Maybe he heard himself say it.

The boy lay there, glassy eyed and panting.

"*Don't hit him with your forearm. You'll kill him!*" echoed inside Emmett.

"You trying to get a better view of the practice, Coach Peterson?"

The familiar voice came down from the sky.

Sam Burke stood over Emmett and spoke to him. "Kuballe can get all worked up with his linemen."

Embarrassed, Emmett scrambled up. He had been down on all fours, back where he was eight years before in a clearing where there were six comrades and a Vietnamese boy dead at his feet. For a brief, unsettled moment, he had been back there.

Burke saw the confusion. "Are you okay?"

"Sure, I'm fine."

Emmett knew that maybe he was not fine because he had the stale taste of war in his mouth. He had been somewhere else. His mouth was dry.

"Texas sun can be a little more severe than Atlanta sun, sometimes, "said Burke."

They decided to call it a day before the end of practice and the concluding ritual. Emmett was glad of that.

Sam told him of another change of plans. He was to meet Mrs. Jeter now at 6PM at the hotel and drive via the airport to pick up her niece, then ride up to the Jeter lake house. He would be interviewed there by Mr. Jeter on Saturday, fly back on Sunday.

"Unusual," said Sam, "but it will be a nice time. I understand his niece has the same name as your old Longstreet girlfriend."

"Really," said Emmett. "Coincidence."

"Mr. Peterson, the world can be a small place sometimes. You can get a shower, and I'll drive you to the hotel, so you can get your things and check out."

Emmett could not shake the strangeness of the moments watching the practice, the nightmare feeling.

He stood in the warm shower for a long time and went over the practice and tried to shove from his mind the memory of the patrol where they lost Racine.

Yeah, he had killed the guy. Yeah, it was a shot to the body like he had been taught when he was in peewee ball, but he was pumped. It was a war.

If he hadn't hit the guy, hadn't poured all his adrenaline into it, the guy would have killed him.

He let the shower water pour over him and turned his face into it to wash away the memory.

It was a football practice where you've been a hundred times. Yeah, it's a new place. And, yeah, it is weird to be taking a look at a job opened by a guy who died on that field. He didn't die in a war. He did a dumb-ass thing.

Put this stuff in perspective. Make a face 'to meet the faces that you meet.' Like Burke said. 'It's the mask.'

Well, find it and wear it, Emmett.

Some of Harry Parson's cologne made him feel better.

The weekend at Hilliard was just unfolding.

Fourteen

Two roads diverged in a yellow wood,
And sorry I could not travel both
And be one traveler, long I stood
And looked down one as far as I could
To where it bent in the undergrowth....

— Frost

Emmett and Maggie established a quick rapport on the drive. She was easy-going, having admitted that Dan Jeter's schedule was like that of a busy squirrel. "His days are never regular days, but full of twists and turns. This one was especially crazy."

"I saw that," said Emmett. "My own time has been pretty intense. I didn't even focus on the fact I hadn't really spoken with the man who invited me here. This will be good, and maybe quieter."

"Oh, the lake house is wonderful. Harry Parsons and his wife are coming up tonight. Harry loves to cook. He treats Barbara like a grandchild. You'll meet Britches, his wife. She's a special person, and she'll check on you, so be ready for that. She might ask you what size socks you wear."

The airport crowd increased at the Houston terminal when the plane was on the ground. An attendant extracted herself from behind the counter, opened a door to the tunnel to the plane. Out of the tunnel came a stream of passengers, women with tired children, some passengers dragging roller luggage, and military personnel, disheveled and sleepy, rushing to make connections on out west.

The lull was the cue for Maggie to move to where passengers would emerge. Emmett followed. What had he gotten himself into? He would let Maggie greet her niece and call him over. He straightened the collar of his Polo shirt, shuffled his shoulders, and looked down at his own pants. He felt conspicuous, like and an ill-prepared actor who had no time to learn his lines.

"There she is!" exclaimed Maggie.

Emmett watched the tunnel exit. A large, perspiring woman heaved her way up the incline. He saw no one else until a slender blonde emerged from the corridor. To him, she looked vaguely familiar. She wore camel hair slacks and a loose navy blue blouse. A handbag was slung over her shoulder. She didn't notice him at all. She moved easily, and Emmett followed her familiar motion into the light. When she saw her Aunt Maggie, she beamed.

"Barbara Lynne! Hi! Over here!" Maggie waved.

Emmett felt his chest tighten. His heart rate quickened.

Barbara Lynne waved.

Emmett stood with his legs embedded in the floor. He heard the lap of lake water and the swaying of trees from a long time ago.

After embracing her niece, Maggie turned to Emmett.

Emmett and Barbara Lynne saw each other. A lingering…recognition and… trees beside a lake…faces…eyes…a possibility…a likelihood.

"Emmett," Barbara said with a tentative voice. "Emmett Peterson!"

"Hi, Barbara."

***

Up at the Jeter place, Harry stood over a large smoker with a chimney, as Maggie wheeled the Mercedes into the yard. He had driven out early and put brisket on the grill to slow-cook.

Emmett stood for a moment holding Barbara Lynne's two bags and wondered how such a coincidence had occurred. He had traveled to interview for a job, not a reunion. Barbara walked into the cabin ahead of him.

Harry watched the two young people. The coach was tall and muscular. He followed the woman he hadn't seen since high school. Had to be ten or twelve years.

From behind them, Britches, mouthed to Harry, "They know each other." Rubbing his hands on his pants, he shook the hand of the Coach. "I seen you out at school a lot, ain't I?"

"One of the few folks I've spoken to at length," smiled Emmett.

"Just throw everything beside the fireplace, Coach," said Maggie. "We can decide on sleeping arrangements later. The day is so grand. Why don't you two go for a walk. Let Barbara stretch her legs. You can get reacquainted. This is too unreal." She beamed at them, and turned to Britches with raised eyebrows and a triumphant smile.

The reunited lovers looked at one another and laughed. Neither seemed to know what to say.

As they walked down a path to the lake, Emmett held on to Barbara Lynne's hand and thought it felt just as he remembered from fifteen years ago, small and soft. He thought he smelled her hair, a scent he knew from movies and popcorn and times under shade trees on her campus.

After a few steps, she giggled. "Raymond Kingsley said this would happen."

"Kingsley?"

"Raymond Kingsley, the Ghost Who Walks. Your idol."

Emmett just shook his head.

Back at the house, Maggie worked in the kitchen, checking the refrigerator and searching through the cabinets. Britches, who looked after the place, had stocked everything, and put place settings out. They quickly added another one for their guest.

"Everything is spotless," Maggie said. "I couldn't manage this without you."

Everyone at Hilliard knew Harry and Britches Parsons, who lived a mile or two from the lake and a dozen miles from the school. Britches let Harry work at the school. He loved to fish and used the lake property to do so. Sometimes, when there was a night game, he would stay in town. They had looked after the lake place for more than twenty-five years and had known Dan Jeter since before he married Maggie, or took the headmaster's job.

"Why don't I show you the dock?" said Barbara Lynne.

Emmett was in tow.

"Aunt Maggie will send Harry after us when supper's ready. He and Britches will be curious anyway. They are so funny. This whole thing is ridiculous!" They turned down another path through the woods.

Back at the house, Harry was checking the smoker. His figure appeared in the window above the kitchen sink where Maggie was chopping vegetables for salad.

Harry yelled through the window. "I put a big brisket on slow at 7:30 this morning. It's done enough. Let her rest in a cooler for a few minutes. We can eat anytime. Britches cooked up some beans." He heaved himself up onto a step on the porch stoop, and said loudly, "So, Ms. Maggie, how you like that new fellow?" He pulled out a pipe and dampened the tobacco in preparation for a smoke.

"Oh, I like him. I'm just bowled over he knew Barbara Lynne from high school, when she was a freshman at the woman's college." Her voice went almost to a whisper. "I think they were serious back then," she said.

"Serious? You mean like serious serious?" he exclaimed. "Young folks know more about serious these days than we were." Harry knew there was intrigue in the kitchen among the women.

"Harry Parsons, don't let your imagination ruin it," she cautioned. She pulled a bread pan from the warming oven and moved them to the porch railing to cool.

"How much you know about this coach?" Harry asked.

Maggie knew that Harry fancied himself a cool reader of personality.

"I know that Sam Burke recommended him highly. He works in Atlanta as a teacher and coach. He served in Vietnam. He's a very polite young man." She never looked at him. "And, he's handsome."

"Had to be a pretty special fellow to invite him up here to meet the niece!"

"Dan is the one who invited him. I had nothing to do with it. Harry, you think too much."

"And, that boy knew Barbara Lynne. Dan had to have known. It's too good. Britches is going to get a kick out of this one. She will pester them two to-a-month- from-Sunday. She'll say it's just like in the dang movies. I got to get ready for this because I'm going to hear about it five or six ways."

Harry climbed up from the first porch step and knocked his pipe on the porch railing, then went back down the steps and out to the grill.

"Thanks for doing the brisket, Harry. "You and Britches have to stay with us and help us eat it, and, of course, chaperone."

"I think we can do that. Just ask the boss."

"I already have," said Maggie. "One thing. Stay away from the dock!"

The lake was a long, thin crease in a limestone rock-fall, fed by a creek at the north end. From the wooded path below the house, the lake stretched for a mile into two directions. A dock of gray planks jutted into the water for forty feet with a bench on the end of it. Across the lake on the opposite bank, a meadow behind a stand of rocks spread up a hill toward a stand of trees.

Emmett pondered the inlets and coves as his eyes followed the shoreline. He followed Barbara Lynne out to the bench, where they sat down.

"I just love this place," she said. The breeze lifted her hair. "What are the odds, Emmett, of our meeting like this?"

"Inevitable, I think. In the cards, like Kingsley said." He smiled at her. "The Ghost knows all." He laughed.

Sitting there was easy. He turned to watch the woodcocks floating on the water. "This is an incredible place. When I thought of you, I always saw you in places like this, the lake, the trees. Remember the lake?"

"Of course," she said softly. "You said 'inevitable.' You really think so?"

They both stared beyond the water, feeling the breeze and watching the bobbing woodcocks. Water lapped against the pilings of the dock. Twittering swallows swooped and dove, skimming the surface, then disappearing and flying upward.

"Tell me," she said. "Where have you been? Doing what?"

Emmett safeguarded his emotions. "The script in the movie says that when the man comes over the fence into the girl's backyard he isn't supposed to be first one to talk."

"Oh, really?"

"Oh, really," he said. "She's supposed to confess how lonely she is doing chores, cleaning house, ironing, going to church meetings, singing in the choir, and stuff. She's longing to escape and become the wife of some house painter-handyman, and live behind a picket fence and keep cats, five of them.

"Remember the man who came in on the westbound train, jumped off, and went looking for work in this small town. He saw this blonde woman standing at a clothesline and paused outside the fence to look at her, then asked her for a drink of water. The music swells. They meet, and it is magic."

Barbara Lynne smiled at him and took up the description. "She was wearing a printed apron and holding a dish towel. Isn't that how it happened in the movie?"

"Of course," Emmett said. "I told you it is in the script. William Holden, Kim Novak, *Picnic*. We saw that, remember?"

She looked down at the water. "You might be teasing me!" she exclaimed.

"What does that mean, 'teasing'? It was our first movie."

"What I remember is the popcorn and all," she laughed. "It was a pretty romantic movie, wasn't it?"

The breeze lifted her hair again. She brushed it out of her face. She was pretty.

"You bought me so much pop corn." Her voice was light and easy.

"So..." he said, "you tell me about you, first."

"Okay," she began, "I am a nurse in Jacksonville. I finished at Wesleyan in Macon, and went into nurse's training. I've worked at the Medical Center in Jacksonville in the pediatric ward for six years. Now, I'm an operating room supervisor in neonatal care. I have an apartment and a cat named Pollack. I guess, my life is rather simple. I play tennis in a ladies group on Saturday mornings, and I visit my folks in Macon."

A swallow made a swift pass right in front of them. His darting made tiny ripples on the water.

"Then, that's it?" exclaimed Emmett. "No adventures, no proposals, no desperate love affairs or trips to exotic places? No boyfriends?" He smiled. "I would have thought that Barbara Lynne Jenkins would have swept some young intern off his feet."

She laughed. "Maybe a few. Nothing special. Yet! Now, it's your turn. I want the full Emmett Peterson story, adventures, thrills and spills!"

Emmett felt like standing up.

"Me. Well, after you left and went to Macon, I graduated. I...." He stopped abruptly and explored the banks beyond the dock. "I went into the priesthood." He tried to be serious, but he really couldn't. "I lasted about two weeks. I did, however, commit myself to a lifetime of celibacy and quiet. I never spoke for seven years. Seven being a sacred number. I visited monasteries around the country, but they expelled me for bad grammar and over sleeping. So, I came out to Texas to change my life, when I met your aunt in the Houston airport in the bar. She said, 'I'm seeing my niece. She is nice. You would like her.' Here I am."

He looked at her, waiting for the familiar elbow or slap on the shoulder.

It came, harder than he remembered, the slap on the shoulder.

"You haven't changed a bit, liar!"

She loved his tease, how his eyes danced. "Be serious. About as monkish or priestly as you ever got was at Longstreet when your daddy made you go there to keep you from reform school. Tell the truth. What have you *really* done? Tell me you got married and have seven children."

"Just five actually!"

When she laughed at him, she looked like the school girl he had known. He could barely contain his desire to touch her.

"Will you be serious!" she demanded.

"Okay, okay! You're right. No monasteries or priesthood. No children. I was married for two years. Divorced."

He watched her reaction. She was listening intently.

"You were married?"

"Yes," he said. "I was in college playing football. The school closed. I married a girl I was dating, and got drafted immediately. I went to Vietnam, came home, and divorced. We were together for about eight or nine months total, not counting the war."

For a moment, the sky was sunless.

"Then, I went back to school in Massachusetts, got a Master's Degree, and now teach and coach in Atlanta. Maybe not simple, but that's the true story. I'm interviewing with your uncle." He smiled in a way that made his face crack with the effort.

He waited for her response.

"And no kids," she said.

"No kids. Don't even have a dog."

Barbara almost laughed at that last point. "Well, you are an open book, Emmett."

"I got stuff inside. Don't worry. Your uncle invited me to interview for a job at Hilliard. It is a rare chance, I think. Tough job, considering circumstances of the opening, but I'm hoping."

A strange mixture of mirth and desire made him splatter on the inside when he looked at her.

"And, you are serious?" she said.

"As a judge. I went to the war, Barbara. I saw it up close. That was a long time ago. I'm a coach now. It's what I want to be. I'm a junior varsity coach, aspiring to be a head coach. Sam Burke taught me at Longstreet. He got me the interview. We've kept up."

The stuff of his past kept rolling out of him. "I've been a light-hearted guy most of my life. More serious now, I think. This trip is a real eye-opener, the private school and all. Like nothing I'm familiar with except the football."

Barbara gazed across the lake. "That's good, Emmett. You were a great player. You found yourself. I knew you were married because Raymond told me, and I knew about the college shutting down. Later, he told me you were drafted and serving in the Army. I figured, maybe, it was Vietnam."

"You talked to Raymond about me?"

"I called him after the Longstreet thing. We got to be telephone friends."

"You didn't know Raymond when we were kids. At least, I didn't think you did." Emmett was amazed.

"No," said Barbara, turning to him. "I didn't know him, but I felt like I did. You talked about him all the time. When I thought of you, I'd call him. He sells jail bonds and life insurance. I know that. Honestly, I haven't talked to him in several years. I thought you had just moved on."

"Kinglsey never mentioned any of this, the bastard!" exclaimed Emmett. "I wonder if he ever sold himself a jail bond?"

"I almost called your parents when you were in Vietnam," she said, "but didn't because I knew you were married. It would have seemed awkward to them. Maybe, even to me."

"You thought about me?" Emmett felt warm.

"Of course, I thought about you. You were in a dangerous place. I knew your mentality, how you pretended to be fearless. Of course, I was concerned. We had been close friends." She was looking straight at him.

Emmett's mind doubled back-and forth. He wanted to hug her. She was prompting him to love her again. Whisperings were finding their way deep inside of him.

"I wondered about how you felt about us," he said quietly.

"Oh, Emmett, you never would believe me about the lake incident, or that the affair between Rodman and Evans had anything whatever to do with us. You just had to blame yourself for slipping up on them. They were in the wrong. We were so scared of them in those last days before you finished school. It was just crazy. We just let it, what we had, drift apart too easily. I thought about that a lot, and thought of you for a long, long time."

She laid her hand on his, and looked deeply at him. "You know what?" she said softly. "We are at another lake right now. And, they are nowhere around." Her easy tone skimmed over time and dove into Emmett.

"So, all along you had called Raymond Kingsley, and he told you I married the dance hall queen, didn't he? I did that almost the same week I was drafted. I met her on a blind date. We lived together. I was mad about everything back then, parents, school situation, and being drafted. Maybe mad I lost you. The whole thing back then was a big mistake that turned into a mess when I returned from Vietnam. She asked me for a divorce the night I got back to the States."

"Oh, Emmett! I'm so sorry." she said.

"Yeah…I didn't hesitate to give her one. I spent the next five years getting myself together again, finishing my education. So, don't be sorry. Might be the best thing for me now that so much time has passed.

"Actually, I'd like to coach here at Hilliard. The school is great, and the surroundings." He turned and faced her, and she turned toward him. "It's so good to see you. This whole thing is just …."

She didn't allow him to finish, but touched his lips with her gentle fingers.

He wanted to kiss her.

"I'm so glad too," she said softly.

As he leaned toward her, her blouse brushed him.

A piercing whistle made them both jump.

"Supper time!" Harry cried, and was chuckling.

"Dammit," Emmett muttered.

"Come on," she said, pulling his arm around her and holding it there.

Fifteen

I don't think the King is Dead!
— Emmett Peterson

In the weeks that followed his trip to Lofton, Texas, Emmett drove three times to see Barbara Lynne in Jacksonville. To his mind, he belonged to her; she belonged to him. He would eventually marry her. He would bring her to Texas, though the wedding didn't occur until the early winter at Christmas.

The interim time became a healing field for him as Mr. Jeter called him seven days after his interview and offered him the job. He consulted Sarah and Robert Hughes, who told him in no uncertain terms to accept it.

"Why don't you come over tonight?" said Robert. "Sarah is smoking ribs. We'll get a case of beer and talk about the interview. Give you the proper etiquette to use on the Texas school people. By midnight you'll be so polished and polite even the First Lady would want you for an aide."

"Okay," Emmett said.

"Fine, six o'clock. Wear a tie!"

"A tie?"

"Coaches at private schools have to wear ties."

"They do? Maybe I don't want the job. No ties."

"Bring a tie," said Robert. "We'll decide how you look."

Sarah loved Emmett. She enjoyed him as he had swum his way back into their lives. Her personal goal became setting him up with single girls she knew, pushing him out of himself, helping him to enjoy life again. She had teased him into revealing his wit.

He delighted in telling her he had met someone. She could stop playing matchmaker.

When he revealed that it was Barbara Lynne Jenkins, Robert Hughes went nuts. "You called her? Somehow I knew this would happen. You are a bold, romantic son-of-a-bitch. Back in the old 'Barbara Lynne Zone!'"

He had to explain to his wife what the situation was.

"This girl tied Peterson in knots in high school, a beautiful girl from the college. He met her, and he turned into a sheep-dog. Followed her for a year. We got to drink to this, man!"

Beer loosened all of them considerably.

Emmett began to pose first as a head coach, who exercised all the lingo of the game.

"What do you think?" Emmett asked them. "Coach and teacher. Not bad!"

Robert and Sarah laughed at him as Emmett laughed at himself.

He wanted to conclude the evening by admitting he was frightened to death of the prospect of what the people at The Hilliard School might think of him.

"I'm a deathless bastard," he exclaimed.

Sarah and Robert scoffed at his distress.

For him, however, apprehension was quite genuine.

"You know what you must do, Emmett?" Robert said seriously, "Put a Volkswagen in their library! Show them how you planned it, and controlled everything. Lie about keys to the flagpole and pivot shoes.

"What on earth are pivot shoes?" Sarah asked.

"Pivot shoes are a joke Emmett made up for cadets who didn't know any better. You had to have special 'pivot shoes' when you marched. He got a few guys, who didn't know any better, to go to the shoe store and ask for them. Salesman were on to the joke and sold them more black shoes, required for the uniform. It was Emmett's big joke. He even sent a kid to the Commandant's office to apply for a 'Permit to Wear White Underwear.'"

"You were a rascal, Mr. Peterson!" exclaimed Sarah. "You guys are just nuts."

"Want to see my permit to wear white underwear?" Emmett exclaimed and winked at Robert.

After that rollicking evening, Emmett went to Cordele to visit his family. His dad had suffered from angina for the last several years; his parents had reconciled their differences upon his return from Vietnam, but he had still stayed away more than he should.

He spent an afternoon back at Longstreet, looking at two new buildings. They had replaced the old barracks where he had held court with the 'fish.' He did not drive to the school's lake property, but he took a photo of the Longstreet statue to match with Sam Burke.

Several weeks before he left for Texas to find a place to live, he met Barbara Lynne in Macon and drove with her to Cordele for two nights with his folks. He told Barbara how strongly he felt about their finding each other again. It was inevitable, he said, and told her he had loved her since the tenth grade in the movies.

The visit took on special meaning. The effects of his visits were a tonic for his family. His mother, especially, realized her dream of having a married son. He and his father embraced as they left.

On the way back, he pulled the car to the roadside and asked Barbara to marry him. Typical of Emmett. He made her get out of the car on the pretext of viewing a cotton field in full bloom. He knelt beside her and pledged his troth. She didn't hesitate to accept. He kissed her and held her until a passing car blew its horn at them.

In all these proceedings, Robert and Emmett met regularly for breakfasts. Emmett glowed.

"I feel so good," he told Hughes.

"You know what?" Emmett exclaimed one morning. "I don't think the King is Dead! As a matter of fact, he is very much alive and well."

"What are you talking about?" Hughes asked

"Raymond Kingsley, the The King! He lives in south Georgia. Sells jail bonds and life insurance. Barbara Lynne told me. I called him last night. He said to tell you to go to hell. So, Robert, my friend, 'Go to hell!'"

"That is certainly him," laughed Robert. "I hadn't thought about him until you came to town."

"Barbara told me she had phoned him several times to find out about me. I didn't tell you that, did I? So I finally called him. I stayed in touch with him while I was in Nam, and even after I got home. I liked talking to a ghost come alive. We talked for about an hour. I told him I was going to Texas, that I had found Barbara Lynn again. He seemed to know it, so she must have called him like I did.

"Look, I'm going down to see him. He has several kids and a wife! A bail bondsman in Vidalia! Amidst the onions and fertilizer!"

"Whoa!" exclaimed Robert. "I thought that Kingsley would be dead before he reached twenty-five. He'd be the one to go to Vietnam. I should have known hiding among the onions, the draft wouldn't find him. Anyway, he was the King once. King's have special dispensations, don't they? Divine rights!"

They laughed.

Emmett planned for the two of them to drive to Vidalia, take a whole day, have a reunion. They'd see Raymond, meet his wife and kids. "

"Just surprise his scrawny ass!" Emmett exclaimed.

One week later, they did it.

In five hours, they found Raymond, the red-faced, raw-boned replica of the hero of their youth, sitting behind a cluttered desk, an oscillating fan in his window, reading a back issue of *Truck and Driv*er magazine. His hair was thinning, fading yellow. His shirt was stained with perspiration. The sun had burned wrinkles around his eyes, and his jaw hung with loose flesh. He wore baggy khaki pants held up by a floppy, brown belt too long for his thin waist. A ring with many keys jangled from it. Thin like a fence rail, Kingsley had always possessed keen brown eyes, but one of his eyes appeared faded and washed out. It didn't move in its socket like his other eye and gave him a cock-eyed appearance.

When Emmett and Robert entered the room, he looked up. His face flushed with excitement and anticipation because they had called him from a service station forty miles up the road.

"You damned son of a bitches! Get in here!" he exclaimed. The profane greeting sent Emmett howling and wrestling his friend in a bear hug.

It had to have been fifteen years since the three of them had been together. No one really remembered, and no one really cared.

"Son of a bitch, if this ain't two wet puppies. I'll be damned! Look at you, old men. Robert Hughes, a teacher, you smooth-tongued bastard. I knew you back when.

"And Peterson! Crazy-assed! Like two old ghosts walking in the room. Pale as milk. Peterson, I remember you shining my shoes in that god-forsaken barracks at Longstreet. Whatever the name of that place was, it was a hell hole. You was a little scrawny bastard, who thought he was a linebacker. But, a pretty good one. And Robert Hughes! How old are you now? Must be about sixty-five! You were forty, fifteen years ago - old as hell! Son-of-a-bitch, it is good to see I am not growing older than I am. This is a treat. Set down. Set down!" He offered folding chairs. He flung the magazine into a corner.

For an hour, they stayed, listening to Raymond hold court on the fall of man. He felt he had to give his life's history, beginning with his first year home after expulsion from Longstreet, how angry his dad had been, how he had gotten into trouble trying to drive a bulldozer for fun on a construction lot, how the judge had given him probation. He went to work at the Goodall Medical liquid plant, checking vacuum seals, spent two years in junior college and earned an insurance license. He had a bout with alcohol for several years, then lost his eye in a boating accident, when he hit a dock water skiing.

"Damn near killed the girl I was with. Only jabbed a splinter in my eye.

Can't see out of it now. Got one more that still works good. God was pretty smart to give us organ pairs, eyes, ears, an' a couple a balls!"

Then, he met Lauren Margaret Nichols.

"First thing she did was hit me! Knocked me silly in the front seat of my own car. When I come to, I was in love with that woman. Rawboned love. Couldn't walk straight what I wasn't with her. Couldn't speak or make do without her. Drenched in love. That made me take stock of everything. Realized I had made monkey shit most of my life and played in it. If I weren't impersonating somebody, or lying to 'em, I was sneaking off to get drunk.

"She made me reproduce myself in a reformed fashion, like a make-over." Emmett and Hughes laughed at Raymond's honest story. It was distinctly Kingsley in rare form, his anointed-of-the-devil form, now reformed as a bail bondsman.

"I took stock of all that I done. Went to church, got myself baptized. And, I married her. Now I'm a deacon. Still full of sin. Some shit you don't live down. I know that God is watching old Raymond. He has made me a thankful human being!

"Best thing that ever happened to me is getting bailed out of that goddamned Longstreet Military prison, shedding that Rodman bastard. You get the Silver Star for busting that son-of-a-bitch's ass! He was fired for hosing that Evans woman." He waved his hand at Emmett.

"I almost put a bushel of corn cobs in his room one night with a whole tube of Vaseline, so he could put one up his ass one at a time. It wasn't much surprise to me when I heard he had tried to frame you and that girl.

"Banging Gloria Evans! You have to admit she might a' been a handful. Even you, Hughes, you thought she was a piece!

"Sorry-assed bastard Rodman. That was a real event there with Gloria Evans! God Almighty! Only thing at Longstreet I'm sorry I missed."

Kingsley was rolling.

"And Barbara Lynne. I wish I'd a-met her more. Talked on the phone a bunch a times. You know that? She was hung-up on you, Peterson. You realize she called here to know if you was alive and well. You was in her love-craw. What a fine piece of work she was, Peterson. She just loved you, son. A good woman is hard to find."

Emmett smiled.

Kingsley folded his thin arms on his desk and leaned into his stories.

"So, Emmett's got hisself a job teaching and coaching in Texas. Hughes, you remember how old Peterson could play football, stalk the middle of the line like a damn wild cat? You played some ball at college after Longstreet. I heard about that. Barbara Lynne wasn't the only one. I was checking up with the ones who counted to old Raymond."

His extravagance was his charm.

"It was just over a year after we left Longstreet I went to Vietnam, Raymond. You got my letters.

"Oh, hell, yes, I got them.," he said.

"Vietnam! Vietnam! God's little late century turd. I kept my ass clear out of that one. One-eyed jackass, an' I don't march, I told 'em! They said to me it don't matter. I could work at a desk. Real quick, I got my butt busy. Married Lauren and had babies. I hid them birth control pills on my honeymoon and told her that with the war on, the fertility rites were in season! How long we in that war, six years, ten years? Had one kid ever two years! One year in the chute; one year out! I got four babies, who could cry all at the same time. Their noise carried over to the courthouse to the Draft Board Office. I was ready for that, my man. Four fine girls. Each of them is eighteen months apart regular on the clock."

His eye twinkled. "If you behave yourselves, and don't drool in the plates at the lunch I'm gonna buy you, I'll introduce you to 'em."

Emmett and Robert were in stitches.

In the Tomb of the Soul 195

"They have reformed my mind, reformed my abilities, and changed my attitude. Little women will do that. And, their mother is the angel of Gawd. A real pretty, stout woman. Old Kingsley didn't marry no ugly, trashy woman, like you all thought he would. No sir, my man, no sir! I'm married to an angel of God!"

Emmett watched the ruddy face of Raymond Kingsley alive with storytelling.

"Kingsley, you have girls?" Emmett observed. "I thought you'd make boys!" hoping for another uprising.

"Boys!" exclaimed Kingsley. "What do you mean, 'make boys?'" He laughed raucously "I'm a stud all right; a natural, long-night, Brasstown-ball-stud! I'll tell you, even a brass-balled-stud like me can't call that boy-girl shot!"

They roared.

"The Lord Gawd in His infinite wisdom controls how they come out. I reckon He figured me for a gentle soul beneath this leather and sweat, which is the old me. He give me girls, and we ain't sad a bit about it. Beautiful girls. You'll see 'em."

Kingsley had not changed. There was the ribald rogue they had known.

Raymond took them to lunch, then drove them home to meet his wife, Lauren Margaret Nichols Kingsley. She was not the huge woman they had imagined, that Kingsley himself had alluded to, but beautiful, with dark straight hair down her back. She wore blue jeans and a white Polo shirt tucked in and loafers with no socks. She was gracious and gentle.

Emmett knew this was the angel of God Raymond had alluded to earlier. Her manner altered his disposition. In her presence he became gentle, quiet, focused, and serious.

"I want you to meet my baby, Marge. Named for her mother."

Raymond took Robert's arm and guiding his friends toward the side door porch.

"You can say hello to her while Lauren gets the others together. A little like herding up sheep. They come when you call or ring a bell."

Nandina bushes full of red berries surrounded the porch and made it shady. In the heat the cicadas sawed away in his yard, yet the porch was cool, and a giant pecan tree, growing ten feet from the side of the porch helped to make more shade.

Marge was seated in a metal chair with a tray in front of it. She was nine years old. Metal braces on her legs hung lamely down; her head was twisted permanently to the left at an angle, and she peered oddly at the three of them with squinted eyes. A distorted grin creased her face when she saw her father. She had been eating her lunch and much of it was spread on her mouth. A plastic apron she wore spread over a tee shirt with a 'Charley's Angels' logo on it partially covered her shorts. She made gurgling sounds and banged her spoon on the metal tray in a display of joy.

Quickly and gently, Raymond wiped her face and kissed her forehead.

"Hello, Margie. You are the best thing since ice cream. Yes, you are." Raymond's voice was soft and endearing. He bent toward her, unsnapped the apron, wiped her legs and removed the bowl of peaches she was eating.

"Say hello to two of my oldest friends. This is Mr. Hughes and Coach Peterson. I knew them when I was just a little older than you. I haven't seen them in a long time. They're grown up men now.

"This is Margie, the prettiest little girl in south Georgia."

Raymond stooped beside her stroking her hair, brushing it away from her face.

Margie grinned and waved her spoon in a circle. The noises she made were of ecstasy. All of her attention was on her father. She didn't turn to look at Emmett or Robert Hughes.

Emmett, trying to reconcile this moment, stood glancing first at the child then at Raymond Kingsley.

"She is doing so well eating her lunch here," said Raymond. He leaned close to her. "Have you been reading that book I brought you last night? You can read, can't you, dearie. This sweet thing reads all the time, then tells her daddy the stories, one smart girl. I bought her that tee shirt. She likes TV shows a lot.

"Don't you, Margie? You and Daddy watch them Charlie's Angels."

Margie's eyes batted with interest. She screwed her body up in the chair and banged her legs on the metal rings.

"She's got lots of personality. An' this girl can read and do math up a storm. We got this teacher from Special Education at the public school comes over here three times a week year-round to keep her up. Her momma and me have read to her since she was four days old. About four years ago she started doing it herself. Her right arm works pretty good, so she turns the pages okay. She loves that television. She has little motor skill problems, but it don't matter.

"Marge's is in the second grade too. Does beautiful work!"

Raymond's eyes shown with a special glow.

Emmett always thought of Kingsley as coarse and off-color. They had joked about it on the way to Vidalia. He had displayed it back in his office. At Raymond's home, Emmett saw a different side of his old friend, pride in his child, his special child. Emmett stood there letting necessary angels light up Raymond Kingsley, who had once been anointed by the devil, but changed now, burying that tempestuous self somewhere in the tomb of the soul.

"Coach Peterson, here, was a football player, Margie," Raymond said. "A real good football player. Now he is a coach. Mr. Hughes is a teacher. He teaches history. I hated history, but you like it don't you, Margie? Who invented the electric light? Tell em."

Margie waved her hand about and stammered. Her little blue eyes batted and seemed to burst from their sockets as she struggled to speak.

"Tee-Edison!" she blurted.

"She's something special. She don't forget nothing. Just last week we showed her this book of inventors, and she remembers them all. The speech therapy lady said to make her say the words and names. So we do it. Listen to this one.

"Who made the telegraph, Margie? Who invented the telegraph?"

Again she wound herself up in a small ball then burst out the word, 'Marr-cone-ee!"

They laughed.

"See what I mean. She knows 'em all. We only read it once, then she took that book and drove us nuts, hollering out names, and screaming for questions. She don't make many sentences yet, but she knows lots of words, and she laughs like hell."

"Hell! Hell! Not hell!" She pounded her spoon on the metal tray.

"She don't like it when I swear. Gets that from her momma. Lauren don't allow it either. We got this swear box. Daddy has to put a quarter in each time I cuss. Margie, she won't let me forget." He reached in his pocket and laid the quarter on her tray, and she smiled a twisted, ecstatic grin.

He stroked hair out of her face.

She tried to laugh and talk with us, but only sounds spewed out with a few words; nevertheless, they clearly communicated to Raymond Kingsley. His face glowed. Each of his admonitions to her were returned with animated expressions from this paraplegic child.

"She loves them Washington Redskins and that John Riggins. We watch pro-ball on Monday night regular. You like Howard Cosell, Margie?"

She banged her spoon on her tray, bobbing and weaving her torso.

"She don't like him so much. He talks too much like a Yankee. But, she loves Dandy Don."

They laughed with him, and she banged her tray and smiled.

Emmett continued to watch her and his friend, trying to comprehend this irony of Raymond, the raw hero of his youth, and now, this father of the special angel of a child.

In a few minutes Lauren Kingsley returned with three younger children, and Raymond became a human jungle gym. He sat on the swinging couch and let the girls crawl all over him. He introduced each of them: Marylee was the youngest, who loved her thumb as much as her dad. Muriel, the kisser, constantly pushed her face into her dad's neck, caressing him. And, Mona, who had discovered the baton and wanted to demonstrate her skill twirling it. She went cart wheeling awkwardly around the room, flipping and dropping it repeatedly.

Lauren offered cold drinks, took the orders, and left them to play with the girls.

"She's a twirler, like her Mom was. Margie, she's a good twirler, ain't she?" Margie banged her good hand on the medal tray in glorious approval.

They sat with Raymond Kingsley until four in the afternoon.

"He was The King, alright. And a dad. Damn combination for Kingsley," Emmett said later as they drove away.

Life had changed Kingsley. He still hurled foul language and paid the swear box, but he was settled, content with his five girls and Charlie's Angels, the Redskins, and all the inventors.

Late in the afternoon, they said their goodbyes, and left for Atlanta.

On the drive home, Emmett asked Robert to be in his wedding and wondered if Raymond Kingsley would come too.

"Of course, we will come. That's a given."

"I'll need a prompter," Emmett said.

"You should get Margie. She'd be great at it. Prompt you and Kingsley both!"

Emmett pushed the accelerator, peered into the glowing dusk, and drove up the interstate.

***

In August Emmett and Barbara took her savings, and a bit of his own GI money, and made a down payment on a corner house with three bedrooms in Lofton, Texas, a ten minute drive from his school. He would bring Barbara Lynn and her cat, Pollack, to Texas. She was hired at the local medical hospital immediately. At Christmas they were married in Macon. Raymond Hughes and Kingsley were in the wedding; Sarah Hughes, Sam Burke, the Jeters, and the Parsons came to the wedding. So did Nathan Kuballe and his wife, Evelyn. Emmett thought that was a special sign for friendship.

Sixteen

I don't need no salvation. I got me a good car!
— Flannery O'Connor

Over the next three years, the experiences for Emmett and Barbara Lynne were fulfilling. The team he inherited had success the first season, 9-1. It lost by a field goal in the league championship. To the surprise of everyone, even Harry Parsons, the offense of Kuballe meshed with the flex defense of Peterson. Jeter was happy. People liked Emmett and his new wife. Barbara tried hard to grow close to Evelyn Kuballe, and pitched into the social life of coaches, games, and after parties.

The flashbacks Emmett had experienced did not recur.

Nathan seemed, at school, to be reconciled with his position and with the easy-going thoroughness of Coach Peterson. He seemed to allow the loss of Hal Rivers to fade somewhat. The ritual of practice and homage to the dried and pathetic wreath beside the field ended at the beginning of the next season when Coach Peterson took over. The wreath mysteriously disappeared.

Another school year came and went.

The marital issues between Nathan and Evelyn also seemed to be less volatile. He had tried Hal's advice after their fight about sexual fulfillment and surprised her with a meal at the swanky local restaurant. They tried to find things to do together. Several trips out west, even a school trip with students helped their relationship.

They made love even on a school trip. She thought Nathan had heard her admonition to love her better. With his assured caresses, she sank into his arms, whispering, "I'm so thankful."

"For what?" he asked.

"For the Lord returning you to me."

He smirked, hoping she didn't see it, but he teased her. "I didn't know you allowed the Lord to watch us."

"Nathan! You heathen," she exclaimed. "That's sacrilege."

"Maybe so," said Nathan.

She thought his tone was humdrum.

For the last six months, she had attended regular services at the Bethel Baptist Church, recommended to her by some co-workers. She asked him to go with her. He refused.

"I'm not churchy. You go ahead. Pray for the wretchedness of my soul," and laughed, so she went alone, praying all the while that he would accompany her.

She announced one day her Sunday School class was having a retreat to Lake O' the Pines. It was for two nights. Every couple had a private cabin.

"Let's go together. We've never done anything like that. The people are so nice. The Youth minister is going to lead us. He is so gifted. For me, please, Nathan, will you do this? It might do you more good than you know."

At first, Nathan was adamant, growling his refusal, but she persisted. He finally relented.

"Okay," Evelyn said. "To have you along will be wonderful. We can drive."

She had never pressed Nathan on his religious beliefs. He had never shared. She knew with his brooding nature, he needed some inner faith, some kind of peace, or at least she sensed it. She had not joined the faith fellowship of Bethel Church, but she had been invited to give herself to the Lord.

"If my husband will, I will," she had said. She prayed that Nathan would be 'turned.' He might open himself.

He rejected her request.

A church-life seemed to him an invitation to a waste of time. *After all, wasn't the football team full of faith and prayer? Hal prayed with the boys before every game. Nathan wondered if God really cared about football games or scores.*

The only time he earnestly prayed was in Vietnam when the VC fired on the boat when they went skiing. He prayed for his life. It was an automatic reflex at the time. He got through that. He counted it as luck, not God's intervention.

Look what happened. I met Chris Aston. What kind of God leads guys like me to the Chris Astons of the world?

Nathan struggled to conceal his fears. *I've done things I know are not right, but I did them. The only forgiveness I need is from myself. I've done that okay. Hal taught me to forgive myself. I've worked at it. I've won battles with Evelyn more times than I've lost. I'm not living daily hating the guy that Jeter brought in to take my job. I'm okay. I'll do this for Evelyn once, but to buy more time to do what I like to do, and with whoever I like to do it.*

He refused to ride to the camp ground on the church bus.

"I do buses all the time with the football teams. I'm not riding a church bus, even if Billy Graham is driving." That made Evelyn laugh. She was delighted they'd spend a weekend together doing what she loved to do.

After dinner, at the first worship service, the Youth Minister talked about commitment. He urged everyone present to give his or her life to God in Christ Jesus. "For he who is full of sin may come to me," he said. "God calls 'sinners to repentance.' Our God knew us and gave his life for us, so that through his death, we might be saved."

When Nathan heard the message, he was visibly moving in his seat.

Saved from what? If God cares so much, then why did Hal Rivers die?

The question burned through his mind.

God took Hal...he's not getting me. I'm beyond salvation."

The minister was persistent, displaying a vast knowledge of scriptures. He was handsome in a fraternity boy sort of way, Nathan thought.

"Peter says, in Acts 2:38, 'Repent and be baptized, every one of you, in the name of Jesus Christ for the forgiveness of your sins. And you will receive the gift of the Holy Spirit.'"

Nathan thought the man looked right at him. He turned and peered at the people on his right and left, who were enraptured.

"'Repent and be baptized, so that your sins can be washed away.' Be baptized. For immersion in this water means you join the flock of the Saved, baptized out of this ugly, perverse, and unfair world into a new world, one of salvation and unconditional love. Jesus died for us, all sinners. He wants to give his love to you.

"Each of you want that, from housewives, mothers, and mechanics, to the, coaches, lawyers, doctors, teachers, and the merchants to the farmers. God makes it possible through the waters of Holy Baptism and the gift of his son Jesus, for He, as scripture tells us in Acts 5:31, 'exalted to his own right hand as Prince and Savior that he might give repentance and forgiveness….'

"Some of us try to run from our sins, like Noah ran. Even the hero Moses ran, crying, 'I am not the one, Lord.' Even on the cross, our dear Savior cried out, 'Lord, let this cup pass from me.' He, even he, was frightened at the great weight upon him.

"If you feel a great weight upon you, some dark secret, some sin you can't face, give it to Christ. Let him carry it for you, and be free."

The minister lifted one hand in a dramatic blessing. With his other, he dipped his fingers into the water, a great vat that had been imported from town, a portable pool. The waters trickled though his fingers. He paused, gazing at the congregation, waiting to note who would be the first to come forward.

None came.

"As Jesus's own cousin, John, did for his Savior, John baptized Jesus with water. 'There is a river whose streams make glad' those of heavy of heart, those with burdens too great to be lifted, those whose souls contain secrets so defiant and terrible that none can utter, God knows them. God will heal them. God will lift the burden and lighten the load. He will make clear the pathway to glory and peace."

Nathan's mind whirled. He felt himself swaying, as though caught in an inexplicable vortex. He felt consumed with an anger unlike what he had ever felt in his life, a pure revulsion.

Why am I exposing myself? Evelyn has no right do this. This little, lying preacher, spewing guilt and veiled threats, has no right to level this faith and love stuff on people, prompt them to confess, to come do something as stupid as climb into a vat of water with him, and expect a miracle.

Evelyn sensed the tension gripping Nathan. She thought he was moved by the words and might rise to go down and be baptized. Her heart beat in premature excitement.

Then, she saw the pulsing in Nathan's neck, and a streak of red that she had seen many times when they argued.

"Are you okay?" she whispered.

"Why'd *you* do this?" he hissed.

Wide-eyed, she shook her head in denial without opening her mouth.

Nathan rose from his chair and stalked up the aisle.

Evelyn pursued him. Reaching him outside, she demanded, "What on earth is wrong with you?"

Nathan whirled to stare at her. "Wrong with me? Not a god-damned thing."

"Hush," she said harshly. "You sound like a child."

"That's tough," he said. "Why'd you make me come here? What were you thinking?"

"I simply wanted to be with you, and have you experience some of the kindness and joy that I've known." She was at the point of tears, not so much from fear, but from disappointment.

"That guy, Evelyn, is nothing but some kind of a slick-talking shyster. He gets people in here, works them up to get saved, whatever that means, and then probably asks for a lot of money."

"Not true, not at all! He isn't selling anything. He hasn't asked for money."

"Not yet, he hasn't, but you can bet as soon as he gets a group of folks to jump in the pool with him, he is going to charge 'em.

"He uses guilt, that stuff about burdens and sin. He's this golden boy with a smooth tongue. He gets everyone goggle-eyed and scared, then he springs it on them. Get baptized. If he had a flowing river, he'd be in the middle of it.

"I'd like to drown his sniveling ass!" Nathan declared.

"My God, Nathan, where is this coming from? I've never seen you like this!" She stepped back from him.

His face contained a fury she didn't know. He glared at her with pain and anger. "Where does it come from? I'll tell you where. From all the people who have pretended I'm immersed in my own sorrow; from all the people who want to drain away my independence from you, who measure me against some secret, god-damned standard of husband who is a depiction of what you read about in romance novels, plastic men.

"I don't need saving. What I need is to get away from this bible-beating phony. I can't stand this stuff he is saying. I can't stand these people who allow themselves to be dazzled by that crap.

"It comes from my deranged soul, the mixed up place where the wolves howl when I hear phonies like him."

He is literally raving, she thought.

"Please, Nathan, be quiet."

Several people had turned to see them outside.

"Let them hear me," he said loudly. "I don't care. I'm not sitting there anymore listening to his version of Jesus or salvation, or damnation, or whatever else he can drag up from his bible talk. It's folklore, anyway."

Evelyn didn't recognize him or his outrage. His face changed, a fractured and painful face.

"So you don't recognize me? Of course not, because *you never took me to church*."

Evelyn shook her head baffled by his anger. "This is evil. I never saw you like this."

"Sure you don't know me," Nathan said, "because Johnny double-talk taught you to know his version of the truth. I'm one of his lost souls. Can't you see. Old two-tongued-double-talk-Johnny, who believes in two kinds of people, those who have his version of Jesus, and the rest, who are damned to Hell.

"Well, Evelyn, let me tell you something, and you can share it with that preacher. Satan talks to me all the time. I know about the devil. I own his washcloth. I wash myself daily with Satan's suds. I'm covered in them. See me covered in them?" He opened his arms exposing his chest.

Evelyn was revolted, and frightened. She backed away and walked inside. When she slipped into her seat, a woman asked if she were okay.

"Yes," she lied, trying to calm herself. "My husband ate something that disagreed with him."

The curiosity subsided.

Nathan went to their cabin, gathered his things, and waited until she returned.

"I'm leaving," he said, defiantly.

"Fine," Her voice was cold as she could muster. "I'll drive you to the bus station."

"You're not coming?" he said.

"Of course not?" she replied. "Maybe *if I stay here*, you'll come to your senses."

"Oh, I've got plenty of sense," said Nathan. "Enough to know that I can't stay here surrounded by folks who want to listen to that bull crap."

He paused before getting out of his chair. "I know some Bible verses. Did you know that?" he said.

She feared he was going off on another rant.

"How about this, 'Honesty is like a kiss on the lips.'" He leaned forward to kiss her, but she pulled back.

"I've got my car keys. You've ruined it," she said.

He smirked and picked up his bags.

On a bus ride, that ended later with an expensive cab to his house, Nathan, the leader of double lives, thought about losses and failures, and realized that a collection of instances grew out of a morass of confusion. From the time he was a kid on an Alabama farm, watching his dad pull a dead calf from its moaning, pathetic mother cow, through his years at the University of Alabama, service in Vietnam, marriage to Evelyn, and love for Hal Rivers, he had been a prevaricator. These memories, these fragments in time where he had been another person, were colored by confusing identity issues. Each had its own wonderful and dreadful confusion. He sank into each of his exploitations, sensing a kind of perverse excitement, a fascination and thirst for their own peculiarity. The stimulation of his experiences in athletics at Bama thrilled him viscerally - the human body swollen from weight training, glistening from sweat, gave way to a lovely weekend beach rendezvous with a strange blonde surfer, whose smooth touch invigorated him, gave him deep pleasure that throbbed in his thighs. Searing memories of fears, flashing gun fire, screams of wounded men on a foreign river accompanied by a gauzy sense of making love to a stranger beneath a mosquito net enveloped him, and haunted him.

The bumping, rolling rhythm of the bus wheels spinning beneath him made him dizzy and sick. He had been tough on Evelyn, who was revoltingly soft and cloying in her desire to make him into what he was not, a lover of women. He loved Hal Rivers.

Mistakes were not mistakes when love is involved, the dubious, giddy, exotic, and forbidden love.

Could a man live in a double world? Or must he choose? How can such a choice be forced on him by another?

Evelyn, desirable, but demanding, all-consuming, and, always presuming, and intruding. She was the epitome of pressure, of nagging with 'we never,' 'why can't you,' 'won't you' or 'damm it, Nathan.' He was 'damn it Nathan!' What flows from one to the other was not love, but misconception. What flowed back is more misconception, pretending that leads to indifference, longing to escape, and finally weakness. Well, he wasn't weak, and he was not seeking escape, especially into the pathetic idiocy of that preacher's crummy solutions.

The hiss of the bus's airbrakes woke him. He grabbed his bag and climbed down onto the sidewalk beside an all-night diner that doubled as the Lofton bus depot. He made a call for a taxi and decided to get coffee to clear his head.

The cook, heavy-set, with a head of curly hair, covered with a hair net and a white baseball cap, smiled at him. It was 1:10AM.

"Evenin'," he said. "You want it black or with cream?"

"Black," said Nathan. He pushed his leg over one of the counter stools.

The coffee was steaming hot.

"I seen you use the pay phone. You want I should put the coffee in a paper cup?" He transferred the coffee from china to a paper cup with a napkin around it.

"Watch that thing. It can be hot." He waited, then said, "Hey, ain't you one of them coaches out to the private school?"

"I am," answered Nathan. His mind was still sifting through images that haunted his ride into town.

"I thought I seen you before.

"Say, that was terrible about that other coach who died out there. I read that in the papers couple years ago. What happened?"

Nathan's mind quickened at the question. "Accident," he said.

"Paper said the guy was hit in face by a discus some kid throwed."

"That's right," said Nathan, blowing into the coffee to cool it.

"Whew. Shit! That's bad. What I don't get is why a guy who's around sports

In the Tomb of the Soul 211

would stand where he could get hit with something like that. Don't add up."

Nathan struggled to remain composed and didn't face the man.

"Well, you can't tell nothing about what's in a man's mind, can you?"

"Nope," said Nathan. He refused to indulge a discussion of Hal with this dolt.

"I seen a lot of folks come off the bus late at night, who want to spec-cue-late on all kinds of things. I hate that kinda talk, so I ain't gonna ask you how well you knew him?"

The man's clever needle for gossip was not going to probe Nathan's skin. He had enough in his own head to suffice.

"Hardly, at all," he lied. He felt a cold sensation in his throat.

"You ain't that new guy that they got out there are you? The Yankee coach. Somebody said he played in Massachusetts. You him?"

"Nope," said Nathan. The flatness of he response had its effect. The cook turned to his counter and busied himself with other things. When the taxi rolled up, the cook said, "Well, now. You have a good one. I see them lights of your taxi."

Nathan paid for the coffee and left.

Outside the humid air stifled him. His mind slipped into black guilt.

He held Hal's bleeding head in his arms.

He saw that Hal had opened his eyes, "Why did ya have to lie about it?" Hal asked.

Nathan couldn't form an answer.

Seventeen

In Xanadu did Kubla Khan
A stately pleasure dome decree....
— *S.T. Coleridge*

On Saturday morning, Nathan called Davis Wallace, his friend who owned a sporting apparel and equipment shop. Davis had become a more constant companion in the last year. Not a replacement for Hal Rivers, but a friendly, open sort of man, who wrote big ticket items for the school's sporting needs. He always gave nice discounts, especially when Nathan Kuballe made the orders.

They agreed to meet in the late morning, have lunch, and play golf.

"Just stop in, buddy," he said in his cheery voice.

Davis was tall and thin, unmarried, and more bookish than athletic. He loved hiking and biking. He didn't do weight training like Nathan, but he admired heavy workouts, preferring to assist rather than participate. He was a regular golfer and could beat Nathan handily. Knowing that Nathan had pride in his football days at Alabama, Davis needled him on the golf course when they played skins against each other. More often, they preferred playing twosomes, avoiding other partners so they could engage in their banter.

Davis was in form when Nathan got to the store.

"You look like some stray cat dragged you in," Davis exclaimed. "What's the score? Wife beating, hung over, or wrung out?"

"Wrung out," said Nathan. "Evelyn dragged me to some church retreat thing. It wasn't for me, so I caught a late night bus home."

"Obviously," said Davis. "You look like you need coffee and hair-of-the-dog."

"Just didn't sleep. I drank some rot-gut coffee at the diner by the bus station. I think it was two days old. Kept me up."

"Well, you just missed your boss," said Davis.

"Who, Jeter?"

"Nope, Coach Peterson. He came by to select some new uniforms for fall football, the 9th grade, JV, and varsity teams. Big buy. He was just looking at color combinations. He said he wasn't sure about sizes. Spent about 90 minutes pouring over catalogues.

"Nice ticket for the business, I thought," said Davis. He could see Nathan had no idea such plans were in place.

"I wasn't consulted," Nathan said.

"Really? I'd have thought the one guy who had been with the boys for the longest would be included in a decision of that magnitude. Guess he was going to select some combinations, then get with you. If you guys go through with that, I'm off to Florida to fish for two weeks." Davis was beaming. "How'd a guy who is new on the job pull a budget buster like that?"

Nathan snorted, "Hum, when you marry the headmaster's niece, you can command most anything."

Davis thought the joke was good. "I guess so. Mr. Jeter has a reputation for tight-assed finances at the school. Maybe Coach's wife has leverage. She's a pretty thing. The guy marches in here a short time ago, interviews, gets Hal's job, marries the boss's niece, and owns the team. He's an operator."

Nathan didn't answer.

Davis was always friendly. "If your wife's gone for the day, we ought to go to the club and play golf. Maybe I can take some of the money Jeter's paying you?"

The dark mood from the night before ballooned in him. Davis could not see it, but like a cloud, it had descended. The mention of Hal and Peterson in the same breath, crowned by the thought of his bolting from Evelyn's retreat, made him turn away and pretend to study a rack of sweat suits that had just arrived.

"How 'bout it?" asked Davis, "or you got to get a note of permission."

"I can play," answered Nathan. "Be nice to beat your scrawny ass and a few balls."

"Oh, I can attest to beating balls. Whipping my ass isn't in the cards. Davis Wallace has a magic putter," Davis said, referring to himself in third person.

"I'll bet he does," said Nathan, sarcastically.

Davis was called to the phone in his office and gone for a few minutes. When he returned, he was smiling.

"Hey, that was a sales rep for Tasmanian outerwear, who's in town at the motel. He's a business friend of mine, a real sporty guy. I mentioned I was playing golf with you. He said he wanted to meet you and wondered if he could hook up with us for eighteen holes. I told him sure thing.

"Says he has a seven handicap. I don't believe that, but I didn't argue. I think he's a pigeon. What do you say?" Davis' excitement was obvious. "I want a piece of this guy."

"I don't think you come close to a seven handicap," said Nathan.

"Not a problem. He's a big talker. Always going on about what he owns, who he knows that you know. He is one of those. We get him down one bet, and he refreshes the bet. We get to make some change. You in?"

"I'm in," said Nathan. He managed to be as enthusiastic as he could. Golf would relax, suppress some of the shadows that crowded his mind.

"You got to promise me something. When we get to the range before we play, you will concentrate on not looping your club on your back swing. When you swing too quick, it circles at the top and cuts the ball. That's why you slice it.

"I won't have to play that tape of Robert Frost, 'whose woods these are/ I think I know....'" Davis laughed at his own joke.

Nathan had heard it before.

"You treat the golf club like you treat your pecker. Hold it gently, that way you don't roll your wrists, but let the balance of the club take over and keep itself square to the ball. Otherwise, out it goes, slicing to 'whose woods these are....'"

"Go to hell, Wallace!" Nathan said.

Davis Wallace grinned at him. "I sense the old coach had a long night with the little woman and badly needs some man-time. Carl Desmon and I can bring that. Perk up the old, dead willy."

How Davis could bomb a golf ball was a mystery to Nathan. He had no definition in his chest, utterly flat torso back and front. His body reminded Nathan of a two iron, no apparent difference between where his chest ended and his abdomen began. His legs were like shafts and stuck out of his pants. He never wore shorts because the spindles he stood on were too brittle. Nevertheless, he hit shot after shot down the middle of the fairway with an admirable efficiency.

He wasn't at all like Hal Rivers, Nathan thought quickly and drove it from his mind.

At the store Nathan found a pair of slacks and changed into them in a fitting room before a full length mirror. Even in a shirt, the definition of his body was evident. His legs were muscular from running, his arms were fully defined, and his chest had a sculpted strength that showed through a Polo shirt.

He thought he was neither useless, nor hot-headed. *No guilt-stricken person, or strange behaving brute. He was good, well developed, even handsome.*

"'Who do you think you are?'" Evelyn had said.

"I'm the Cube!" he thought."I don't need you today."

To kill time before Davis Wallace could leave for the course, he took a glass and a putter from a rack at the front of the store, placed it in the aisle and backed off ten feet. He began to practice his putting. He liked this putter, how the ball came off as he stroked it. The floor was even, and the ball traveled straight and true, entered the glass with a clink before it bounced out.

After several good putts, Davis came to watch.

"Give you a good deal on that putter, Babe. It suits your hand and stroke real well. You know the funny thing about people and putters?'

"Is this going to be another pecker joke?" Nathan said.

"No, no, just wisdom from a better golfer. Most guys select putters that are too long in the shaft. Now, I could make a pecker joke, but I won't. That putter is shorter than the one you use. That's my point. I'm not making a pecker joke, but if I were, I'd also address length, and, maybe, grip size."

"I knew you'd get that pecker thing in there somehow," said Nathan. "I'll tell you what, you get that Tasmanian rep what's-his-name on the first tee. I'll show you both some putting." He placed the putter back on the rack.

"You're on, partner," said Davis Wallace.

Nathan wasn't disappointed by Davis's description of Carl Desmon. He was the eager, talkative type. He was an instant best friend, tall, head full of blonde hair, a bit too thick and flipped up in curls above his neck, beneath a white golf cap that he pulled low to shade his ruddy face. In dark glasses, a Polo shirt, tight slacks, small waist, he looked strong and tanned. He laughed, then cursed when shots didn't fly correctly, mocking his own mistakes, which were plentiful. After nine holes, with Carl down a hole each to Nathan and Davis, they went for beer. The club was not crowded, so they lingered in the bar while Carl discussed his ski boat at Blue Marline Arena near Galveston.

"Great little marina, good snapper fishing right off-shore. You and Wallace should drive down and see me, Nathan. Got the buddy who owns a restaurant. We'll hit a few balls, water ski, and eat right. I'll show you the nightlife of Galveston without oil refineries."

On the back nine, Carl's game soured completely. Davis won skins from him and from Nathan. On the eighteenth Carl proved the gracious loser.

"You got me this trip, but next month, I'm taking you both to the cleaners. Now, I'm taking you to dinner. I know this steak place over in Grant. Nathan, I'll treat you to the best steak and shrimp you ever tasted, and I owe Wallace a treat or two, as well. How about it?" He slapped Davis Wallace on the shoulder.

They agreed, cleaned up at the club, and drove a large black Buick with

Carl to Grant, Texas, thirty miles away.

Losing again to Davis made Nathan sore-headed.

"Leave the game on the course, Kuballe. Face it, you can't putt a lick," said Davis. "I just kicked your butt. Sit back and enjoy the ride."

"Go to Hell, Wallace," said Nathan. "Don't turn back." He slouched in the back seat, his beer on his lap.

The car rolled on, until Carl Desmon said, "Hey, partner, don't go to sleep back there. Ever do any surf fishing?"

Nathan swam up from his thoughts. "Yeah, once," he answered.

"Snapper in shallow water is a complete blast. I've even seined 'em. Can you believe that? Seining red snapper!"

"Complete bullshit," laughed Davis. "Desmon, you are so full of shit, it's no wonder you don't completely drown yourself."

"Oh, come on!" exclaimed Desmon. "You can have that heavy rod and reel stuff deep sea fishing. Give me a seine net and a shallow cove and I'm a happy bastard."

The sun cast burnished orange on the marshes as they flashed up the coast.

"Alright, coach, where did you do your fishing?"

"In the Gulf when I was a kid," answered Nathan, "with my dad."

"Was it good?" asked Desmon, leaning forward to see Nathan in the rear-view mirror.

Nathan recalled the time his family went down to the beach at St. Petersburg. His father had bought two Zebco outfits, just plain spinner reels to surf fish for whiting. The poles were a surprise birthday present for Nathan. He was 13. His dad rigged them with heavy lead weights and bass hooks. They took along a stinky bag of shrimp for bait.

He had walked with his dad out into the water at low tide. His dad showed him how to cock his wrist and cast.

'Flick your arm and wrist forward, release the button on the reel at that same time. Let her fly.'"

Nathan had done it perfectly. The lead weight carried the hook, baited with shrimp, far out into the breaking surf. Delighted with the distance of each cast, he lost interest in catching fish. He loved throwing the line.

Behind him his father stood apart and was preparing his own baited hook.

Nathan had made a long backswing, looping the weight on the line to make it fly farther.

He remembered the thud as his lead weight struck his father's jaw. The quizzical look on his dad's face was burned into his mind, as the man fell face-first into the shallow surf. He was out cold.

Nathan had rolled his dad onto his back and cradled his head. Together they crawled out of the water and up onto the beach.

"I almost killed my dad fishing in the surf. Just never went back," said Nathan. He couldn't remember ocean fishing at all, only fresh water fishing with Hal Rivers.

"Damn," said Carl Desmon. "You actually cold-cocked your own dad with a lead fishing weight? That's some shit. No wonder you don't go out. How heavy was that weight, man?"

"Heavy," said Nathan

"You better know I always say to my fishing partners to stand away when they cast. You hook somebody, it can be nasty as hell."

After twenty minutes, they pulled off the highway and up a black driveway into a parking lot half-full of cars. They pulled to the side of a white, ranch-style house, bearing a large green sign, "Spooner's Restaurant and Bar."

"If you like steak and seafood, this is the joint," he said.

They took a table near a large, plate-glass window overlooking a marshy woods of palmetto fans, sawgrass and cyprus trees. Someone had decorated the edge of the woods with some ceramic deer and several pink flamingoes, one of which was fallen over.

Carl ordered a round of drinks. Nathan was hungry and studied the menu.

"Hey, Coach, I've been meaning to ask. How's the school doing with the death of that coach?" Carl paused, then said, "How you doing with it? Davis told me you guys were close."

The last thing Nathan wanted to hear was a reference to Hal's death. He shrugged his shoulders.

"That is some tough shit, man. I'm sorry for you and that school."

"They made a good hire," said Davis Wallace. "A guy from Atlanta. Knew a couple people at the school. Nice fellow."

"Ain't that the way it is?" said Desmon. "Guy like the Coach here gives six or eight years to the place, and they run off and hire some dude from somewhere else. Sort of pisses me off."

"It could, if we talk about it," said Nathan, feeling his face turn dark from the incessant Desmon conversation and the effects of beer and scotch.

"Well, fine with me," said Desmon, affably. "Just drop the subject. You guys make me happy. Take money off me in golf, but make me happy. I appreciate you, pal," he said, and cuffed Davis Wallace on the shoulder.

He raised his drink. "Here's to golf, fishing, friendship, and whatever else three squires can find to add to the pleasure of life, shrimp cocktails, and steak, not included." He laughed at his own suggestive exuberance.

They drank. Their meals arrived, and they absorbed themselves in the food.

The steak was excellent, and Nathan had his third scotch. He was finishing it when he saw a couple take a table nearby. A tall brunette in a black cocktail dress, deep opening in the front, revealing ample cleavage, slipped into her chair across from a jowly, shorter man, whose face looked loose. The woman squeezed her legs under the table. Her eyes swept over the three of them seated eight feet away. She gave a gentle smile and turned toward her escort. On his right hand, the man wore a gold ring with a red rhinestone in it. She wore pearls. They studied their menus without speaking.

Carl was drinking bourbon. He leaned over and in a loud whisper said, "How'd you like to have that for supper?" He gave a slight nod toward the woman.

He sipped his drink and gave a long glance at her, then turned and said, "That is de-lec-table."

Nathan shook his head slightly, suggesting more incredulity than agreement.

Desmon had a devious expression. Being clever, he whispered, "Cheesecake."

Davis smiled into his glass in delinquent agreement.

"I'd like a little cheesecake tonight, sweet and delectable. How about you guys? Maybe recreational cheesecake?" He giggled as he sipped.

Nathan's head felt full of gauze.

Desmon kept it up.

"A thin, sweet piece of that cheesecake." He was proud of his metaphor.

Davis picked up the banter. "Very sweet, and a very sweet idea. Maybe a bit of whipped cream, or some dark chocolate." He let his voice slip into a low register and lascivious laugh.

"How 'bout it, Kuballe? Interest you in some cheesecake?" Desmon's eyes were glassy.

Nathan turned his full attention to the woman, who glanced back at him, and smiled. She moved her legs toward him.

Hooker, he thought.

The woman in the black gown turned her head, and Davis caught her eye. Her escort was looking at his menu. Davis smiled, a deliberate, provocative smile. Nathan watched and thought he caught a slight crease in her red mouth.

He turned back to find Carl Desmon, with his glass to his lips, studying first Nathan, then Davis.

He returned Nathan's gaze and raised his eyebrows. "Coach might be horny," he said lightly. "Hmm? It's the shank of the evening, gentlemen, the soft, tender and delicate part." He nodded toward the woman at the table and smiled.

"I know the city of Grant and the haunts for those of us with discriminating tastes. Shall we have another drink and depart, or, just depart?" Nathan was just drunk enough to think Desmon was funny.

"Definitely depart," said Davis Wallace.

Nathan stood, steadied himself by holding the back of the chair, and walked out of the restaurant.

"Nathan, take the front seat this time," ordered Davis.

They got in the car.

"What's your pleasure?" asked Desmon, "a little pulchritude or a little pussy and pulchritude?"

Nathan suddenly felt that Desmon was obnoxious, but he said nothing.

"Let's get laid," said Davis.

"My sentiments exactly. See Miss Peggy Peckerwood."

"So, Kuballe, what's your current? Direct. Indirect. Alternating. Offensive or defensive? Into the backfield. What do you say?"

Nathan avoided looking at him. "I say you're driving, Desmon, be careful. It's your game plan." He felt dizzy and rolled the window down. Air hit him in the face.

In a short time, Desmon pulled into a nightclub with cars double-parked. The thump of heavy music pulsed even outside. A neon sign flashed, "Welcome to The Overdrive - Dancing, Dinner and Fun." A pair of stocking legs on alternating current gave the impression of kick-dancing.

Carl paid the cover and ushered them into a loud, raucous room. On a small stage were three girls, undulating in boozy rhythm. The air was raw with smoke and stale liquor. The floor was sticky, and the crowd rolled about in various stages of intoxication. Men stumbled, and faceless women glowed in the dim light. The blare of the music staggered them until their ears adjusted. They joined in the smoky crowd and made their way to a table in the corner by the stage. Each table featured a pole through the center. Hypnotized men leered at girls, who were grinding themselves around each pole on the stage. Occasionally, a man handed dollar bills to one of the girls, who stepped from the stage onto the table to move on the pole in sensuous, suggestive rhythm.

If you want some of my pie,
You better look in my eye;
This ain't yo' momma no mo'.

Nathan's eyes focused enough to see a topless waitress, her breasts quivering, attempting to take drink orders above the din. Two large bouncers roamed among the tables, watching for men who got too frisky with the girls.

He thought he heard one growl, "You want more, buddy, move to the end of the bar."

The music changed from the reverberating grind of the first tune to a more melodious one that floated in sensuous harmony. The lights changed from orange to blue, and three girls in gauzy gowns began to sway in unison.

Nathan, Desmon, and Davis shifted their chairs to watch the show.

Smoothly, suggestively immodest, one of the girls danced away from the other two and floated toward Nathan's table. Her blonde hair curled about her face, her eyes were dark with heavy mascara. She bumped her hips and allowed her gown to slip off one shoulder. When she dipped her knees, turned and allowed the men to see between her knees and thighs. She lifted the gown almost to her waist. They could see her dark crotch and the outline of her vulva.

Nathan sipped his drink and inexplicable feelings washed over him. *Evelyn would not like this.*

The girl's abdomen, so pale, so inviting, yet so unfulfilling, smelled of smoke and stale beer.

He shook his head to clear the vision.

Desmon and Davis mimicked each other, rocking unsteadily in their seats, their mouths damp and soggy, their lips spongy. Davis's eyes fluttered as the dancing girl swirled above him, reaching her arms and hands into the light, and letting her gown slip to the floor.

She was completely nude.

She put her hands on her hips and moved them back and forth suggestively, her stomach, white and smooth, expanding back and forth, as she slowly rubbed her crotch on the pole and slid down to stare straight at Davis.

"Holy shit," he mouthed.

"Go for it, go for it!" Desmon whispered.

She turned to Nathan and smiled sensuously. She mouthed the words, "I like you," and stepped nimbly back onto the stage, leaving her slipper lying on their table, a dark invitation.

Desmon fished a five dollar bill from his wallet as did Davis. "Damn," he said. "I want that one."

Nathan nursed his drink, his eyes on the slipper. His legs felt heavy beneath the table. He knew if either of them touched the slipper, it was a signal for the bouncer to come and usher one of them to the end of the bar. The action seemed to be on the second floor. Nathan knew he was drunk.

The music ended. The girl grabbed her gown from the floor of the stage, and with the others disappeared behind a curtain, and lights raised to a smattering of applause, leaving the three of them squinting at each other.

Desmon leaned toward the stage, hanging on to the table. He was very drunk. "I think I'll get laid tonight!" he laughed.

"Another drink for you, Carl, and you'll be 'docile-dick' Desmon, unable to fish in the pond." Davis thought his own joke was hilarious.

Desmon's eyes bulged so that Nathan thought he looked like a blonde catfish. His head, round, his face flat, nostrils that flared and ears protruded, as though they made way for his gills. Nathan snickered at him. "Fuckin' catfish."

Before the remark had time to sink in on Desmon, the girl reappeared.

"Well, damn," said Davis. "Cinderella has returned for her slipper."

"Hello, sweet thing," burbled Desmon. "I kinda like your little boobies."

She paid no attention to his compliment.

Nathan continued to laugh because Carl looked like a catfish opening and closing his mouth.

They all began to laugh, blubbery, drunken laughter.

The girl grinned at them.

Carl was swaying on his chair. "Hey, you know what? My nuts are aching. Honey, you want to know what that means?"

They all looked at the girl as Carl made his hands into orbs on his chest.

"Catfish," said Nathan.

"Yeah," said Carl, "catfish smells like pussy."

The girl, accustomed to drunken babble, ignored their remarks. "My shoe," she said, "slipped off when I was performing."

"Cinderella has lost her slipper," Desmon said.

Davis laughed.

She was wearing a tee shirt and a dark mini-skirt. She slipped around Nathan, leaned over him, placing her hand on his neck, brushing his face with her breasts, picked up her shoe and slipped it on, dancing on one foot.

Nathan recoiled from her touch.

"So, you fellows from around here?" she said.

Davis smiled intensely. "We are three squires of the night's body."

"Huh." She looked at them. "That's crazy. You want I should get you some more drinks?"

"Sure," said Davis.

Nathan saw her walk away how she accentuated her hips as she moved.

"Wallace is horny," Desmon sang. "Wallace is horny."

Davis Wallace straightened his back, lifted his eyebrows, affecting agreement. He opened his eyes very wide and belched. "Hey, I'm the horny bullfrog." He laughed and let his body go slack.

Desmon turned his bulbous eyes on Nathan. "Hey, Coach, are you in heat? Want a little toss with the dancing girl. She likes you."

Nathan stared at Carl Desmon, knowing his own eyes were dilating into spheres of anger.

I hate the guy. I hate his happy-go-lucky, bragging, money flashing son-of-a-bitch, he thought, with his ski boats and stupid jokes. I hate ski boats. His lousy, lying golf game, mouthy crudeness. I hate the guy.

Alternately hot and cold, Nathan sat staring at Carl Desmon, seeing a catfish and a slobbering idiot.

"You all like for me to dance on your table n'pay for this drink?" She sat three glasses of scotch in front of Nathan.

She is just a kid, Nathan thought.

"What else you do for five dollars?" asked Desmon.

Won't the son-of-a-bitch shut up. Shut the fuck up.

Nathan cut his red eyes at Carl and let them bore into him.

"I ain't that kind o' girl," she said.

"Then, what? A ballerina," Carl Desmon said in a mocking tone. "We want a little action, baby. You know buck-a-fuck-in-the-bed action."

"I ain't no ballerina. I'm a good go-go dancer."

"I'll bet you can go-go," sneered Carl. "We ain't really interested in your dancing. My friend here wants a good lay!"

Carl sipped his drink.

Nathan saw bubbles rise from Carl's choking on his on words.

Come on, Nathan, Evelyn said.

"Shut up," Nathan blurted.

To Carl, the words came from nowhere.

Nathan stared, visualizing Carl's mouth working like a catfish gulping air. His eyes were closer together than Nathan had realized.

"What?" said Desmon.

"I said, 'Shut up! Leave her alone. She said she's a dancer." Nathan's voice was as cold as the ice in his glass. His stare made Carl melt.

"I just thought …we'd have a few … laughs," stammered Desmon.

Not taking his eyes off of Desmon, Nathan drained his drink, reached into his pocket, and slapped a twenty dollar bill on the table hard enough to upset his glass and spill ice. He turned on the girl.

"There!" he said, "Go dance your ass off."

Getting really sick, Nathan lurched from his chair.

The suddenness of his movement startled Davis, who grabbed at Nathan's arm. "Wait a minute, Coach!" he said.

Nathan's rush was too quick. He bolted for the exit.

"Nathan! Wait! What's wrong?"

Carl sat at the table too drunk to notice anything but the girl.

Outside, Nathan leaned between two cars and vomited.

Eighteen

For I have known them all already, known them all:
Have known the evenings, mornings, afternoons,
I have measured out my life with coffee spoons...
— *T.S. Eliot*

Emmett and Barbara Lynne had settled as a married couple, in a new house, on a lovely street. After two seasons his life became immersed in the life of The Hilliard School and new friends. He worked hard to integrate Kuballe's philosophy with his own, aware of special tension, but comfortable enough to believe that Nathan was relaxing. His second year unfolded prosperously for the football team. Emmett's spirit infected the players and the faculty. In fact, he had the impression he and Nathan made a good team as they worked to make football central for the players and important to the school.

Emmett, in the meantime, never considered Kuballe's unhappiness or noted any strain in the colleague's marriage. They worked on building the boys, fostering a winning tradition, and enjoying the success. Emmett worked on his cars as a hobby at home, and a vegetable garden. Barbara Lynne excelled at home decorating. The community embraced his humor, his storytelling, and his general enthusiasm. Her kindness radiated to others and she flourished at the hospital.

Nathan secretly glowered in envy and glum resentment, except when the team won games, which it did more frequently than when Hal Rivers was alive. He saw life as divided between school and home. Davis was his diversion. Misery haunted him. It showed at home, where he endured, despite Evelyn's attempts to facilitate, cajole and support him. She forgave his outburst at the church retreat, even pledging to leave her religion out of his life. He was thankful for that.

The Jeters had an opening-of-school party in the fall of the Emmett's third year. Held in the school courtyard beneath old oak trees, the party was festive with checkered table clothes that fluttered in the evening breeze. The Texas barbecue, salads, and beer were standard fare, as the faculty gathered with husbands, wives, and a few older children to celebrate the opening of a new school year.

No one took note that Coach Kuballe had come without Evelyn. She was, he said, visiting her sister. Mingling with only a few people, he stayed inconspicuously apart from Barbara Lynne and Emmett. He had a habit of feigning excuses to miss social functions, especially if they included spouses. He had even missed the reception that followed Emmett's wedding, saying Evelyn had to rush back to be ready for a large court case the next day that her boss required her to attend.

At the party, Maggie, Dan Jeter, Sam Burke, Barbara Lynne, and co-coaches gathered around Emmett, who was in rare form.

"Swear to God!" he exclaimed. "Somebody was in my dad's fruit trees throwing apples at the house windows."

"Where was this?" Maggie Jeter asked.

"In Cochran, Georgia, my parents' home. My dad was out of town."

"We know you're going to tell us what happened," Sam Burke said.

"My mother called the sheriff," Emmett began, "saying that someone was throwing things at the house. The sheriff came, along with another squad car. It as eight o'clock on Sunday evening in the summer time. I was about ten years old."

Maggie knew from Emmett's expression how much he loved an audience.

"The sheriff knew my dad wasn't at home, so he came up the front steps to the door to talk to mom. She told him someone was throwing stuff at the house. At that moment an apple splattered on the front porch. It was just about dark. The sheriff deputy shined his spot light in the direction of the apple trees.

Three monkeys scampered higher to avoid the light."

"Monkeys?" Maggie Jeter exclaimed. People laughed.

"Three monkeys," Emmett said, "sitting in the apple tree armed. When the light went out, they grabbed more apples and threw them at the deputy sheriff and his men. I remember one of them yelling, 'Horace, it's raining apples! It's a bunch of monkeys.'

"'What you mean?'"

Emmett imitated their southern accents.

"'I mean there's three monkeys in the tree throwin' apples at us!'"

Emmett had everyone's attention as they waited for the punch line.

"About that time," he continued, "a couple more hit the walls of the house. One or two fell short of the squad car. These weren't soft tosses, these were real zingers. Smushed apples were everywhere."

"Then one of the deputies yelled, 'Duck, Sheriff, don't let 'em hit yew!'"

Emmett was enjoying the attention as he sipped his beer and laughed at his own story.

"What happened?" someone asked.

"They ran off," he replied, matter-of-factly. He looked at the group, as if monkeys in his family's fruit trees was an ordinary occurrence in south Georgia.

"You mean the Sheriff didn't go after them?"

"Did you ever try to catch a monkey? Can't be done by fat deputies in a squad car. Required nets and things."

"They didn't shoot 'em, did they?" Maggie asked.

"Why, the town would have had a fit, if they did," said Emmett.

"Something happened. What happened?" Maggie had to know.

Without smiling, Emmett looked right at her and said, "Well, there's just a whole bunch of monkeys in the county now."

The seriousness of his expression held them long enough to allow the joke to settle in.

The group howled.

"Maybe that's why you are in Texas monkeying around with our football team," Mr. Sam teased.

"Just maybe. Seriously, I think someone reported a troupe of monkeys escaped from a carnival a few miles away. They had been on the loose for awhile. Must have found my dad's fruit tees and had a feast. I don't think our sheriff ever caught them."

"Too busy ducking," someone said.

The group disbanded and went to the buffet for barbeque.

Nathan Kuballe had stood apart. Barbara Lynne went to him and took his arm.

"I've come to escort you to the table, Coach," she said, shining her most endearing smile on him.

He smiled back. "I have some other plans, so I'm not eating. I got to leave."

"Well, that's too bad. Where's Evelyn?" she asked.

"Visiting her sister in Houston. It's a regular trip for her. Sister is sort of sick," he said, knowing full well that Evelyn was there because their time together had grown so awkward and difficult they decided not to do the faculty party routines, except after games. In fact, he wasn't so sure she would come to those parties either.

"Oh, you can come and have a nibble. Harry worked all day on this beef, and you know as well as I what an expert he is."

"No, I really can't. This guy's picking me up out front of the school. Have fun. Tell Coach Peterson I enjoyed his story." He pulled away and walked toward the front drive of the school. She turned back to Emmett and the others.

"No luck," said Emmett.

"Nope," she said. "He's got other plans."

"He is a bit of a loner," said Emmett. "Too bad because Harry's barbecue is to die for." They glanced at the figure of Nathan walking briskly to the front campus.

Harry Parsons limped over to them. "What's this? Coach Q is turning down my beef I worked on for eleven hours! I'm getting after him on Monday. That guy is one strange hombre. He ain't the same, just ain't the same."

"Well, losing a best friend," said Emmett, "can make a man different."

"I reckon so on that one. Time to move on ain't it? Three years. It's time."

"I just really like his wife. I wish she were here," said Barbara Lynne.

"He mentioned her sister being sick," said Emmett.

"Hmm!" said Harry. "I heard that one before. I could'a used that too, but Britches will find out. Somethin' ain't right." He turned back to his place behind the serving table.

Nathan, as he walked away, thought to himself, *there was a time I might have matched Peterson story-for-story. I miss Hal a lot.*

He tossed his beer can in a trash can. He had lied about someone meeting him. He got into his own car and drove home in a gloom. He did not bother to turn on the lights, but sat in the dark, letting his mind wander over his life. It seemed to him that at every turn he was met with some sense of being blocked or failing.

As a small boy he had watched his father pull a dead calf breached inside its mother. The boy had followed at a distance as his father, who drove a John Deere tractor to the edge of the woods.

The cow, unmoving, lay on the ground. Discharge from her backside had pooled beneath her. She lay on a wet matt of leaves and sticks that had stuck to her side.

Nathan remembered exactly how his father had looped a rope around the cow's front legs and tied it to a tree. Around the back of her where the gray sack lay on the ground, he had looped another rope to a pair of tiny legs and attached the rope to the tractor.

"Stand way back," he had said. "She may bolt. I don't want her to run you down."

How could she run him down, this sick cow?

He remembered the bulging cow's eyes grow wider as his father pulled the tractor away, and the cow's front legs lifted. A small, wet body sloshed on the ground and water ran out of the cow.

His own mouth had quivered as he gazed at the mess of death on the ground.

Today, nearly thirty years later, gorge rose in his throat. He heard the flies gather quickly and swarm over the body of the calf. He felt flies on his own flesh.

Death came so indifferently, he thought, *so disgustingly grotesque.*

The flash of the speeding motor boat at the old Vietnamese river. *What was the name of it, where Lipsky died in the water? Dong Nai, or something like that. Shots slapped the water, a flailing ski rope, and clatter of a .50 cal. machine gun. When they pulled him over the side, he had been sawed in half, as blood had run down his legs gathering in pools on the riddled deck, the screaming of a wounded lieutenant, "I'm hit. I'm hit."*

Hit, shit! thought Nathan. *You don't know what hit means. Gut shot.*

He had shot a hole in his father's porch ceiling, being careless with a shotgun. He was fifteen. He spent a frantic week trying to cover the ceiling and roof damage.

That frigging car that I backed into a ditch hauling the shingles. I couldn't even drive a car. I fucked up the whole thing, the car, the paint job, the cover up. I was caught and locked up. Later, the car I backed into the ditch had a broke axle. My dad might have killed me had mom not intervened.

She knew how to save me. Only she and Hal could save me.

Nathan sat watching the lights of cars light up his living room. He heard the blaring of a few horns in the distance, then the quiet. The silence seemed to roar in his mind, like the sound of surf at a beach in Cocoa, where he had met the surfer, and let himself go utterly into the arms of a man for the first time.

The other times were sick times, but a lover in Vietnam had comforted him after Lipsky died water skiing.

Hands beneath a sheet had soothed him.

He could never look at Chris Aston again.

Evelyn appeared to him, as a mixture of boyish stiffness and sexual ardor. There were flies. One was crawling on his face. He slapped at it, and heard her voice, summing up his assessment of himself. He saw her naked vulva before his face. Smelled its pungent and putrid odor.

You useless bastard, she whispered. *Lick me.*

Carl Desmon had baited him. Desmon knew him. 'What'll you have, Coach? Catfish smells like pussy.' Dead calf in the woods smells like pussy. Evelyn smells like pussy rubbed in his face. Sick.

Hal...Hal, you never complained but once, only once.

Nathan compelled himself to move and went into the bathroom. It smelled of perfume and hair spray. He heaved, as though he had run sprints for hours. He hung over the toilet.

"What is this?" he said, staring into the mirror, dim from only a yard light coming through the window from the neighbor's backyard. He saw the face of a cow with bulging eyes, his own eyes, and felt a strain inside him and heard his father's voice spoken to his mother.

We lost it, but I'm glad I didn't have to shoot her.

'Kuballe,' can't say I ever heard that name before.

Well, son, Coach Bryant tells me you can dress with us, but you ain't quite ready to play. Maybe when we get a score, you can have a few downs. 'Nough to get that Kuballe name in the books before you get out of here. Keep working.

Coach Bryant, at least, had not said what Evelyn had said. *You are a pretty quick boy, but Petty has beat you out, son. We're going for a national title. You gotta wait.*

At least he didn't call me 'useless.'

And he didn't have to shoot you, Hal had said. *Hell, you made the team. Ain't another coach in a hundred miles of here can say they played for the Bear.*

Nathan had savored the story. He told it to Hal, but not to Emmett Peterson.

After all, Emmett didn't need to hear it, or deserve to hear it. Evelyn might have known it.

She doesn't give a crap for football or what I do. Not one piece of crap.

Evelyn's face came into the mirror, hair over her forehead, sweat glistening on her forehead.

Go deeper into me, Nathan, deeper,. There, oh God, God! That's so good. Yes, yes!

He saw his fist strike her.

Isn't that good for you? Oh, God, God! Isn't that good? Did you come? Did you come?

His neighbor's back door slammed shut. A sharp bang caused the images in his bathroom mirror to disappear.

Evelyn returned the next night. When he said that he had not gone to the school faculty party, they argued. It turned into a shouting match over his alleged envy of Emmett, the bright-eyed pride of Mr. Jeter, and his ponytailed-wife.

Nathan left the house again, slamming the door, and ran for two miles all the way to Davis Wallace's home. He did not return home that night.

Nineteen

Ware's Cafe

THE YEAR UNFOLDED PROSPEROUSLY FOR THE FOOTBALL TEAM. They won nine of ten games for a second time. Enthusiasm was everywhere, or so it seemed. The community fully embraced the Hilliard athletic program, itching for a league championship to come.

In a spring rain, Emmett drove four blocks to Shorty's Garage to have his oil changed.

Sixteen fifty is outrageous! It would take less than an hour. I hate submitting something so simple to a garage. Can't budge the oil nut without stripping it!

Barbara Lynne, tired of his profanity, sent him off to Shorty's. It was Saturday morning. Taking her umbrella, and leaving the car, he jogged to Ware's Cafe, a small downtown coffee shop, to spend an hour, read the paper and a magazine.

He slipped into a booth and began reading *The Sporting News*. The waitress knew him, so he didn't have to order. She brought him black coffee. He thanked her and buried himself in an article. He had not noticed that Evelyn Kuballe sat in another booth. She had noticed him jog to the door with that brightly colored umbrella and sit in a booth.

She felt she needed to talk to Emmett, but he would notice she had been crying. *He was a kind man*, she thought.

Outside the rain increased and sizzled on the sidewalk.

My hair's a mess. I should go home. Don't wives stay home on Saturdays?

She could not remember when she last spent a Saturday with Nathan. The retreat weekend had been a fiasco. He was out with Davis Wallace or at the school. Always, he seemed angry about something.

What was happening to him? To us? He refused every attempt to get some help from somewhere. Our marriage has collapsed.

She took a deep breath, and it caught in her throat.

"I'm meeting Davis at the school to work out. I'll be home late," he would say.

Same thing week after week. Football film, workouts, golf. Why couldn't he fix cars, wash them, putter around in the garage? Never speaks, never has time for me. It has changed so much.

What did I do?

The air in my house isn't fit to breath anymore.

She felt the fears her sister had spoken of in Houston. *You need to see somebody. See a lawyer, Evelyn. See a doctor. You can't let this go on. You deserve so much more from him. Don't wind up like my friend, who found her husband in bed with another woman.*

I don't believe Nathan is seeing another woman. He has his work. It isn't women. He doesn't like me. He avoids other people, except for Davis Wallace, this sporting goods store owner. Except this friendship is different from what he had with Hal Rivers. Hal was like an older brother. Davis Wallace is a single man, who seems to pay excessive attention to Nathan.

When Emmett Peterson took Hal's position, it cut Nathan's heart out. He wanted that team so badly. He talked about how he and Hal had something special. He thinks he can leave a legacy for Hal. It has grown to be obsessive and pitiful.

I blame the Headmaster for a lot of this. He went for the new fellow and sweet-talked Nathan out of the job. Gave him a big raise. I couldn't believe it. Nathan gave ten years to that team and that school, and to be treated like it didn't matter? No regard at all for the man's pride. He wants the team so bad. I understand that. But, he can't let Jeter's choice go.

Jeter introduced the new guy to his niece. He's a nice fellow, married his niece in less than a year after he was hired. She is a sweet girl. He is very nice, very easy-going, but it leaves Nathan lost and sad, always angry. He turned his anger on me for some reason. He is so far away from the man I knew when I married him.

These thoughts raced through Evelyn's mind.

She sat in the booth until her coffee grew cold.

"Want me to heat your coffee for you, Mrs. Kuballe?" the waitress asked. She poured her a fresh cup and moved to do the same for Emmett at the next booth.

He still had not noticed Evelyn sitting close by.

When Nathan and I stopped having sex, the coldness was hard on me. He had no regard at all. I saw it coming, this creeping distance. Stopped greeting me when he came home, never kissed me. We didn't go anywhere, see anyone one, attend the parties at the school. We argue all the time.

When he moved to the guest bedroom, I was devastated. 'Let's see a counselor. This isn't working,' I said.

He got so mad at me that he stormed out of the house, shouting, 'What's with you? We don't need to see any one.'

'You are scaring me, Nathan!'

'Then I'll wear a mask and you won't have to look at me. Maybe I'll get me some earplugs, and I won't have to listen to you. If you'd shut up, and tell the other imbeciles to shut up, all those people trying to analyze me, who want to tell me how to live, who want to tell me who I should associate with, that would help, you included!'

For some reason she wanted to talk to Emmett. He was oblivious to her presence. The rain outside the Cafe subsided. *It would be nice to talk to a man whose temper wasn't on edge.*

She imagined rising to leave and pretending she had not noticed him. He'd invite her to join him, and they could talk. Emmett didn't seem to take life seriously like Nathan. He had just worked at the school for a few years. He adored his wife.

The thought of the two of them gave her a shiver.

She sipped her coffee, took a deep breath, found two dollars in her purse and slipped them under cup, and turned out of the booth.

Emmett looked up.

"Evelyn, hello!" He rose.

He had a nice face. She pushed her hair over her ear.

"Coach, I didn't see you sitting there. How are you?" She was happy for the diversion, she thought.

"I'm just fine, "said Emmett. "Killing time while they wrestle the oil nut and take the filter off my car. I have skinned my knuckles for an hour struggling with it. You probably never got whipped by an oil nut? Barbara made me come in and get Shorty to take care of it. 'No mechanical touch,' she said. Makes me mad. Sit down. I'll buy you coffee."

"I really need to get to the grocery."

"Well, if you have to go, I'll be sitting here for another forty-five minutes."

She warmed to his kindness and slipped into the booth. The waitress came with the coffee pot.

Yes, it was good not to have to run to school to watch film on Saturday. "Just stay in bed until after eight in the morning," he said. They were pleased with the fall planting, the condition of the yard, and the house.

It was all small-talk. She didn't betray what was really on her mind.

"That landscaper Dan Jeter recommended was excellent. He charged us a fortune. If the fertilizer works, I'll be busy all this spring, especially with all the rain we've had."

Suddenly just as the conversation had begun, it sagged, and for no obvious reason. They sat looking at each other, until he fingered the article he had been reading.

"I was reading a track article by Kenny Moore," he said. "He's the guy who ran in the '76 Olympics with Frank Shorter. Moore is a terrific writer. University of Texas, I think. I'm not much of a track man, like Nathan, but I like to read this guy's work."

Emmett could not be aware of the fluttering in Evelyn's mind. He had spoken to her often. This was the first time the two of them had chatted together, just the two of them.

She's an attractive woman. Must be a smoky room to make her eyes that red.

He wondered what life must be like with Kuballe. He knew the guy just tolerated him, or so he thought. *It didn't matter.* They produced good teams as long as he catered to Nathan's whims regarding offensive plays. He was great with the boys, but he played favorites too much. He was hard-nosed, even excessive at times.

I think Kuballe is afraid of something, he had once told Barbara. *Those mood swings are obvious. At school just today the new guy in the Lower School tried to tease him, and Nathan jumped him with a short fuse. Offended at some little wisecrack about Bama football. Nathan said, 'Just spare it, son.' We all laughed, but it was more than a little weird. Awkward actually.*

'He's a proud man, Emmett,' Barbara had said. 'After all… he lost a friend. Of all people you should know about that.'

Emmett looked at Evelyn over his magazine as she studied her coffee. The sun made momentary weak streaks in the cafe front glass.

"Well," he said, laying his magazine down. "How are things over at the Kuballe household? Life's got to be more sane now that we don't spend Saturdays running out to school every minute studying film. I can't keep up with Nathan. He is Superman in the gym."

"I guess he's at the gym working out. He left early and didn't say." She wasn't about to admit that he left without her knowing because he was in another bed. "He goes with Davis Wallace and hits golf balls if he isn't spending mornings at the school. Says he grades papers. He's sure not the work-around-the-house type. He calls it his 'private time.' He announced that the second week after we moved in."

She tried to laugh weakly.

"So, I know my place on the weekends. I just steer clear."

Emmett studied her face as she spoke, but he was faintly aware of shifting clouds moving over the sun streaks.

Evelyn paid no attention to a customer entering the coffee shop, wearing a sleazy brown windbreaker, dark glasses, and fleece cap pulled low over his face. It was raining, but it wasn't cold.

Emmett had glanced down at his article when the first shot was fired, like the clatter of a heavy skillet hitting the floor. Evelyn jumped, but Emmett was quicker, and crawled over the table on top of her, pushing her, and forcing her head down with his own body crushing her shoulders. The moment became electric with firing and shrieking, falling dishes, burning grease, glass breaking, and the howling.

Emmett felt the air go out of Evelyn like an inner tube losing air, a sound he had once known. He lay on top of her, and she clutched his neck, pressed between the seat and the table leg. A pool of blood formed within reach of his hand. Not Evelyn's, but the blood of another woman. The waitress, who had been walking toward their table, had been hit in the gunfire. She was howling in pain. He saw blood pooling from her neck and gathering on the floor.

The assailant leaped for the door and crashed through the glass, fleeing.

Emmett, without thought, scrambled from beneath the table, as it lurched above him. The odor of smoke and grease pinched his nose. He flung himself toward the door and out, down the street. The crying of the wounded woman rang in his ears.

"Emmett! Emmett!" Evelyn screamed.

He was out of the door and running.

He glanced both ways. A man in a brown windbreaker streaked away in the rain as it began to fall heavily again. Emmett dashed after him through puddles of water that splashed up as he sprinted.

He tucked his chin and began his pursuit, running low, pumping his elbows, trying to relax his shoulders.

No one was on the street. He could fly; he was in condition.

Run the shooter down. Gun or no gun. Run the bastard down!

The ran fell harder. His jeans were soaked. Space began to close as he gained ground. Acid mounted in his thighs.

Run through the pain. Catch 'em. Go. Go.

The man glanced back quickly and increased his pace

What if he shoots me? Catch him.

Emmett ran off the sidewalk onto the street, pushing faster.

Out of the hardware store, a woman pushed a baby in a stroller, dipping it down the curb into the empty street, hurrying to avoid the rain. She didn't see him. He saw her and tried to cut around her and slipped, lost his balance, and slid on the sidewalk.

The brown-coated figure darted up an alley. Emmett went dancing after him again, skipping on one leg, feeling his knee twist. He fell a second time, skidding and bashing his elbow, and skinning his head. Rain water covered his face and mouth. His chin was bleeding from the pavement. He was a bloody mess.

A person screamed.

Emmett lay stunned in the gutter. The child in the stroller screamed.

A person shouted, "He's been shot! I heard a shot."

Standing at the curb, an older man seemed to grasp the situation.

"I saw the whole thing. Your running and falling."

He handed him a cloth to staunch the blood.

Yowling sirens and voices tossed around him. It made him dizzy.

With the man at his side, he stood up and stared back to the cafe.

"There was a shooting," he stammered.

"I heard it. You chased the guy."

"People are hit." Emmett tried to jog and limp along toward Ware's.

"I saw you chasing the guy. I thought he shot you the way you fell," the old man said.

Others followed him along the street, gawking and staring.

Emmett remembered Evelyn lying on the floor. The blood, the three or four shots, the shattering of glasses. He had not heard gunfire since the war. It was surreal.

An old hag with candy eyes flashed and burned in front of him. He had seen her, felt her. The howling of pain and agony, the smell inexplicably came into his nostrils. He blinked his eyes. The hag disappeared. There stood the old man.

Emmett's knee stung and ached.

"Evelyn Kuballe's in that cafe!" he said abruptly.

He broke free from the man's side and hurried back. An ambulance arrived as Emmett pushed through the crowd. He heard his name, "Coach! Coach!"

Evelyn sat in a booth, her head bleeding. She held it with a towel. Medics scrambled to the side of the bleeding waitress.

Emmett felt the strong grip of a police officer clamp down on his arm. "Okay, Mister, you can't be in here."

"Please, Officer," said Evelyn, looking up, "he was with me. He went after the man with the gun. Please. Let him stay."

"Is this your husband ma'am?"

Evelyn was haggard and bruised.

"No. He just saved my life!" she blurted.

A paramedic came to her side. "Let me see that cut, m'am. Are you all right?"

"I am. This man saved my life. He saved me!" she kept repeating.

Emmett felt himself growing dizzy. He had hit his head on the concrete.

The Hag appeared again, her eyes like bright candles, leered at Emmett, bobbing her haggard, blood-stained head.

"I've seen you," Emmett said to no one.

Instinctively, he helped Evelyn sit up. The paramedic put a compress bandage on her head.

"We need to get her to the ER, mister. Her head needs a stitch or two. You don't look too stable yourself. Get in the ambulance with her. We will take a look at both of you." The medic meant it as an order, but Emmett refused.

"Take her. I work with her husband. I'll contact him."

"Ma'am, you have ID?" the policeman said.

"I do." She found her purse. "He saved my life, you know."

"I realize that ma'am. This is a crime scene. You both were witnesses."

"You, sir?"

Emmett gave him his driver's license. He slumped on a chair.

"I'm telling you, sir, that leg doesn't look so good. Your chin is bleeding. You better come."

"It's an old injury. I'm fine. It'll stop. Take her. Her husband is at The Hilliard School. I work with him. I'm coaching there." He turned to the policeman. "I'll give a statement."

The policeman agreed. "I'll drive you out to the school," the cop said.

As they got into the squad car, the ambulance took Evelyn away. A second ambulance took the waitress away with sirens blaring.

A crowd had gathered outside. Already, the police had cordoned off the scene.

In the squad car, the policeman handed Emmett a metal first aid kit. "Clean up your chin, and that skinned elbow," he ordered. "Scrape is nasty. You shoulda let them stitch that chin.

"Now, what happened?"

Emmett told him.

"You are taking a big chance, Coach, chasing after any guy with a gun. He could have shot you."

"I guess so, but he didn't. He was wearing a brown windbreaker, old one, and wool cap. Maybe dark glasses. He could run like sprinter."

"That's what I mean. Crazy guy like that. Might shoot you and other folks too. Must have had it in for that waitress, you guess?"

"Maybe.

"I just chased him. I got Mrs. Kuballe under the table and took off. It's training. I ran and fell on the curb running, when this lady with a kid came out of no where."

"Were you meeting Mrs. Kuballe?"

"No, sir. She was having coffee. I was waiting on my car at Shorty's. We were just visiting. I work every day with her husband at The Hilliard School. I was in the military. I was reacting to the shots. It's the way I was taught."

"In the war? Vietnam?"

"Yes," said Emmett, "three years."

"Lot of combat?"

"More than enough."

The policeman nodded agreeably. "People in the cafe'll give a good description. We'll pick him up. Bank on that."

"I hope so. The girl was hurt bad. I saw the blood. Evelyn was lucky."

"Reckon he was shooting at her or the waitress?"

"Hard to say. More than one shot. I never saw him come in."

"Who got hit first?"

"Can't say. Maybe the waitress. I don't know. Stuff happened so fast. I just reacted."

The squad car pulled onto the campus and sped under the line of trees to the library and around to the gym. Kuballe's car was parked in its usual spot.

"He's there," said Emmett. "I need to call my wife, too."

"Sure," said the policeman, who got out with him.

Inside the locker room the clink of weights signaled where Nathan was. Emmett noticed how wet he was, how sweat was pouring off him. He was dressed in red gym shorts and a Hilliard teeshirt. He appeared haggard, like he hadn't slept all night. Nathan wiped himself off with a towel as he saw Emmett approaching with a policeman following.

"Evelyn was in a shooting at Ware's. She's okay," Emmett said.

The policeman stepped around him and told him what had occurred. Emmett went into the office and called Barbara Lynne. He could hear the policeman say, "Coach Peterson saved her. All she's got is a small cut on her forehead. Another woman was shot."

Kuballe showed little emotion "Are you are alright?" he said to Emmett.

"We got under the table. That's how she cut her head. I guess I shoved her too hard."

Nathan's eyes flashed.

"You and Evelyn at Ware's for coffee?" he remarked.

"My car's at Shorty's getting an oil change. I stopped off to wait it out. She was sitting there. We were chatting when it happened. I chased the guy, fell on the curb, and ripped myself up pretty good."

"You were lucky," said Nathan, without looking at him. "Let me get on some other clothes."

Emmett thought Nathan was shivering. Maybe he had been in the shower because water was standing in the aisle near his locker.

"I'm taking Coach here to the ER to get that chin taken care of. I can drive you too, Coach Kuballe."

"I'll follow you," he said.

Nathan was a blank slate. How was that?

His own head was pounding. Emmett knew he had a concussion because he was a little dizzy.

At the hospital Barbara Lynne was waiting outside the examining room where they were working on Evelyn's forehead.

Nathan arrived and was admitted to the room where Evelyn lay with a bandage round her head.

"You came," she said.

"Of course," he answered. "You and Peterson got yourselves into a fix. What did you do, slip off and have coffee with him?"

"Stop it, Nathan. Hold it right there!" Her voice was sharp. "We happened to be there at the same time. He invited me to sit down. He was waiting on his car to be ready. We were just killing time."

"Okay. Okay," Nathan said. He looked sullen, his eyes burned. She thought he was shivering.

Evelyn's elbow had a raw scrape on it. Her thigh hurt from a deep bruise.

"I guess you want me to wait around?" he said.

"You can, but you don't have to. The police want me to make a statement. They may come in here in a minute. They can bring me home."

Nathan studied the wall above her head. He didn't say anything more.

"Then you won't stay?" she asked.

"I've got things to do at home. "

"Since when did you ever have anything to do at home?" she said with some scorn. "I just got shot at, you know."

He ignored her. "Why don't you call me when you're done here. I'll come get you. There's a phone in the hall."

"So...you are going home?"

"I got papers and stuff. I'll be there. Call me."

"Why did I know you wouldn't stay?" she said with tired resignation.

He left the room without answering.

Outside in his car Nathan felt the warmth of tears on his cheeks. Weeping had become a habit for him. It had been nearly three years. He found himself still doing it almost daily, sometimes unconsciously when someone would say something to remind him, or after a clash with Evelyn. Some melancholy tone of voice would play inside him like an oboe. He would fill with emotion and pledge himself to Hal's memory.

In his soul he was a dewy mess. He lived there, a place Evelyn could never visit. He entered that place where Hal should have been but was not. Hal would never come again. *Could Davis Wallace go into that place? Maybe. Evelyn will never go there. Ever. She would never understand.*

With both palms, he wiped his eyes, and blinked. It was just misting rain. No one was in the hospital parking lot. He wished he had a handkerchief. Instead, he wiped his hands on his jeans and backed out of his parking place. He drove straight to Davis Wallace's home. Davis wasn't there, so he went home and sat in a cane-backed chair on the porch and waited for the next hour.

Twenty

Let us sit upon the ground and tell sad tales....
— (Richard II), Shakespeare

The week before the shooting Nathan had gone to Davis' apartment and waited on him. He could not bare to be at home.

Davis drove in and dashed up the steps. When he walked in, he saw Nathan's red eyes and drawn face. He had seen it before. A month earlier after their night on the town when they had both been drunk, Nathan had gotten sick. They rode together to Davis's house, where Davis put him to bed.

Nathan had been too drunk to protest against anything that happened, so Davis had gotten into the bed beside him and held him like a child. Nathan had complained that his stomach hurt, so Davis got him a damp, cool towel. With it, he stroked his forehead to stop the nausea.

Once that night, in a dream, Nathan had thought Evelyn came into his head to shame him, to tell him he was cracking up. He woke Davis, shouting to Evelyn, "It's your fucking fault!"

Davis sat up. "What did I do?" he said.

"Nothing. Nothing. It's her." Nathan lay back down and faced the wall. He had felt her tearing his shirt, but it was his heart. She was breaking it. It crushed him. He had retched as she relentlessly reminded him of what he was not, and would never be.

When his restlessness subsided, Davis held him hard.

At dawn, they had gotten up. The darkness reminded Nathan of a thick, inexorable gloom.

"Shower?" asked Davis.

"What?" said Nathan.

"Let's take a shower. That'll fix us both up. Then, some hot, dark coffee. Clear our heads. Does mine."

When they had finished, the first drops of rain began falling again in large plops making round stains on the window. Rain drops made odd, queer shapes, like fish and cow's heads. Stomach cramps made Nathan bend over.

"I'm glad she isn't here," he muttered.

"Me, too," said Wallace, massaging Nathan's neck. "You need food. You are hung over really bad." He fixed a grilled cheese sandwich that made Nathan feel better. He drank warm coffee.

"If she came in here, you know, I'd probably kill her," said Nathan.

"No, you wouldn't."

"Oh, yeah? And what do you know?" He sat his cup on the table. "I'd hear her come in, click her heels on the garage floor, fumble in her purse for the goddamned keys and open the door. I'm sitting there drunk. I'd hear her, and grab her. Watch her fall. Hear her fucking shriek. 'Nathan, what are you trying to do?' she'd shout. 'What are you doing?

"'I'm killing you,' I'd say. And, I'd do it. Straddle her like she rides me, and do it. Hands on her throat. Put out her lights." His eyes had been wide open and his neck showed strains from his imagined effort.

What do you do? wondered Davis. *Just love the guy. Just love the guy until he settles this in his mind.*

"That's enough," said Davis, struggling to keep his voice even. "You just had too much to drink. Stop talking like that. Let me get Aspirin." He went to the bathroom.

———

That episode had been several weeks ago. Davis had tried to forget it.

Now, Kuballe was sitting in Davis's kitchen again, having let himself in with the key Davis had given him. He made coffee and waited, looking grim, confused and lost.

Nathan was staring into his coffee mug when Davis came in.

Davis stirred around the kitchen saying how good it was that Kuballe felt comfortable enough to let himself in.

"You know something, Davis?" Kuballe said. "I'm very fucked up. I think we both are fucked up, you and me."

"Now, how is that, man? You drove over here to tell me that. If you are talking about that other thing, and it embarrassed you, you got to remember we were both drunk as skunks that night. That's what I know."

Nathan looked at him with blank, tired eyes.

Davis has no idea how I am. What I've done. No idea.

Davis kept on talking. "Hey, Carl Desmon is crazy. I took care of you, that's all. That's not fucked up in my book. I thought you'd want to kill Desmon. Now, you want to kill Evelyn? Make up your mind, or let 'em all live." He laughed weakly, standing at the window by the sink running water into a glass. Somehow this moment with Nathan seemed different. He could not figure it out, but he thought, *If you can't understand somebody, just be nice to 'em.*

Distant thunder rolled, and the coffeepot puckered. "Desmon is really a pathetic bastard, isn't he?" Davis said. "I took care of you, man. That is what I did, and I'd do it again."

Nathan was looking out the window. Tears were in his eyes. "He tried to be with me once, you..." he muttered, not saying who he meant, but Davis knew that he meant Hal Rivers. "God, how he tried." Nathan held his head in his hands. He got so mad at me the day before he died. We sort of fought. I forced myself on him. He did it, saying, 'I'm okay, Nathan. I'm okay.' I just didn't know it could kill him. Can you understand that? I didn't know he wasn't okay."

Davis remained quiet. He hoped the confession would help Nathan. *God, he is still depressed about a guy, whose been gone for three years. He is like a rollercoaster. Jus' let him talk.*

Nathan heaved a sigh, and sat still for more than ten minutes. Nothing was said.

In the Tomb of the Soul 253

"Shit," he finally said. "Last time I got that fucking drunk and depressed was in the Army. Met a guy on China Beach. He had a fifth of vodka. We drank it all. Bought another one, he puked so much he couldn't talk. That was in Da Nang on leave before I shipped out. We slept together on the beach, just drunk as hell."

"Hell, everybody does that. It was a war on," Davis said. *I'm just letting him talk. He is confessing to me. That's a good thing.* Davis felt this deep sympathy for Nathan's pain.

"Other guy, named Rondell, died in Vietnam. Scared to death," said Nathan.

"I really loved that guy, too."

"Really?" said Davis.

"Yeah, I loved him. He loved me too."

They were quiet. They sat drinking their coffee.

Davis looked at him sympathetically. "You know what, Kuballe?"

Nathan looked at him. "What?"

"You are all right," Davis said. "Not a good golfer, but all right." He touched his shoulder. "You never told me about yourself. About other guys. Somethings I just knew. But, how did you get to be a teacher?" *I'll just draw him out.*

"When the war ended, I just wanted to hide out. I needed to escape the other life. It was nasty in ways you could never know. I need to forget. Teaching was a way to hide out, coach, do what I do in athletics. I was good at it, you know. I could coach and teach a little. Just hide out. Just forget.

"Hilliard was pretty new. They needed people. I signed up. Met Hal. We were a pair. Not complicated. We had the ball, the boys. We were good together. He was simple, clean, honest. Just good." Tears trickled down his face.

Davis watched him.

"Then Evelyn came along?"

"What about her?" Nathan's reaction shocked Davis. It shifted Nathan's demeanor to a more edgy tone. "I met her jogging one day. She was athletic. Nice. Good looking. We dated. It was okay. I never touched her. We just dated. She didn't understand shit about shit!"

Davis felt like he was seeing Nathan's other side, a very attractive side he hadn't known, a double side. "So what happened? You married her."

"Hal liked her. She liked me, that's for sure. Marriage seemed okay. It seemed right. What normal people do. I thought I could handle it. Hal made it easy. He expected it. He never gave a thought in the world about me being a cover-up guy, or so I thought," he said hesitantly, "I was over the other stuff, the war and all, you know.

"We were never lovers, me and Hal. Just coaching brothers. Best friends."

Nathan's face was about as sad as any man's face Davis Wallace had ever seen.

Davis smiled. "Sure, I know. What did Hal say?" he asked softly. *Be careful, Davis. Don't go to deep with this. You are helping this guy.*

"Hal? He's probably the reason I married her. 'You need to complete yourself, Kuballe,' he said. 'Man needs to complete himself.'

"He was my best friend. We were never lovers. But, God, I loved him, and he knew it."

Nathan sat looking longingly out the window.

Davis thought he had broken open a place in Nathan Kuballe that had been dark in him for a long, long time. *This is good.*

"I knew that," Davis whispered. "I just knew that about you."

They sat listening to the rain fall. With a paper towel, Nathan wiped his face.

"You're okay, Kuballe?"

"He was just my friend," Nathan said, looking at Davis with a longing that spoke of strange, wonderful love, a love Davis felt he knew in himself.

"God, it was such a beautiful thing, Cubes. You loved him. He knew it. Believe me he knew it, and it was a beautiful thing." he said.

"Yeah, it was, but - why did he have to die like that?"

"It's the way it is," said Davis. "Some can live double. Some can't. It's the way it is. You are okay. You are a straight velvet, man. Straight velvet."

The rain fell for the second day.

Nathan gave Davis a sad, sick smile and kissed him, putting his forehead on Nathan's forehead. He loved him.

You are no Hal Rivers, Davis.

Twenty-One

Death's second self...seals up all the rest.
— William Shakespeare

It was well after 3PM when Mr. Sam got the phone call from Dan Jeter that Emmett and Evelyn had been at Ware's Cafe when there had been a shooting. Emmett had apparently chased the shooter, tripped, and hit his head on the sidewalk. Sam sat back in his chair and stared at the rain out the window. *That would be Emmett's choice exactly, chase down someone with a gun,* he thought.

He recalled conversation with Harry Parsons in that first year Emmett had come to the school.

"He's a good one," Harry had said. "Ain't but four of us veterans at Hilliard School. You, me, Peterson, and Kuballe. But he don't count because he is too damn private about it. Now, Coach Peterson will come by for a talk now and then."

That also would be Emmett. Drop over and check on him later in the day.

A few months after Emmett's arrival at the Hilliard School, Sam had sat in the coaches' locker room with Harry. Burke often helped Harry with uniforms on game days. He would wash and fold. Picking up game uniforms was an elaborate ritual for the young players, and Harry had made it so. They had discussed Peterson's emerging role at the school and the way he conducted himself.

"Them is special pants," Harry would say to a player, or, "That number 33 was wore by one of the best. Make sure you do right by the number."

After the flurry and the noise, the two men had sat and solved problems in Harry's make-shift office under the gymnasium. The odor of Icy Hot tainted the air.

The second home football game of the season was to begin in a few hours. Players were in meetings before dressing. Coach Peterson had instituted a strict schedule before games. The atmosphere was thick with anticipation, and the two old fellows liked it.

"There's something to be said for order," observed Mr. Sam.

"Got that right," agreed Harry. "Not enough order or respect in this world. Things get pushed around all the time. I like my ducks in a row. So does Coach Peterson. Comes from that military school background, then them Army years. Can't have no clutter going after the bad guys. Learned that one in my time."

Mr. Sam agreed.

Harry liked that a history teacher would spend time with him, would value his judgment. Having Burke talk history made him feel his own past was part of something larger. Likewise, Burke prided himself on his breadth of knowledge, but he had read up on World War II to be able to answer some of Harry's questions. He also liked Harry's earnest serious judge of character.

"Seen that movie about the Burma Tigers last weekend on late night television," Harry said.

"Ah," said Mr. Sam. "'Merrill's Marauders.' That's a good one. What do you think?"

"Well, it was okay. Not too real. Too damn easy. Burma triangle and the Japs. That was something else, for real. Them actors pretended they was in jungle warfare. They don't know nothing about that, all them clean-shaven boys, them uniforms sort of straight and too clean. Ain't even close to being real. Bothered me some. I can't sink into to a war movie without the dirt and slime. Jungle warfare is mean business."

Harry took his cane and pushed back in his chair and squinted at Burke.

"You was in the European theatre. Totally different from the shit holes I was in."

"How's that? We were pretty lowdown on our side, plus I spent the winter of '44 freezing my bottom off. Below zero."

"Don't know which is worse, then," said Harry, "the rain sweat, bugs, blood and itch, or the freezing cold. All very bad. Very bad. Didn't see no real blood in that movie either, no bones, no guts. Fake. Not one of them actors had the jungle rot. You think jock-itch is jungle rot? What these boys get in them jock straps is mild compared to living two, three weeks in salt-soaked fatigues at a hundred and six degrees heat and humidity. You'll find out about the itch when your skin peels off in your hand. Guys' tally-whackers shrink in jungle heat.

"I can tell you now that pants' rabbits would have chewed my leg off if a sniper didn't shoot it off.

"There weren't no real pain in that movie either. Maybe a little screaming, but it weren't real pain.

"War is nasty business. Sometimes feels like *'Death's second self'* getting us through it."

They sat in silence until the big fans in the ceiling snapped on.

Around the corner hurried a large boy with shoe in his hand. "Mr. Parsons, can I have a cleat wrench?"

"Can you say 'please'?" Harry said. "Come in here for my cleat wrench all the time. What happens if I need it? You better ask nice and stand right there an' use it." He reached into his drawer and laid it on the desk.

"Please, sir, can I borrow your cleat wrench?" the boy asked.

"Not until you say 'may I borrow,'" said Mr. Sam.

The boy shuffled his feet. "Sir, may I please borrow the cleat wrench?"

"Well, now," said Harry. "I think so, if Coach Burke here don't need it first. You need it, Coach?"

"I think he can use it," Sam said.

The boy took the wrench and leaned against the wall to screw new cleats into his high tops.

In the Tomb of the Soul 259

The older men watched.

The boy returned the wrench, thanked them, and left.

"Coach likes that kid. Reckon he will grow into them cleats. Peterson is a pretty good coach and recognizer of talent."

"Well, he was a helluva player. He should know a thing or two," said Sam.

"That's the truth. He's been in here a time or two, and we done shared a few stories, being veterans and all."

"When was that?" asked Sam. To some degree, Sam knew of Emmett's service record. He had alluded to a dark story but had given no details. "He's pretty closed up about the war."

Harry looked at him. "Mr. Burke, you know how it is. You don't come sailing home full a campfire stories and all, especially if you done pinned the tail on some Vietnamese donkey.

"He come in here a while back during two-a-days, and we got to talking. He hadn't been here but for that first season, and I see he was struggling to get some things together. Kuballe and all the new organizing wasn't easy, if you know what I mean."

"I know," said Mr. Sam. "He spoke to me about it once or twice. I think he got it straight."

"Yes, he did. We had one those 'how you doing' kinda talks. I had my leg off. I had forgotten my shoe horn, so I had to get him to help me push down on the stump to run the shoe into the foot. Damnedest thing.

"He seen my leg. I knew he wanted to know how it happened, so I told him. He got this funny look in his eye. It were a look I hadn't seen in a long while, that far-away, long time ago, shot-to-hell look."

"We had quite a talk that afternoon," Harry said.

"He talked about Vietnam?" Sam asked.

"Oh, yeah," said Harry. "Told me a helluva story. Bad things, and you heard a few of my stories."

Sam knew better than to demand that Harry share Emmett's story. *One doesn't intrude on the memories of a warrior.*

Once Emmett had mentioned a mission where several in his squad had been left behind after a furious action, saying that he went back for them. Dak To, November 1967. Harry knew the event had shaken him. Emmett was fiercely loyal. *He displayed that at Longstreet. He got respect from it and demanded it in return. His friends gave it. He'd go back. Such a moment would sit on his mind forever, especially if what he found wasn't what he expected to find. He found his point man shot up in the legs, a good kid they called 'Hero.' Got jumped in the bush. Emmett drug him out and called in a helicopter. We didn't have no choppers on Iwo.*

"You know the one thing about combat, Mr. Sam, that I can't shake?"

Sam had looked quizzically at Harry.

"It's the timing. It's how in one flick of a second, the shot or the blast can change a life forever. So damn fast. The terror of it. Your hearing, seeing, smelling and all gets so intense like a quick burn. Ain't nothing like it in this world. Not even car wrecks. Then you lose some buddy who's right next to you. Whop, gone!"

Showers had begun to drip as Harry told Sam another of Emmett's stories about losing a couple a guys, and Emmett's having a hand-to-hand encounter with a young kid in the same action. "The blow he delivered killed the kid. Slap broke his neck.

"Telling me that story was like lifting a rock for him. I knowed it by the way he tole it to me. You know what I mean? The thought of it had hung on him a long time."

Harry continued, "Coach got all intense and quiet and said he heard the guy grunting and struggling to breathe. When the squad leader got to 'em, the kid was dead. Broke neck. His forearm shivered him and killed him. Emmett said he couldn't stab the guy when the sergeant tole him to. Next thing he knew he and others was on a chopper out, leaving some guys from his unit on purpose. They cleared out because the damn place was so hot. Wasn't like that other time when he went in and found his point man. This last time they left folks in there. Tough shit!

"When he finished the story," said Harry, "Coach just sat there looking at the floor. 'I can't leave that story alone, Harry. Back then, I wasn't paid to think. It became my motto. Don't think. Don't talk about it. Don't remember. If they go and find bodies, I don't know. Later, they gave me a Bronze Star for Valor for killing a kid, by power-driving him, and saving another kid by hauling him out. Not very courageous, is it? Ugly, as a matter of fact.

'Now, I'm a fucking football coach.'

"That's exactly what Coach said." Harry shook his head, knowingly. "Done him some good. Later that night, we beat hell out of some team. He was happy. War's a see-saw, ain't it?"

"Emmett's a strong guy," said Mr. Sam. "I suppose he's carrying a lot of that war around in his head. I don't know if any of those men ever shake it.

"Harry, you familiar with any Greek myths?"

Harry looked startled. "Who? Me? Hell, no. Only myth I know is the one Britches tells me. She says, 'You're a beautiful, man, Harry Parsons.' I just look at her and wonder how I'm beautiful wearing a god-damned hickory leg?"

"Beauty is in the eye of the beholder, Harry. I was thinking of the Greek warrior, Odysseus, who received a wound when he was young. His uncle took him on a boar hunt. The boy was wounded by a wild animal. The young man was left with a terrible scar. The uncle told him it was a sign of manhood, a battle wound."

"He didn't have no hickory leg, did he?"

"Nope," said Sam, "but he was left with a memory and a scar to remind him. War leaves scars, and a soldier needs to say, as the author Robert Graves wrote, in his *Goodbye To All That* book."

"No shit!" Harry agreed. "But, you can't sometimes just walk away. Takes a lot of distance and a lot of reflection. I don't know nothing about Greek myths, but I do know to think about it day-in and day-out, it's a very hard thing. That boy is working it out so he can stand up to it.

"Yes, sir, on the day, when he told me about the medal and all, I knowed, we had the right coach. He is deep and true. He's a warrior, that's for sure. I don't know much about deep literature, or no Greek myths, but I can read a character. He'll be good to these boys. Teach 'em you don't give up. You keep going back till the higher authority tells you, no more. Ain't no soldier ever gonna run up the score neither."

Harry was emphatic. His voice rose emotionally.

"Now teaching and coaching is noble things for him. In war you do stuff that requires the dirty, *but necessary things*. Ain't nothing noble about it. His'n might have seemed un-noble that day, but he saved more'n he let get killed. The reports said that."

Sam Burke nodded his agreement.

"And, the other thing, that sergeant who wouldn't let him go back in, done the right thing. Coach's here now because of that horse's-ass-sergeant. Might a laid a scar on him, like you said, but Coach put his own life on the line and found a place now to pay out the knowledge. Got his point man back. Saved people knockin' down an enemy soldier. I believe you pay out what war teaches."

Harry paused.

Sam smiled, "You got it, Mr. Parsons."

"That's a deep one, Harry. Right out of Greek myth whether you know it or not."

Harry slowly sat upright. "That sergeant weren't no fool-horse's-ass, you know. I met a few of them tough bucks. When the heat is on, a good leader is a voice of truth. Might be the voice of the Man Upstairs talking through him. Saved Emmett's life pulling back."

Sam Burke smiled warmly. "You can tell a good one, Harry," he said. "Be sure to know, I'm not saying a word that we talked about the Coach."

"Shouldn't have to. It's in the tomb. Deep in the tomb."

Harry had smacked himself on his chest above his heart. Mr. Sam did the same.

After he remembered that conversation with Harry, Sam knocked out his pipe and decided he'd drive over and see Emmett. The events of the morning seemed to portend some kind of inexplicable shift in the school's posture. He was not sure, but the events contained some kind of dread, perhaps.

He spent a bit of time brooding over his old student, and, later, drove to Emmett's home. He didn't call ahead, but went by his office and pulled down a collection of poems by Robert Graves. He leafed through the book until he found what he wanted, a poem written in 1916, following the battle of the Somme in WWI. Graves was severely wounded in the battle. It was the end of the war for him. He had written:

> *And have we done with War at last?*
> *Well, we've been lucky devils both,*
> *And there's no need of pledge or oath*
> *To bind our lovely friendship fast,*
> *By firmer stuff*
> *Close bound enough.*
> *— Robert Graves*

Twenty-Two

The force that through the green fuse drives the flower
Drives my green age: that blasts the roots of trees
Is my destroyer.
And I am dumb to tell the crooked rose
My youth is bent by the same wintry fever.
— Dylan Thomas

Following the shooting, Emmett and Barbara got to their home after 2PM. Emmett lay on the couch with an ice pack on his knee and listened to the rain pound his roof. The doctor told him he had a mild concussion. At the ER, they had put two stitches in his chin that stung.

For a minute, he tried to read the newspaper, but his head hurt. When he closed his eyes, he replayed the events at Ware's Cafe. He wasn't supposed to sleep, but he felt so peculiar and groggy.

His dreams gave way to a heavy sadness. He could hear Barbara Lynne rattling dishes in the kitchen, followed by silence. She emptied the dishwasher and dropped a pan she intended to place under a cabinet. It clattered on the floor.

He sat upright. He was sweating and looked around. He was in his own living room. Barbara was standing over him.

"Nightmares?" she asked.

"Not really. I'm trying to keep awake, but I feel like sleeping."

"It's your head. You have a concussion. You mustn't sleep just yet. You're sure everything is okay? Ice has melted in that bag? Doctor said keep your leg elevated and iced for a few hours. Keeps the swelling down. I'm going to wash the kitchen floor. You just rest."

She left him staring at the ceiling.

The swirls in the plaster of the ceiling moved to resemble some old places he had visited. The rain increased. His eyes fluttered.

Back then, Gina Peterson had seemed warm toward him when she met him at the airport upon his return. He was stiff and dirty. They went straight to a hotel she had booked. *Was he glad to see her?*

She worn a black, strapless night gown. It was an awkward night, ages ago. In his memory of her, she looked so severe with her bobbed hair and dark eyes, eyes he had seen somewhere else.

Probably, he had thought, *she was just tired from a long flight.*

He remembered how the lights in the hotel dining room later had dazzled him. He had felt dizzy from no sleep. Gina sat and stared into her wine glass.

Evelyn was doing the same thing at Ware's Cafe. Wasn't she doing that? Didn't she have a similar look in her eyes, like she was a million miles away?

Remembering his return from Vietnam seemed to make every joint in his body ache, especially his knee and chin.

That was years ago.

Not sprinting in several years will do that.

Gina's words stung him. *'I want a divorce, Emmett! I've got the papers with me.'*

Outside, lightning flashed, and he sat up again.

"You are kidding!" he said out loud.

'I'm not kidding,' Gina seemed to say. *'We aren't going to string this out. It would be harder than it is now. I want a divorce.'*

So strange, he thought. *A million years have passed. Didn't even happen, did it?*

Emmett tried to smile, as he lay on his sofa, listening to thunder rumble and remembering meeting Barbara Lynne at a movie. *Lots of popcorn.*

That night when Gina asked me for the divorce did my face turn purple? Did the ceiling lamps sway? 'More wine, Sir?' *Sure, we should drink a toast to a break-up.*

No popcorn. No movie.

In his imagination, Gina's hair began to part to make curious licks like a curtain closing on a time that melted before him.

He had allowed his newspaper to slide to the floor.

"Don't go to sleep, honey," he heard Barbara call. "I'll make some lemonade. Would that be nice?"

"That's okay. I'm trying to stay awake."

"I know. I thought you were going to wiggle off the sofa."

He smiled. "I just want to sleep."

On the sofa, he felt the sun baking his neck, a post-rain sun, began shining between clouds.

Isn't that odd? Outside, aren't I? On a field somewhere.

The smack of shoulder pads and leather-on-leather, vaguely reminded him of some kind of assault. Just like that, he said to himself. He felt he was on hands and knees in grass clipped short, not like brush in a ravine, but short grass, wet and slick. Across his vision, lying behind a blocking sled, brambles of vine. He saw boys. Football helmets, green jerseys full of sweat and dirt, thin, small boys. Peering through the support ribs of the blocking sled, he heard the crackling of thunder, like the mortar fire.

Wasn't this football? Or war? He braced himself for the charge.

After all, it was a dream, he thought.

He wasn't supposed to sleep.

He couldn't help it.

On his knees, ducking for cover, he heard the slapping of leather, the firing and popping. The grunting and yelling full of struggle. He gasped for air, and wanted to scramble up, entangled in arms and legs.

Some larger boy had knocked the wind out of Larry Ballard. Several players stood over him.

'What's going on, Ballard? Are you hurt...are you hit son? Kuballe's voice distinctive and sharp. "Stay low. How many times.... How many times.... React! React!'

'You hit, Peterson?' Sharp voices, agonized moaning.

The Ballard boy came to his knees and stood up.

'Don't hit him with your forearm, Springfield. You'll kill him. Drive with your shoulder, son. Put your shoulder into his chest.'

The boy didn't get up, did he? In the dream, it was football. In the war, he didn't get up. His legs were shot up. His neck was broken.

'Peterson, what did you do? Hit him with a bat? You knocked his neck clean out of its socket."

Who said that? All mixed up.

Emmett sat up so quickly he felt his head jerk.

It was the doorbell.

For a minute he had been back to places he had not visited in years, places where his memory was plastered over. Now, it had been cracked open.

"I came to check on the coach!" Sam's voice boomed from the outer hall.

"Hey, Sam, that's a good thing" exclaimed Barbara Lynne. "I can't keep him awake. Go talk to him. He is part of the walking wounded."

Mr. Sam entered the room with a six-pack under his arm.

"I've come to keep you company. You have, sir, decided to save lives for a weekend hobby."

Emmett smiled at the lameness of the joke.

"It was a surprising morning. Some oil change."

Sam forced a laugh. "I'll say. It made the evening news. You are a hero according to the account on FM-81, your own kind of Waterloo," said Sam, aware of the allusion. His humor was intentionally light.

"I'm wondering about Evelyn Kuballe," said Emmett. "She had a close call. I got her under the table, but I busted her face doing it. You know me. Hell-bent-for-leather Peterson," Emmett sat more upright.

"I think it was your open field run and being tackled by a baby carriage that captured the highlight reel," said Mr. Sam. "Looks like you have to go on injured reserve, Coach."

"I called Evelyn and Nathan right before I came here. He hasn't come home, or at least he hadn't when I reached her on the phone. A policeman brought her home from the hospital. She was resting."

"Not good!" said Emmett.

"Strange that Nathan wasn't with her," Sam said. "Something's going on."

Barbara Lynne came into the living room with three glasses of lemonade. "I'm keeping the Coach off the beer for a day. You are going to have to settle for some very tart lemonade."

"That's fine."

The door bell rang a second time. It was Harry and Britches Parsons.

"I done brought over the chicken soup. Harry says when things get upset, Emmett needs his chicken soup." Britches entered the kitchen without even looking at the folks in the living room, and went straight to the refrigerator. "You just heat up a bowl of that, and he will be feeling real chipper real soon. Cures hangovers, hiccups, and hang-ups, so I guess it'll cure knees, heads and chins. Does on Harry Parsons."

Harry was still shaking out an umbrella on the front porch and removing his drowned, floppy tennis shoes.

"I'm telling you now, when it gets to raining in Texas, it don't stop until it has drowned a bunch a cats."

He stood there reviewing the situation. "Well, Coach, you ain't running the ball tomorrow, I can tell you that."

"Nope, I need to sit out a few plays," Emmett smiled. "I tried and failed."

"I'm gonna tell you, can't no one blame you for it, but it wasn't no finest hour for you to be chasing after people with guns. You done enough of that."

"I guess so," said Emmett. "Reaction. I was taught that. Just never forgot it."

"You get a good look at him?" Harry asked.

"Harry, damn it! Stop!" exclaimed Britches. "Police done ask him a lot of times. Don't make him do a full review for you."

Harry looked a bit sheepish at her rebuke. "I guess they did. It's okay. I heard a little."

Emmett saw a wink and knew the conversation would continue when Britches was out of the room.

The doorbell rang for a third time. It was Dan and Maggie Jeter. She had sandwiches and took them into the kitchen.

"Maybe, it's a Hilliard assault!" exclaimed Sam, laughing.

"My goodness," said Barbara Lynne, "we have enough food to feed an army."

"Don't need an army. We can handle the beef later. And we got Britches' soup!" exclaimed Harry

"How's my football coach?" Dan Jeter looked at Emmett, who seemed fully awake. He had swung his wet knee off the sofa and onto the floor.

"You put that knee back up, Emmett," said Barbara Lynne. "I want you walking around tomorrow without a limp. We got to get your car from Shorty's. I called him."

Dan stood over him. "I'll go get it on Monday.

"Well, the radio said you went chasing after criminals and saved the life of your assistant coach's wife. Nathan should appreciate that when he comes in. God only knows where that guy is."

"You mean he isn't at home, yet?" asked Barbara Lynne. "We saw him with Evelyn at the hospital."

"You know Kuballe. He is an island to himself on all occasions," said Maggie.

"Anyone heard if the police caught the shooter?" asked Maggie.

"Nope," said Harry. "Ain't nothing in the wind but cordite."

"Stop it, Harry!" said Britches. "Honestly, he cannot leave it alone. I told him we would do 'small talk' and not discuss the cafe." She glared at him.

"Look," said Emmett. "I'm fine. I'm a little light in the head because I butted the concrete. I'll be fine. I'll heal."

"I don't give a rat's ass what anyone says. This is a messy thing, and it don't go away easy. Am I right, son?" Harry looked at Emmett.

"I appreciate it," said Emmett."

Barbara Lynne smiled. He knew she had invited them to keep him awake.

"I have an idea," she said. "You boys talk, and the women can come with me. I got some potato salad, we got chips, sandwiches and soup. I believe in feeding concussions. We'll have early supper."

They three women trailed her into the kitchen and shut the door.

As it closed, Maggie said, "I know I shouldn't say a thing, but I can't believe that Nathan didn't stay with his wife at the hospital. It's brazen."

Barbara didn't engage the moment, but Britches weighed in. "I been saying to Harry for a year or two there is something strange about that man. You got to admit that keeping a dead wreath on the field for nine months ain't normal."

No one commented.

Britches took up the subject again. "He never goes home, Harry says. Harry will go to the gym late on Saturday to wash out dirty towels and get a head start, and there would be Kuballe with some friend doing something. He don't go home. That ain't right."

Maggie said, "I can't comment, but you won't say a word if I do. Evelyn told me she had to visit her sister most weekends. She and Nathan have been fighting."

"Fighting!" exclaimed Britches. "What kinda fighting?"

"Arguing," said Maggie.

"Over what? He ain't never home, honey. You don't think he has himself a little sweetie, do you?" She let the thought sit there.

Barbara Lynne listened.

"I don't think he's the type," said Maggie. "He's just fiercely independent, I told her. I suggested they go see someone, some kind of counseling."

Barbara Lynne said, "She asked me for some names. I gave her a name or two. I have to stay out of it."

"So do I," said Maggie.

"Well," said Britches, "I just know one thing. It ain't right. Something is going on with that couple. It can't be but one of three things: the bed, boredom or the brothel. Any one of them three leads to heartbreak. You better know it."

Most of the food was laid out on the table. Barbara made more lemonade.

"I'm betting it ain't the bed. I'm telling you that's one handsome couple. Might be some boredom. Ain't no brothel in forty miles of here...of course, he might have a fast car."

"Britches!" said Maggie. "Your imagination outruns your common sense. They will work it out."

"Harrumph!" Britches said.

In the other room, the boys had settled into chairs. Harry rolled his eyes toward the kitchen to indicate he was the recipient of an order.

"I'm not talking about this morning. I'm gonna talk about my theory on it."

Sam glanced at Harry. "So, you got a theory on the shooting? Let's hear it."

"Marital strife! Got to be marital strife." Harry hit the arm of his chair. "Man feels his wife's cheating on him, decides to shoot her." He looked at his audience. "She don't come home, so he goes to the place she works at. Takes his gun and haves at her, full bore and all. That waitress's husband or boyfriend done it. That's what I think."

He had a captive audience.

"Coach, here thinks he is a cowboy. Chases the guy to kingdom come. Like a movie! A gol-darn movie!" It was his final word.

Dan was amused. "You figure that out?" he said. "I'm just thankful we didn't lose Evelyn or the Coach."

"Look at it," said Harry. "Waitress hit in two places. Guy's shooting at her. Clear to me."

"I never thought about it," said Emmett. "It was real stupid. I just left Evelyn there and hauled ass after the shooter."

Sam saw where this conversation was going. "Reaction is what you do, Emmett. Not stupid. Maybe a bit foolhardy."

"Not stupid at all," said Barbara Lynne, bursting through the door with snacks. "I'm with Mr. Sam. I don't see my husband hiding when there is action. We have been together long enough for me to know that just isn't his way of doing things."

Britches followed, full of indignation. "I thought we wasn't talking about shootings or chasin'.

"Harry Parsons, you need to stow all them theories you. Just stow 'em! The man is trying to forget that mess."

"It's okay," said Emmett. "No one needs to second guess anything. I'm impulsive. A reactor. It's why I played football. I teach it to kids to react, not to hesitate."

"That's what I always say. 'He who hesitates is lost!'" said Harry. "Ain't that Shakespeare, Mr. Sam?"

"Might be, if you say," laughed Mr. Sam. "It isn't *Hamlet*."

Barbara Lynne was excited. "I loved your fearlessness the minute I saw it. And, you know what I mean."

"Well," said Britches, less animated. "I do know a man has got to do what he's got to do. Shoving that woman under the table before the guy shot 'em all! Wild, but right!"

"Got that right," said Harry.

"And," she said, "if Harry had been there, and even half able, he'd have done the same thing, one leg an' all." She looked at her husband. "Now, change the subject."

Harry popped open a bottle of beer, leaned back in the chair and sat the bottle on his stomach.

Maggie began to laugh at him. "Mr. Harry doesn't look too vigorous to me."

Harry smiled, but didn't open his eyes.

"Emmett, we are just glad you're here," said Dan.

All of them agreed.

Emmett lay back on the sofa and sipped lemonade. *God, I am tired*, he thought.

Jeter began to talk about school work, spending eight thousand dollars on percussion for the school band, a science building addition, and new landscaping to begin in the summer time.

Emmett closed his eyes and listened vaguely. Maggie was talking about her daughter's desire to go off to a summer camp for majorettes. "And, we don't have a marching band. She still wants to go."

Emmett saw wounded images set off by Maggie's dreamy talk about her little girl's Brownie troop raising money for the animal shelter. Vague remarks touched a deep, vague place in his mind, a place he hadn't visited in years: a little girl named Melea, decked out with silver chains, lived there.

"She won four ribbons for baking," said Maggie. "She worked all day over the stove. Covered it with chocolate and icing, sugar and flour spread all over the place. Looked like a pastry battlefield. She had a chocolate chain of blobs around her neck."

Her voice trailed away, as Emmett saw a child he had refused to remember. *Evelyn Kuballe's bloody forehead mixed with Melea's blood. He had seen it before he leaped to run for his life. He had carried her before he tripped and fell, feeling air rush out of her lungs.*

He saw a man in a brown windbreaker break loose and run in the rain.

Had a knee touched his knee beneath the table when the shooting began? A pool of blood.

Emmett heard Harry answering a question.

"A' course, I don't wear no other leg. You ought to know that, Capt'n, because I can use the same tack to keep up my sock. I don't have to change very often. My foot don't sweat." He was laughing.

"I don't think I ever knew that, Harry," said Dan.

Everyone was laughing.

"Probably, you ain't never inquired," Harry said.

Melea left Emmett's mind. He tried to be jovial.

"Is it really hickory?" Emmett asked.

"Hell yes, it's hickory. It sure ain't no white pine. White pine is too soft for a wooden leg. It'd get all chipped up and rot. It's pure hickory."

"It's the only one he ever got," said Britches proudly, "and it was a gift. Wasn't it, Harry?"

"Oh, yeah," he said. "I got it from this Indiana man, friend of mine who was with me in the Solomon Islands and on Iwo before any of you was born, except Mr. Sam.

"We was lying up in a rock outcropping on Mt. Sara-botch-a. I was all shot up from my shin to my foot, bleeding and crying like Christ on the cross. This feller, named Hopkins, took action. Didn't wait at all, but filled me full a morphine. When we blowed the cave and killed them bastards, he hauled me all the way down the mountain on his back

"You want to talk about reaction. He done reacted, even swearing I weighed too much, but he didn't let drop my sorry ass. He got me down.

"God bless him! I didn't know nothing."

In the Tomb of the Soul 275

The group listened intently, staring at Harry's leg.

"He might could have left me to bleed to death. Been fine with me at the time, too. Just let my blood pour out, not try to carry my ass down to the CP (Command Post)." Harry looked at Emmett, knowingly. "But he didn't do that. Didn't hesitate at all."

Everyone seemed to grasp Harry's point. Harry had lived because of the daring courage of a comrade.

"His name was Hopkins. I always thought that was funny. 'Hop-along' Hopkins, we called him because of the cowboy in the movies. Hopkins rounded up a medic, who shot me up again, tied me down to a stretcher, and put me out on a LST boat and on out to a hospital ship with all the other shot-up boys.

"I don't remember any of it, except Hopkins saying to me, 'I'll make you an Indiana hickory leg if you lose that one, Parsons. I swear to God, I will.'

"Then, just as they was about to give me the shot, he winked at me and patted me on the arm. That's what I remember, that danged wink. Didn't see him again for five years. Should give him a medal for putting up with my fat-ass."

Dan was amused at the story. "Well, don't worry Harry, when has any other man winked at you?"

Everyone laughed and looked at Harry's leg.

"I remember two winks, Mr. Jeter. One was from Hop-along Hopkins. The other was from my little lady, Britches. She did the same thing at me. I'm more of a sucker for woman's wink, you can bet that. Them winks speaks words, don't you know.

"Years later, I have this plastic piece of crap tied on my leg, slipping and sliding all over the place. Me and Britches had been married about five or six weeks at the time. I get this telegram in the mail. I didn't want to see nobody. I had been miserable for awhile, inside and outside VA hospitals. I didn't want to be bothered.

"About four days later, here come Hop-along Hopkins driving a beat up Chevy truck. He had a smile on his face, a lathe tied down in the truck-bed, and a bunch a flowers for Britches. He winked at her.

"He hauled out this hickory log about as big as a man's waist and drug that strap lathe out too.

"'This here wood I will make into your leg,'" he said. "'Like I promised you I'd do, Parsons.'"

"He stayed with us for a week. I borrowed a better lathe from a farmer up the road, who made me show him my stump to prove why I needed it. Happy to have his machine make a guy a leg, I guess.

"'Hoppy' measured me ever-which-way-to-Sunday with calipers and tape. Insisted that Britches fix him chili and beans. I bought him a fifth of Four Roses whiskey, and we let him loose to work. On the fourth day, three short of the Lord's week, he produced this here leg for me. Screwed a wooden hinge to the knee, a steel bolt and plate thing he invented on the spot, and a foot on the end of the hinge that he had carved at home. He mounted a little six gauge spring in the joint, gave me some 3-and-1 oil, and left back out of here for Mt. Vernon, Indiana. Works for the US Post Office up there on the Ohio River."

Britches was beaming as Harry told the story. "I'm telling you one thing for sure," she said. "He might have been a powerful drinker, but he was the sweetest man I ever saw outside of my man right here." She laid her hand on Harry's shoulder.

He reached up and patted it.

"That there is the story of my hickory leg," he said. He lifted up his trouser leg to reveal the faded, slick, white, wooden prosthesis. With his thumb and middle finger, he gave it a good thump. "That'll be thirty years ago, or more. This here hickory will outlive me."

Dan said it was a great story and asked, "You really do keep your sock up with a tack?"

In the Tomb of the Soul 277

"Damn right," Harry said, "A brass tack. Only had to use about three, 'three since '53! That ain't poetry, son!"

"I take my leg off at night and stand it beside the bed. Know what two things I like about it best? It don't smell or rot, and it'll float good! Damn thing will float just as pretty, so it serves when I fish in the lake. Never have to worry about my ass sinking if I fall in. Just depend on my leg. Float around, paddle a little 'til the help comes. Another thing, I don't have to change my sock much.

"Now, ain't that good?"

As everyone laughed, he rapped his leg again. "Only thing that war give me was this leg. I learned to appreciate it a lot."

He squinted at Emmett. "That damn war was a bad thing. I ain't let it get me down none, though." He nodded at Mr. Sam. "Ain't that right?"

Sam smiled. He knew.

"I got that note you give me with them words, Sam. The one you give me," Harry said.

No one but Sam knew what he meant.

Emmett loved Harry. He was so direct and honest that they all felt it.

"I was thinking about it, the war," Emmett said, "when you came in here Harry. Maybe this morning set me thinking, dragging up stuff I'd pushed down in my mind," Emmett said.

"Of course," said Harry. "I told Britches it would. She didn't want me saying it, but I said it. If a man can't mention it, how can he heal hisself, right? Man don't get around shooting, he don't think about the war if he's been in one. I ain't talking about hunting. There's shootin', and there's shootin'. This here thing at Ware's ain't just shootin'.

"You are a lucky son-of-a-gun, Coach." Harry glanced at Britches. His eyes were watery, and they told her not to say a word. What he had to say needed to be said for the sake of the coach's attitude and for everyone else's understanding.

Emmett looked down at the ice bag on his knee. "I been lucky all my life," he said quietly.

Barbara smiled at him and moved to the edge of the sofa.

Emmett took her hand and gazed at her. "I was lucky to get back here," he said. "We should be done with all that."

The room remained quiet.

Harry leaned forward in his chair. "I'm gonna say one thing, though, and I don't care if it sounds terrible or crude to anyone here. Your shit stinks when you are scared. Don't nobody ever talk about it, but it is true, because you know your life is leaking out of you, and you don't mean it to."

"Harry!" said Britches. "Don't say stuff like that."

"I *will* talk about it. It is something me, Mr. Sam, and Emmett shares and knows about. None of you others knows. We fought and saw dying. Felt it, too!"

He looked hard at Emmett. "You thought you was back there in war this morning. That's why you run out of that cafe.

"Now, I done said it. I'm right, ain't I?"

Emmett let out a sigh that was loud, if not long.

"Yes," he said, "that's the truth. Just for a minute, I was back there. I've dreamed about it. I felt it."

The silence among his friends was deep. No one spoke a word. Only the rain kept up its patter.

Why was it always raining when war dreams came?

"It's been a lot of years for me," said Harry, gazing at Emmett as if he were in a trance himself. "A lot a years, but I dream about it still today."

Harry's voice was barely audible. "People don't realize how dreams come and go for us, how sounds or words can set it off. Sounds late in the night can do it. Remind you. Tires on the pavement...thunder... shower stall dripping,.... slow rain. They can do it.

"That shooting done it for sure to the Coach. It did definitely send you flying back. I had me plenty of dreams, seen plenty of men covered in mud and sand, flies eating on 'em. Them stinkin' with blood and death. I had nightmares so bad once or twice, I'd roll over in the bed and cry."

"Yes, he would," said Britches, reverently. She stroked his arm.

The room grew quiet.

Barbara Lynne shifted her seat closer to Emmett. He moved to let her put her arm about his shoulder. She felt him rigid under her touch.

"One night," said Harry, whispering, "when I as dreaming and cryin', Britches found my hand and put it right on her boob to make me be quiet." He looked at her.

She was gazing back, adoration in her eyes. "Yes," she said simply.

"My brain would get like a swarm of 'a bees. Buzzing and whirling. I know about it, son. Believe me. I have seen the phantom of the night come out and shake its ragged self."

Emmett's ice bag fell off his knee and splattered on the floor, knocking over a half filled glass of lemonade.

Dan leaped for a napkin.

"Oh, God Almighty!" he exclaimed.

"Let me get that," said Britches. She went after the spill with several napkins.

Harry sat up. "Well, hell," he said. "I probably shouldn't have come over here tonight."

"Oh, no, Harry. You should have come. You helped me get it out in the open. I got the dreams. I got plenty of them. I saw stuff. I actually saw it again when the shots were fired. I saw Evelyn's bloody head. I was there for sure. I was running through tangles and vines getting after that shooter. No question about it. I can tell you the jungle is loaded. An' nobody comes away in one piece."

"Can't be helped, can it?" asked Harry. "Little pieces of us stays there. Can't be helped. Am I right, Mr. Sam?"

Sam had not opened his mouth. He was watching Emmett closely. *"Non dolce et decorum est,"* he said. "It's not pretty sometimes to remember."

"No, it ain't," said Harry. "Part of life for some of us, though. We done our job, but it gets us mad in the head and sometimes in the heart, too."

For a moment, Emmett saw a little girl running toward him, her arms flailing. They became wings and lifted her over him. His eyes filled up.

Harry stood up and looked at Britches. "We should saddle up, woman."

"Yes, we should all do that," said Dan. "Tomorrow, Emmett, we'll check back again. I'll get by to see the Kuballes and the waitress. We can hope to know more. Take off Monday if you need to. We'll be thinking about you."

Maggie hugged Emmett and whispered to him, "You did exactly the right thing." She looked at him like a mother looks at her grown child. "Did you call your parents?"

"Not yet," said Emmett.

Mr. Sam had said little. He was watching.

"Call your mothers," said Maggie, and she nodded at Barbara. "You too."

Emmett and Maggie stood at their door while cars backed out of their driveway. The last bit of sun shown on the horizon above their neighbor's garage.

Mr Sam was the last to leave. "Be brave," he said. He smiled at Emmett.

"Maybe, it's clearing," Barbara Lynne said. The rain had stopped.

"Maybe so," said Mr. Sam, as he went down the steps. "See you on Tuesday, Mr. Peterson."

Emmett and Barbara Lynne watched them drive away.

"They are good people, aren't they?" whispered Barbara Lynne.

"Leave it to Harry," said Emmett.

Emmett pulled her to him. She kissed him. The kiss lasted a long time.

They walked down the hall to their bedroom. She left him and went to wash dishes. "You can probably sleep some now," she called.

Emmett felt fatigue creeping over his body and nausea. It was heavy and deep. He peeled off his jeans, damp from the ice bag. He lay in his underwear on the bed with a pillow under his knee. Light glimmered in the bathroom, making a fluorescent patch on the carpet.

He could hear Barbara Lynne putting away dishes and clinking silverware.

He felt himself sinking.

Against the back of his eyes sat the Hag of Vietnam, drooling, and beckoning him back into the gloomy jungle of torn and twisted bamboo and trees. She went along whispering and moaning. He followed, reluctantly. She forced him to watch grotesque shapes flicker in lurid light and to hear the dull artillery, heaving the earth in the smoky distance. Before him shrouds of troopers gathered on soggy ground. He grew sick to his stomach.

In the bathroom, all of his dinner came up. He felt lighter and returned to his bed.

He could see better now, behind his eyes, an ancestry of loss, graceless and pale, wavering like a mirror. Roscoe, Racine, his squad leader, a lieutenant without a name, and other faces, whose hobbling walk left litter and scraps in their wake. In candlelight their white hands and fingers wiggled. Their hands waved before them, unconsumed by the fire around their feet. They pointed at him. He seemed to be a man he did not know.

An unnamed force compelled him to move forward, to leave the Hag and the luminary chamber of lost, crippled souls. He kept tripping over debris, the cast off stuff of soldiering, groundsheets, water bottles, shelter halves, entrenching tools, rain gear, knives unsheathed, cartridge belts, and torn jungle rubble. He saw a trooper he remembered, Boozler Ledbetter, a cigarette hanging from his mouth. He had died in a rain of mortar fire falling around his bunker.

Ain't no hell like a 105! Harry Parsons had said.

Ledbetter leered at him, his face cloudy and blood speckled. Henre, an old Frenchman, with no legs below the knees, mouthed inarticulately at him, his bald head and wispy hair waved in the breeze caused by billowing smoke rising from the ground. Hurricane Fox stumbled about blind from phosphorous smoke, his eyes pale and white, uniform burned, and streaming white smoke. Cordite hung in the air.

Emmett saw a soldier like himself, or at least a guy with the same name, groping in the debris, searching for wires for claymore (mines) and detonators, mortar shells, cursing to himself for a lost radio transmitter. Furtive animals pawed at the ground, just as he had done.

Who is this? Who was this? Not him.

Old names he had not thought of for years bubbled up into his mind. He listened to a dirge, a lingering, yowling requiem sung by artillery shell fire and popping off of small arms. The racket of combat. The crying voices made a cacophony of anguish out of sobs of the dying.

The little girl, the child he knew, Melea, pushed an empty wagon with bicycles wheels on it. She beckoned him to follow. *Melea. Melea.* He wept her name. Other apparitions mouthed words at him he could not hear. His own voice was lost in the whining shrieks of shelling.

Roll call? He was a leader, their leader. He couldn't answer his own name. *Who was that soldier really? Who? You got a name, soldier?*

Candles illuminated the place. Their wax flowed in gelatinous folds of ten, twelve years, and spread out before him, like napalm jelly, spewing flames over the folds of years, illuminating the killing fields momentarily only to sink and fade into sizzling, waxy pools of burning, smoking debris.

Melea flew above him, her arms like wings, her feet on fire, leaving a smoky trail in the clouds.

A cool breeze pervaded his dream. He was frightened of the change. He wanted to pull a poncho over him like a shroud. His wet pillow was too heavy to move, and the ground quaked under him causing his dizziness. Seeing the Hag's face, feeling her bony leg nudge him made him cry through clinched teeth, "You bitch! You bitch!"

"Shh - shh." The soothing touch of Barbara Lynne woke him.

He felt her hand brush his shoulder, then stroke his neck, gentle kisses on his face clicked softly about his eyes. "Shh - shh. I love you, baby. I love you. I'm here. Shh - shh. I'm here."

He knew she felt his body quaking from his sobs.

She let him cry softly until he was quiet and slept.

It wasn't him. That wasn't him. Not any more.

It took two weeks before Emmett felt like his old self. His knee was better. Whatever trauma the Ware's Cafe shooting caused seemed to slip away with Barbara Lynne's attention and mostly her touch. She took a day off to look after him. He had followed Mr. Jeter's offer of the day off, and lay about the house, reading, and watching the yard dry out, even mowed the grass.

Mr. Sam came over for a dinner. Emmett loved that his old teacher was now a close friend and colleague. Burke said he was teaching *The Odyssey* again.

"At least the twenty-fifth time," he said. "It's better every time. You know, Emmett, you and Odysseus have a lot in common? Do you remember studying it with me?"

Emmett scratched his head. The question was classic Burke. "I know we read it when I was a senior in high school. At least it was in my book bag."

Sam smiled. "Let me tell you something, Emmett. Odysseus is a hunter. He is one tough cookie. He loves dangerous games, loves exposing himself to danger. The thrill of it all. He sought it out.

"Sound familiar?"

Barbara Lynne listened. "You mean the cafe, don't you?"

"I mean the cafe, the Rodman thing, the war stuff. Odysseus lived to take advantage of the dangerous position, the sense of exploit and personal exposure to danger. He killed a boar when he was a boy, but the animal scared him forever before Odysseus finished him off. From that adventure he earned his name, Odysseus, 'inflictor of pain.' After his war travels and many adventures, he goes home to Ithaca. Living up to his name, he killed all of the suitors to his wife in cold blood."

Emmett was dismayed. "And you think that resembles me? I hope not."

Burke smiled. "Of course not. You didn't go seeking the moment of confrontation, except in a game of football. You haven't killed anybody here. But, you know what it is like to expose yourself to danger, to make war. That's in your blood. It's on your heart."

"That's tough to hear," said Emmett. "I don't like it."

"Because you are not living out an adventure tale like Odysseus. *The Odyssey* is a tale. It's a myth. You have to remember Odysseus doesn't always live up to his name. He suffers and fails. That's the lesson.

"We all fail. Odysseus does, but he also survives. You survive. Like him, Emmett, you've exposed yourself to danger in the war, sometimes jumped ship and chased down your own one-eyed monster. For you not to do that means oblivion. It means taking a risk that could lead to death. You must do it. It's how you were taught in the army, and on the football field.

"You can understand that. Maybe that's why football is in your blood. It has its violent and daring side. You stalked the defensive line, seeking out the ball carrier. You hit him, time after time.

"Odysseus is not a perfect comparison, but close. He suffered what's called the 'weariness of rowing.' It's the aching pain of questing."

At this moment, Barbara Lynne saw in Mr. Sam the stuff Emmett loved. He could transform literature into life and back to literature.

Emmett, transfixed, muttered, "I guess so. You make me sound weird."

"You aren't weird. You are human, wired to react, like you told Harry and the rest of us. You did it because of what you are and how you were taught. Certainly, not weird. Not even close. You got courage. You row hard in the prow of the boat. But that's another subject."

"I probably couldn't live with myself, Mr. Sam, if I had not gone after the guy at Ware's. The prow of the boat."

"Exactly. We know that. Accept it, Emmett, for what it is, your nature."

"You know what Odysseus said about himself, 'I have endured at the will of the gods.'"

"Did you ever look at the meaning of your name?" Sam asked.

"Not really. Did you look me up?"

"Didn't have to. It means 'rebellious explorer.' How's that?"

Barbara exclaimed, "You are better than some doctors at the hospital."

"No, I'm not. I'm just well-read."

"My time as shrink and healer is over. I better be headed home or you might make me sit up all night reading *The Odyssey* again."

"You've done that?" asked Barbara Lynne.

"Sure, many times." He smiled, picked up his hat, and left.

Twenty-Three

So she with flattering smiles weak hearts doth guide
Unto her love, and tempt to their decay,
Whom, being caught, she kills with cruel pride,
And feeds at pleasure on the wretched prey.
— Edmund Spenser

When Emmett returned to school, he and Nathan put the finishing touches on the spring football practice plans. Emmett threw himself into his coaching and teaching duties, closing out the school year.

After class one morning, Emmett closed his office door and set to work reviewing practice film and preparing for a spring game to be played at the end of the week.

The telephone startled him.

"Hello, Emmett. This is Evelyn Kuballe."

She sounded dull and far away.

"Hello," he said. "I can barely hear. How are you feeling?" He had not talked to her since the incident at Ware's Cafe. Barbara Lynne and Dan had said she was trying to get back to work. Nathan had never offered one word about her condition or the situation.

"I'm okay."

"I hope those cuts on your forehead are better," he said. "I feel bad about having slammed you down so hard. I didn't mean to."

"You don't need to apologize to me. I'm fine. You probably saved my life. I just need to talk with you. Could you meet me?"

"Right now?" He was surprised.

"I was hoping now. If you aren't too busy." She pled with him. "I need to speak to you about some things. Could you meet me?"

Emmett's mind went tumbling. "Why don't you come over here to the office? I could meet you in about forty minutes. I have a class after lunch, then a staff meeting."

"I can't come to the school," she said. "I was thinking of Radison Park. Do you know it? It's about four miles past the Dairy Queen on the way to Bristol?"

"Sure," said Emmett. "I know it. Picnic tables. Are you okay?"

"I'm okay. I just need to talk to you, please."

Her voice sounded brittle and hesitant. He knew that down in Houston her sister was having a lot of problems, probably marital. Nathan had mentioned she was down there often over the past several months.

"I can probably get away," Emmett said. He couldn't imagine what was going on. "Let's say thirty minutes at Radison Park beside the picnic tables."

When he hung up the phone, he felt a ticklish, skittish uncertainty.

What could Evelyn Kuballe possibly need so urgently? Hadn't the police said they would apprehend the man quickly? I guess they haven't. Don't compromise the investigation by talking to people. Evelyn won't matter.

He could not concentrate on the game plans now.

With his mind racing, he drove to Radison Park.

Evelyn was waiting in a station wagon, slumped in the seat. He pulled into the space beside her, but she didn't seem to notice. On a beautiful spring day, her window was up. She glanced up and nodded to him when he cut his engine. She had a black eye, but she stuck on a pair of sunglasses quickly when she saw him.

She slid into the passenger seat beside him. She wore a beige sweater with one sleeve pushed up. On her left arm a row of costume jewelry covered blue marks and bruises. She gripped the cushion of her seat until her knuckles turned white.

For a moment Emmett thought she might bolt from the car and run away, but she stayed.

"Thank you for coming," she said, avoiding facing him. "I've been wanting to talk to you since last week, but I couldn't make myself call."

Emmett saw bruises on her neck and a red mark below her hairline. When she shifted to face him, he saw her left eye was bruised and dark green, even with dark glasses on. The cut on her forehead looked small and red.

She hadn't been struck in the eye at Ware's.

"I really couldn't think of anyone else to talk to, Emmett. I didn't know what to do, so I called you!" she blurted.

"I didn't realize that I had pushed you down so hard to hurt you this much," he said awkwardly.

"No, no, Emmett." she reached across touching his arm. "You didn't do this. I did it to myself. I hit the back of a chair edge in my kitchen at home when I fainted. It was something that I ate, I guess." She looked away over the picnic tables, blinked tears from her eyes. "I felt dizzy on Sunday night. I guess I fell… in the…kitchen." She found tissue in her pocket to dab her eyes. "I didn't feel so good the week after the shooting."

Emmett felt his face and neck growing warm.

She is lying. What does she want?

His discomfort mounted.

"I'm sorry," he said softly.

She looked into her lap.

After a time, he asked, "Did you want to ask me something?"

She struggled and nodded. "I do. I do."

He waited for her to continue.

"I want to know what is … wrong…with me?"

The words, barely out of her mouth, made Emmett freeze.

"I thought," she continued, "I might be able to talk to you." Her breath came hard as she pulled in sobs as her throat closed.

"I can wait," he said. He really didn't want to be in the car with her.

"Tell me, please, what to do," she blurted.

"About what?" he asked.

"About Nathan! Tell me what to do about Nathan!"

Her words splattered in his mind.

"Nathan?" uttered Emmett. "What about him?"

"I didn't fall on a chair." Her tears flowed.

Has Nathan done this?

"Has he hurt you?" He felt stupid for even asking.

"Yes," she said.

"He hit you?"

She didn't answer him.

He knew it.

Kuballe beat her in the face, smacked her around, choked her!

The thought was like shells bursting in his mind.

"What am I doing wrong?" she asked. "I don't do anything but try to love him, be with him, be his friend. He doesn't want me. Doesn't want to see me. I think he's sick." She faced him, working the tissue in her hand, dabbing her swollen eyes.

Emmett wished he had a handkerchief.

Do I have to deal with this?

"He has never hit me before. We've been fighting a lot since Hal Rivers died. When it happened, Nathan sort of died with him." She sniffed. "I didn't think it was serious at first. Just that he was grieving. But, he didn't get over it. He'd leave me so cold. You can't imagine."

Emmett watched her struggling.

"When I said anything, he would snap at me. Later, he would grow angry for no reason, and get a crazy look in his eye. Once or twice, he broke some things and went tearing out of the house. We got to the point we couldn't have conversation without some kind of argument. It was awful."

She paused and took deep breaths between sobs. She was a wreck.

"Then, he met Davis Wallace."

"The supporting goods guy?" Emmett asked.

"Yes."

Things got a little better. Soon he spent more time with Davis than with me. So I went to Houston."

She gazed out the window.

"I want to know what I'm doing wrong. Does he talk about me? Tell you things … about me? Please tell me if he does, and…if they are bad…tell me that. Please." Her face was red, and she was pleading.

Her red-rimmed eyes reminded him of eyes he had seen in some nightmare. She was heaving in her agony.

"He never has mentioned anything to me," said Emmett. His words sounded cold, even final. "Have you thought about seeing a doctor, a counselor?"

She shook her head, and he watched her hair shaking loose and dangling across her face. She pushed back in the car seat. "When I mentioned a doctor to him, he cursed me and the idea. He keeps telling me to shut-up, that I don't know what I'm talking about. I'm not threatening him, Emmett. At least, I don't think I am. He needs help. I know he does. What do I do? Tell me what to do."

Emmett perspired, and wiped his face. He wanted to get out of car and walk away.

It's not my battle.

Enough of demons.

She was desperate.

Maybe that was the reason she was alone at Ware's looking so forlorn.

Yes, I can see Kuballe hit her. I can see that.

"Every Saturday he leaves the house and goes to the school. At least he says that. He and Hal used to meet there and work. For years they did that. Hal died and he kept doing it. He'd even leave me in bed and go. Or, he'd go to Davis Wallace's place. Stay all day long, then say they played golf. Sometimes he wouldn't even take his clubs, but say he was hitting balls with Davis. 'I used his clubs, he'd say.' He'd be glum or anxious. He'd go into our bedroom and sleep.

"If I tried to touch him…" Her sobs overcame her speech.

She lay her head in her hands. "If I tried to crawl into bed next to him, he'd turn away from me. Later. More recently, he told me to get out, get away, and pushed me out of the room. He moved into the guest room."

Emmett felt the car closing in on him. He glanced at his watch. He had forty minutes until his 1PM class.

"You've not spoken to Wallace?" Emmett said.

"God. No, no," she blurted.

"I think you should arrange to leave town for a while. Go to your sister, but also go see Dr. Childs, the psychologist at the hospital. Tell this to him. Let him advise you. You need to get out of the house. Stay a week or two in Houston. Then come back," he said, intent on getting her out of the car and away. He couldn't focus on this matter.

It's not my battle. I'm not fighting it.

"I've taken off a week already," she said.

"Evelyn, they'd understand if you talked to them," he pleaded.

"But, I could lose my job," she replied.

"Maybe not, especially if you explained what's going on to a doctor. He'd intercede for you, surely your boss would understand. It's the best way. Maybe Nathan will come around. You don't have to subject yourself to his temper."

"Can't you talk to him?"

Her plea was like lightning to his mind.

God, no! No!

"I'm not an expert. It would be awkward." He wanted to say he knew Kuballe could be a son-of-a-bitch if given a reason. He was intensely private. He'd seen it that way. Fly off the handle.

It's not my battle, not my battle.

He stared over the hood of the car.

He could not help himself. "Has he done this often?" he asked. *Police. It's domestic abuse. She should know. She should know.*

"Just once," she said. "That was enough. He was so cruel and mean. I screamed at him, 'Stop it. I haven't done anything to you!' He said that I insulted him. I said I had not, then he did it. He hit me and kept coming at me, grabbing my arms, my hair, and throat. He went wild."

Her intensity was overwhelming.

"It's okay, Evelyn. It's okay," he said as soothingly as he could.

She should call the police.

He didn't say it.

She slid across the seat closer to him, and he let her come into his arms. He held her while she sobbed. He stared out the window. Cars were rolling by unaware of the drama unfolding. Her breath was on his neck, and her breasts were pressing against his side. She was attractive. He responded to her touch as she pressed her face into his neck. Her tears were cool, and he let her lie there until she began to kiss his neck, gentle kisses that grew hungrier.

He pulled back from her, feeling his own heart pounding. "Evelyn," he said gently.

She pulled away, turning her head toward her window, the back of her hand to her lips. "I'm sorry. I'm...so mixed up."

He saw her bite tongue at the corner of her mouth.

"I'm sorry." Her breath caught in her throat.

Emmett struggled with what to do next. "I think you should see the doctor then call your sister and leave town. When you settle down and heal up, you may have a better perspective. Maybe…maybe…we can talk again. I can get Barbara Lynne to find some help for you."

His mind yawed. He pulled the door latch, and popped open the car door to let her out.

"I'm a fool," she said. "I'm such a fool for doing this. I've embarrassed you."

"No!" he said. "I…I have to get back to campus to teach." He lifted her arm. "I'm just sorry, Evelyn. I just think…. I think I have to get back to the school. I'll talk to Barbara Lynne. Go call your sister."

"Maybe," she said. "Thank you." She smiled weakly.

She got back into her car and drove away. He was so hot his shirt stuck to his skin.

I should go to the hospital and tell Barbara Lynne what happened. I have a class to teach and spring football. Damn. Why is this happening?

His mind raced with the speed of his car as he left the park.

That low son-of-a-bitch! How could he push the woman around like that?

As he drove through the city, he thought of the blows, like bullets in his mind. He listened to voices. He wanted to chase them, get them to shut them up.

Evelyn's battle isn't my battle, he kept saying to himself.

Traffic whizzed by him.

No man has a right to smack his wife in the face even if he caught her with another man.

He could hear the thud of blows and her screams. The grunting of her struggle to get away reminded him of Melea, struggling in his arms as he ran with her down a mountain side. She had run to him first, then fled away. Shots were firing around them.

You are hurting me, Nathan. You are hurting me.

Emmett's mind tumbled as the traffic light turned red.

He saw the Hag, hanging before him where the traffic light should be, like a tattered old piece of twisted cloth, red eyes and a yellow mouth.

He tried to clear his head.

In the Texas breeze the light swayed. It was the wavering of her head, leering at him.

He thought about pulling the car over, but he didn't.

That's not me!

"Goddamn it!" he heard himself say. "I've had enough of nightmares and dreams. I have to be sure about this, then get away from it." He drove on.

Get to a beach somewhere. Anywhere with Barbara Lynne. Get away from Nathan Kuballe.

Not my battle.

How was Kuballe capable of hitting anyone, of beating Evelyn? He just wore his temper on his sleeve. Why was that? Why would he hang on for nearly three years to a sorrow over Hal Rivers? Did he love that guy so much it replaced his wife when the guy died? That'd be incredible.

Could Kuballe shoot his wife?

Jesus Christ! The thought popped into his mind like a rifle shot!

I've got a class to teach.

He focused on his getting back to school.

Talk to Barbara, maybe Jeter. That would work. Right now, American history class.

Exactly what was Nathan's relationship with Davis Wallace? Weird stuff. Tell Barbara Lynne to pack a bag. Get on with it, the sooner the better.

He drove past the McDonald's, the Dollar Store, and the Rib Shack, down Lansdale Drive to the school's main driveway. He noticed clouds building to the north like a storm brewing, more late spring rain. God, the rain.

Five more days of spring ball, then the summer. Go to the beach and stay all summer long. Be nice.

Can I face Nathan? Just avoid him. We are far enough in to do that. The son-of-a-bitch. Now, put this shit out of my mind. Don't drive in there.

When he parked the car, his head was clearer. He still had the class, then the football practice.

Clouds hovered.

In his office he had a call from Mr. Sam about dinner on the weekend, which they had promised, and a second call from a reporter.

I'm not fielding any more questions. Newspapers are looking for some angle.

By the time the practice was an hour old, the heavens opened. Rain came in sheets, subsided, and came again with lightning. They broke the practice and ran for shelter of the gym.

Emmett ran in the middle of the pack, heard the clatter of the cleats rattling down on the steps to the locker room, and saw the trail of water and mud. He bounded down the steps, shouting to the his players about entering the building with muddy shoes. He had them return with towels, and in bare feet, clean up their mess. Following his lecture, he realized he had left his clipboard with a collection of new plays and blocking assignments on the field.

Damn. I got to get those blocking schemes before they are ruined.

The rain was so hard it obscured the view of the field. He would just get soaked again. It didn't matter. A raincoat, he needed a waterproof jacket.

At the bottom of the steps, Nathan stood, talking to a few players.

"Coach!" he shouted, breaking his vow to avoid Kuballe, "have you got rain gear in your locker? I left the clipboard on the field with the blocking. I have to get it."

"Get a kid," said Nathan, turning back to his group. "We got a volunteer to run to get Coach's clipboard?"

"No, no," said Emmett. "I'll do it. Don't want to risk lightning, and one of 'em getting hit. Haven't you got gear in your locker?"

"Sure," Nathan said, "hanging on the hook. It's open. Use it."

Emmett went to Nathan's locker. He looked inside. Nathan's slacks, undershirt, and dress shirt with the tie still under the collar hung on one side. On the floor under some towels, a pile of workout cloths lay in a heap. He lifted them, looking for the rain coat.

When he lifted the rain cape, there lay a brown windbreaker and a wool cap. Stunned he took a step back.

Coincidence?

Nathan frequently wore a wool cap. Nathan's cap was usually crimson, Alabama colors. At other times he wore a black one.

The shooter wore a black one, just like this one, didn't he? He forced himself to remember.

Thunder rolled outside. He tore up the gym steps and ran onto the field. Finding the soaked clipboard, he ran back inside, his mind going as fast as he was. Nathan was gone.

It couldn't be that Nathan was after Evelyn. Bury it, Peterson. Bury it.

Driving home, he was consumed in thought. He reviewed step-by-step, frame-by-frame the encounter at Ware's Cafe, the gunman's height, his size, his weight, his gait, his shape.

Nothing resembles Kuballe. Lots of people wear brown jackets. Couldn't be. Who am I to talk about another person's thoughts? I could write a book on strange behavior. I'd be the main character, like Mr. Burke said. Exposure.

Nathan is different. Not a shooter in a cafe. Surely not.

The last two weeks had been a jumble from sore knees, to nightmares, and now Evelyn's situation. He could feel himself becoming consumed by the events. Sam had said tumult at Hilliard was like the boat of Odysseus, one oarsman out of synch, and the boat swerves dangerously toward the rocks.

"It's the weariness of rowing, Emmett, grieves the mind. Remember that. Everyone at the school needs to remember that. I pray Nathan is not too weary of the rowing."

Later, Emmett thought, *Kuballe and Hal Rivers together, hanging around each other on Saturday. Rivers dies, and Nathan meets met someone new. Davis Wallace becomes the next new friend. He's just a guy who sells the school athletic gear. Maybe having a friend outside school ties is a good thing. Who knows?*

Emmett tried to picture Nathan and Davis Wallace hanging around each other Saturdays in the gym, the pool, the weight room. *They seemed only a couple of buddies working out, yet Wallace was always there, except when coaches met to grade film. He would come at noon and pick up Nathan. What would they do?*

The weariness of rowing.

Twenty-Four

Turning and turning in the widening gyre....
— W.B. Yeats

For the rest of afternoon, Emmett mulled the situation, asking himself if Nathan could do the things that Evelyn accused him.

If Evelyn confronted the relationship in a forward way, even a sexual way, Nathan would become angry. He could beat her. Maybe that was the real story, and her confession of innocence was just a ruse to cover herself.

Nathan could be defending his honor as a man. He was intense, opinionated, temperamental when bothered by things that others said and did. Sometimes he would lash out, and mostly at adults, never with children. He wasn't stupid.

Barbara Lynne had to work late, so Emmett ate a sandwich, and sat in his recliner, letting his mind wander.

Sometimes Nathan got carried away. He was a passionate guy, but it always was in the realm of football and the drama of that. He could be loud. He could curse. He never struck a child. He was just demonstrative. A lot more lately, it seemed. He could brood.

That was it! Something was eating him more than losing Hal Rivers. Maybe it was Evelyn, his marriage, or just Nathan's sense of brooding. He was quiet, a loner. Maybe she was his Circe.

God, I'm doing it? I'm doing Major Burke!

He decided the windbreaker was a coincidence. He would talk with Barbara Lynne, lay-out the whole collection of episodes.

Why did things like this have to pile up on his door step? Barbara Lynne got home at midnight. He was in bed waiting for her. He didn't get up when she came in and undressed. Her underclothes lying on a convenient stool reminded him of the way the windbreaker lay in Nathan's locker. He closed his eyes.

Images passed in his mind until she said. "I thought you were asleep."

"Nope," he said, "just thinking."

"Nice thoughts, I hope. You look like a man on a long distance trip. Something wrong?"

"No," he lied.

"Did you notice the flowers on the dining room table?"

He had not.

"They were having a spring plant sale at Molly Mae's Florist. I bought several pots. I couldn't resist."

"I think we need to plant a garden this spring," he said. "We've had a lot of rain, and we need a lot of flowers."

His small talk sounded lame.

"I thought so too," she said. "Notice, please, I didn't buy tomatoes in pots. We will have big red tomatoes in the summer. Kind of romantic, don't you think. Our big garden." She nibbled his ears. She could tell he was tired.

After petting him, she said, "I'll leave you alone. You had a big day."

"You can bank that," he said. "I'll tell you about it later." He felt a great weight lying on him.

In the night, he awoke sweating, having seen a ragged, brown, drooling scarecrow, sitting on his porch deck. It was the Hag again.

That damn coat. Why am I obsessing on that? Kuballe could not have done it.

He lay awake, then got up, leaving Barbara Lynne's side, and went to the living room. The situation with the jacket seemed ludicrous, but he could not shove it from his mind. If the coat were not the very one, he would be a fool.

Nightmares make me into an idiot.

Plenty of times nightmares had tricked him. Allowing imagination to engulf him turning him into a disembodied, wild-assed creature he didn't really know.

He could float outside himself, seek the memory he wanted to penetrate, like a card file in his mind. He could probe it, then be drenched with agonies.

War agonies, work-related situations, twisted events from the past would come to him, in a writhing collection of dreams of ugly contorted, bloody events, war-torn, confusing, thunderous, game-changing events. The fantasies were insane.

Weren't they insane? Shouldn't he talk about them with somebody? Were they really that horrible? Did he need Dr. Childs?

After the war, he had decided to write about the one memory that had torn at him the most, then other writings followed. It had helped, but he stopped as his work-load picked up with college classes. Now this happens. Not nearly the same.

This business with Evelyn and Nathan was shaping up to be a significant ordeal. I should start the diary again. It could help like it did last time. Stop these other thoughts, the nightmares.

Had the pressure of taking on Hal Rivers' job caused them to return. They tricked him?

He felt completely immersed in his own emotions.

Weariness of rowing. I'm sick of it!

Maybe I should wake Barbara Lynne and tell her all the stories, show her the diary from the war. She'd help me. I'm not submitting to more nightmares. I need to deal head-on with all this.

The hall light came on.

"Emmett? Did you call me?" she asked.

"Probably," he said. "Just couldn't sleep. I didn't see any sense in keeping you awake tossing and turning."

"Bad dreams," she asked, snuggling down on the sofa and beckoning him, like a mother calls a child. He slipped in beside her.

"Almost," he said softly. She was in a light bathrobe and felt soft beneath his arm. He gathered her to him.

"Want to talk?" she asked.

"I should," he said.

"Go ahead, I won't say a word."

"Evelyn Kuballe called me today at school and asked me to meet her, so I did." He waited. "I met her at Radison Park. She was black and blue. Nathan, she said, had beaten her."

Barbara turned toward him and looked quizzically.

"She wanted to know if Nathan had said anything to me, or given me indication why he was unhappy with her."

"That's awful," Barbara Lynne said. "What did you do?"

"I told her I'd talk with you. I suggested she get out as soon as possible. We'd find her a doctor or a counselor. It was pretty intense."

Barbara settled back under his arm. "She could call the police. You did the right thing. I know some people. Is that all?"

He was relieved that she didn't probe him for details. He waited.

Windbreaker. What about the windbreaker?

"Are you sure you want to hear all this?" he finally asked.

"If you want to tell me. We're a team, aren't we? I can't solve these things, or help if I don't know how you feel, or what you know." She was resolute. "If they bother you, I want to know. Talk to me."

Emmett shifted his feet to the floor.

"I found a windbreaker in Nathan's locker that matched exactly with the shooter at Ware's." He paused to gage her reaction.

She looked at him. "You did? How?"

He told her about the rain cape and the clip board, how Nathan had offered his own rain gear in his locker.

"Nathan was working with the kids. He sent me to his locker. I found the cap and windbreaker, just like the shooter wore. It's driving me crazy."

She lay limp and silent, breathing steadily.

He knew she was now mulling all this over before she said a word.

They lay together in the dark. A streetlight shown on the carpet making shadows from the trees outside.

She lifted her hand to his neck and pulled his head to her face. "You heard too much," she said. "You and I do that, don't we? We see too much, and sometimes hear too much." She pecked him on the lips.

Emmett smiled to himself. He could hear Mr. Sam say, when they were at Longstreet, *don't let yourself be victims of too much information. It will get you nowhere but trouble. That is why I go to Mass to let it go.*

She had no solutions but to lie in his arms. As moments passed, she whispered, "What are you thinking we should do? We can't not deal with this."

He waited, "I'm just thinking about you - about us," he said.

They lay in each other's arms, but Emmett did not sleep. His mind turned to shootings, his diving under table, under leaves on a jungle floor, a ravine, the wailing sounds of a wounded woman beside them, and his own frantic leap up to run after a shooter, who fled into the rain. Then, today, the windbreaker. Evidence, lying limp under a large rain cape.

"It's all so damned mixed up," he said.

"Sometimes, it is," she said. She was utterly quiet.

In the twilight of his memory, he must have twitched because Barbara Lynne stirred.

"It's okay," she whispered. "Just listen to the rain." Then, later, she said, "What else is there, Emmett? What else?"

He let it come. "Maybe I should tell you how I keep reenacting the moment in the cafe, all the shooting, the smell of it, the moaning. I see it all mixed up with other things, war things. Stuff I had to do, people I knew and depended on. It's all messed up in my head. Every time I try to sleep, I see that stuff. This Kuballe thing and Evelyn are driving me crazy, if I'm not already nuts. I thought I had left it all. Buried it somewhere."

"Shh," she said. "You are not nuts. You care deeply. That's it. You care deeply about her and them." She pressed herself near to him.

"I wish that was all," he said. "I keep feeling Evelyn's leg press against mine under the table, the blood spilling, the wailing of the waitress wounded next to us. It reminded me of a time in the war when there was a young girl I worked with, who died next to me. I felt responsible. I exposed her. I didn't mean to."

He wept and could not help it.

"It was a war, Emmett, a long time ago. This is not war, now. You aren't in the jungle. You kept Evelyn from being exposed."

"I wonder if I failed Evelyn today?"

"You didn't fail her," said Barbara Lynne. "What you did today is so you. Of course, we will confront it, but we will take our time. We will do it together the right way.

"You reacted. It's your nature. I saw it in you years ago. You know it has been seventeen years since I met you - at the movies." She wanted him to laugh.

"*Picnic.*" he said. "I remember."

Silence came over them. They heard more rain.

"This rain is biblical. Forty-days and forty-nights," she said.

"Means there's gonna be a fight!" said Emmett. "We used to say in Vietnam, counting the days of the rainy season until we got to come home. "40-days, 40-nights, look out solider, gonna be a fight."

"It all came back on me when I heard the shots at the cafe. 'Gonna be a fight!' I ran and ran." The intensity of his voice grew stronger.

"I carried a little girl down a mountain. She died in my arms, like I thought Evelyn might have died." He looked at Barbara Lynne with mournful eyes.

Barbara Lynne lifted his hand, just like Britches, and lay it on her breast. "You don't have to be afraid again. Evelyn lived. We are together here. The war was another world. It was another you. We can be together and get through this thing, this time."

Emmett sighed. "I hope for that."

He was seeing the little girl, a half-caste French-Vietnamese child. She walked before him across his carpet in the moonlight, then lifted her arms and flew over the mountains above a trail in the southern Highlands near An Loc village.

"Melea," he said. "Just a kid caught in a war."

"What a lovely name," said Barbara Lynne.

His tears flowed. "I might have caused her death. She saved my life, but I couldn't save her. Its ripping me a part.

"So when the war ended, I tried to write it down. Some guy said it would help. I did forget for a while, until I saw her in a dream. She was like an angel, flying over me."

"It still might help to tell it. Let it come out. We'll learn what to do together." Her pleas prompted him.

A chord inside him sounded.

Maybe. Maybe.

He left her side and returned quickly with a worn, spiral notebook.

"This is the story I wrote of Melea."

"Read it to me," Barbara Lynne said.

The Melea Diary, 1970

In the flickering morning light about 5K from the village of An Loc, a thin line of the mud-crusted troopers, stiff and damp from the night patrol, shuffled across the fire lanes and through the perimeter wire. They ushered along a little prisoner, open-mouthed and breathless. The prisoner wasn't bound. I wondered how they could bring in a captured VC and not have him bound, but the light changed. I could see it was a girl in a loin wrap, naked from the waist up. She couldn't have been more than twelve, and she walked between the men, skipping like an elf when she needed to catch up.

I opened my rations, wondering whether they had found a lost kid on the trail, or captured her. We had learned to fear children, young girls especially. Heard stories of how, while units moved into a clearing or a village, some kids would dart from a hooch, fling a grenade, or open up with a blast from an AK-47. It had happened in the unit bivouacked two clicks over. They had walked into village that seemed friendly enough, but a kid, squatting in front of a dilapidated hooch, had rolled out a live one, and lit the place, incendiary fragments of shrapnel had blown-up troops, who were milling around. All they found were pieces of them and charred boots.

At the THQ (Tactical Headquarters), the girl went inside with some S-2 guys. The patrol broke up, and I went on eating my Ks.

I didn't think much about it until we were asked to assemble at dusk that evening. It was May, just before the rainy season really began. I thought we'd be going out again, the usual stuff. So all day, I had tried to sleep. It was hot as hell.

Sgt. Fox called us together in front of Alpha bunker where the big guns were. We kept 105s concealed beneath canopies.

Sgt. Fox, a hard-assed, platoon sergeant from eastern Kentucky, was a lifer, who drank whisky until the case was empty. He bragged about running liquor before coming to Vietnam, about drinking firewater he burned in the lamp when his kerosene ran low. We called him Hurricane Fox because he had a brown, hypnotic eye and a blue eye. He'd turn his blue eye on a recruit and freeze him like a cold sore. I had been on patrol with him, and knew some stories, how he would sing to himself on the trail, chants that nobody understood, bad, fascinating songs. At night he would whistle soft gospel tunes and rock back and forth on his haunches, watching the wire. He was from holy ground, some said, and a lot of superstitions flew about Fox and his cold blue eye.

S-2 gave Fox special orders that day, a hike into the jungle with the girl I'd seen at dawn. S-2 (intelligence) with support of CIDG (Civilian Irregular Defense Group) people had determined she might know about an NVA staging area. The information came through a special tactical unit that was well-respected. Real solid, they said. She could lead us to her father, a half-breed Frenchman, who had lost both legs when the VC came into his village. He had a contact that would show us where they stashed their supplies: guns, ammo, and other stuff. Lots of stuff. Maybe where mortar ammo was kept, stuff that came in on top of us each night. She swore she could find her father, and he'd arrange for contact for us. He had sent her to find us. S-2 was all over this.

We could take care of the stash. Fox wanted several of us to go with her. A nature hike, he called it. He put his eye on us, the baleful blue one, like the white eye of a hurricane. The point would have to "wear the white suit," he said, meaning go under a flag of truce, but looking like a trader, not a soldier. Sounded crazy.

Fox produced a jacket and laughed, hauling it out in front of us. One guy on point, the others behind for cover. We'd be shadowed by a platoon of SF guys with a Radio Special Ops person from the 405th detachment.

"Okay, girls, one of you want to meet a French queer," he said.

Nobody said a word. We all knew it could be suicide-stupid mission that could get five or six of us killed easy, maybe wipe out a platoon. Nobody said anything. I remember my hair crawling up my neck, the kind you'd get when you're about to run the football just before the snap; they'd call your number, and you'd feel tension in your legs. I might have thought a leech was sucking on me, so I slapped my neck. Like yesterday, I remember I shouldn't have done it. That was all it took for Sgt. Fox to put his eye on me.

"You are a bright-eyed, wild-assed boy, Peterson. You want a medal? You are a sapper! Take the point on this."

I had not said a word, just brushed a damn leech from my neck that wasn't anything but an itch. It had been raining off and on for a week. We were all wet. Wasn't cool.

"You are full of shit, Sarge," said Boozler. His real name was Ledbetter, a tough, skinny kid from Kansas City, who transferred in from Pho Tuc in another zone, a real cherry (transfer), but a bold bastard. I didn't like him.

"Ain't no human in his right mind walks the point in this shit, humping with that girl to find a Frenchman who knows the VC. You asking Peterson to buy the farm himself. You gonna believe that girl's bullshit? I ain't believing no VC girl! I ain't gonna be no part of this. No way. You got to order me to do it. Cluster fuck waiting to happen, that's what I say."

Hurricane straightened up. "You got no say, Ledbetter, so shut your trap. I ain't saying we are taking volunteers either. It's goddamn orders that Peterson, here, is the man. The rest of you cocksuckers, except Peterson, Miller, Berry, Wiseman, and Manning will just sit in your own shit. Peterson'll take point. I'm squad leader. You others will shadow him with the hand-helds. And, Boozler, darlin', go off and play with your dick 'til it gets bigger. Grow balls, man. We got a war on here."

I blinked and didn't say a word. I can't explain it. It was just it. The white suit. On point. Dead as a fish on the beach. I didn't say a word. Like when they called your number in the huddle, and you got to run the ball, knowing the defense is bigger, strong, faster. You just plow into them, living on your knees, twisting and turning. hoping a hole to squirt through opens for a few yards.

I thought about football all the time, in training at all the floating camps we went to. Call my name, I went. Once there was thrill to it, but that had left me quickly. Just react, train, react.

Silence from the men was enough for The Hurricane to look at me and say, "Okay, ladies, Peterson is the point! He knows French. Cojones on parade!"

He looked at us with eyes working like store-bought headlights. Five of us, Special Ops guys, and Sgt. "Hurricane" Fox.

We were close to the monsoon seasons, and the wind had begun to blow in the early morning and evening. You could see the clouds building far off.

Hurricane didn't wait. He had match sticks cut and waiting. Twelve of them. He needed the others to choose a match and pray to God his wouldn't be a short one. We did it all the time.

He wanted a shadow group of six others, and he had them in two minutes, boys with tight lips and sunken cheeks. Boozler Ledbetter had to stay behind, and I was glad. He slunk into a corner like a lizard and lit a cigarette. We sat there sizing each other up, though we'd been in the field dozens of times together. Sharpen the knives time.

I had plenty of experience moving in Indian country, bushwhacking in all kinds of shit, watching for booby traps, little pieces of string, peculiar folds of the leaves, or an unusual piece of trash. On this mission I'd be the one to infiltrate, then destroy. I knew how to hump on point. Legs like pistons. I'd never been a designated hitter before, but I knew how. At AIT I got a fine award. Exercise that training, survival stuff. Using it was a whole other thing. Takes concentration, moving, watching your step, toe poppers, Bouncing Bettys. What you couldn't see bothered you more than what you could. Stay off the trails, off the paths. Move through the bush, thankful each step didn't send you flying through the air like a sack of rags. I thought about hiking with the girl, and how she might lead us two or three clicks. We'd be cooked in our own boots. Left to rot. Some major would shake his head and cut the papers, and we'd be a number on the evening news. The Shit Happens Report.

Melea was waiting.

A fire drill, and I was scared to death. What could I have done, spoken up like Boozler Ledbetter and lived with the knowledge I was scared and admitted it? That I didn't have the balls, like Fox had said. No way. I wasn't Ledbetter. I was a different kind of stupid. I wasn't the guy who took his knife to his foot and whacked off a toe. Got sent home. He seemed crazy, but sometimes in the night in the mortar fire, I'd think about him, and thought he probably had something I didn't. Guts and brains. I was scared. I knew caution, too. I'd take my chances with the girl, and try to see the next sunrise.

"We leave at first light," Fox said. The new Captain stood next to him looking polished. How long had he been in the field?

"This is Captain Kelce."

We had to rise. Kelce had a soft face.

"I'm grateful to you men for this," Captain Kelce said. "We got a chance to knock-out ordinance that has been raising hell up and down the line on this hill. I know you want to end this pounding, back Charlie off. Now's the chance. Intel says this is solid. They know the girl's father. We found her on a patrol last night. You men are to follow her out. Your cover, Peterson, is as a trader, a black market Frenchman, coming to bring some silver to the girl's father, who wants it as a trade for information. So, Mr. Peterson, you're the French trader. You know a little French, but you shouldn't have to use it much if things go right.

I had to laugh. Longstreet Military French wasn't passable, but I had no choice on this night.

You got to carry these silver chains in a leather satchel," the Captain said. "That's the ticket to get in. Here's the operational plan. We won't take more than five M-16's and a M-79, a night scope, extra grenades, and bandoleers of ammo, five whites, and three reds of power each. I got you six flares each. We'll take two radios in case one gets hit. The shadow platoon will have a VHF attachment.

"Lt. Craig's 3rd platoon with his CIDG guys at 500 meters will be your tactical shadow," said Capt. Kelce. "If anything happens, and you get into trouble, we have two gunships and tactical aircraft ready to move in fast for an extraction. We hope no shit hits the fan.

"If you are hit, do what you can, and 3rd platoon will move in. The handheld I'm giving Peterson has a locator so we can find him the whole time. The other five guys stay close behind. You and Sgt. Fox will check in." He nodded to them.

"Here are maps. Fox will continue the briefing. Good luck, and good hunting."

The maps were old French tracking maps. Half of them were wrong and difficult to read. Our map had been marked with a red grease pencil.

Capt. Kelce left, and Sgt. Fox wasted no time giving orientation.

"You can read coordinates wrote on the map. The dark one is the Landing Zone for your pick up at 0600 day after tomorrow. Use Zulu Orange Bravo for your signal tomorrow. Your point is Baby Bear, the girl is Goldilocks. I'm Poppa Bear, and 3rd platoon is Momma Bear. Radio code is 6-9er-2. Peterson and the girl will move together and find the old man, get him to hand Peterson off to his contact, who will lead him to the place where he can recon the stockpile and light it if he can.

"Peterson, you hang on to that radio. Don't lose it. Lose that little fucker, and we could lose you. The rest of us will rendezvous with Peterson at the location marked A on the map. We'll signal 3rd platoon. If it's right, Peterson'll coordinate a strike, or set out charges, and blow the place, all in the dark of night, ladies. That's where we operate and love to be. It's fucking Halloween. We have two gunships on standby. Lt. Craig, me, and Peterson can call in strikes if we need. Use Ladybug One and Ladybug Two for air cover same code.

"Now, every one of you night-crawlers look at them LZ coordinates, 2-5-7, Hill 9. Memorize it. We'd like to bring out the girl and Peterson on the bird, and maybe pick up the old man and his wife, too. He's the girl's father.

"Peterson, pick up the bag of tricks. You got twelve pounds of C-4 to haul with you. Enough explosive to blow up Coney Island.

"Assemble back here at 0400 ready to review and roll.

"Put that radio in your shirt pocket and button it down. Don't lose it. Lose that little black prick, and we lose you. Get deep into bunker six and pull some Z's. You are going to need 'em. Questions?"

"We gonna carry food?" someone asked.

"Three days rations. Grab the rations on the way out. Get some rest, ladies."

Rest, he said. Hell, I hadn't slept for six months. I remember going into a small bunker thinking I'd take three Aspirins and stuff my ears with my tee shirts and opt for some sleep, but it would be skeleton sleep. We called it 'spook sleep' before a mission, where you don't know if you'll be the trick or the treat. I'd wake-up and find myself sweating, swollen, and soggy. I'd have to pee, and I'd go outside, and the hot sun would blind me, humidity would suffocate me, then back inside I'd sweat myself into oblivion and watch goblins dance in my brain. I'd see things crawling out of the dark, and floundering around, fouling the place where I lay. My pants would always get damp when I slept during the day, and my crotch would itch. I'd rub myself and the skin might get raw. I had a sugar craving in Vietnam I can't explain, but the only thing that would make it go away was milk. What we had was either warm or sour. I wanted sweet Halloween candy, red apples, candy corns, but what I always got was that damn sour milk taste. It was hot as hell.

I remember dreaming about swinging on a rope over a wide rocky ditch, feeling cool air on my face as I stretched, giving my body to the free-fall arc of the rope tied to a tree branch. The breeze would cool me as I swung, out and back. It was nice. But, I let go of the rope and tumbled down toward rocks at the bottom of the ditch and hit my head. It ached.

I awoke in a bunker, and it was 0300. Dried mud in my nostrils.

I ate and packed my gear, damn white jacket. *Why did I have to wear it?* It was too tight and smelled like chlorine bleach. It had obviously been dried on a tin roof at the HQ. I'd pull it on later.

The leather sack was full of all kinds of silver chains, bracelets, anklets, necklaces, and ear ring loops, pins, broaches, all kinds of stuff. I had expected bars of silver, not jewelry. A small treasure, enough to make a high school girl pretty happy and rich. I pulled on my combat boots over a new pair of socks, figuring if I was to get hit, I'd at least have on clean socks. I stuffed the EE8 prick into my lapel pocket and buttoned it in. (We called them pocket pricks because of their shape.) Then, I headed out, loaded for the hunt, even a bag of C-4, a couple of Claymores slung over my shoulder. I knew if I got hit, I'd go off like a human sparkler, guts and shell fragments.

At the assembly area, Melea waited, tramping the ground. Her dress was different, a kind of sack that went just below her knees, and she was barefoot. On a moonless, clear night, she looked celestial. Her hair was long enough to be tied, and hung between her shoulders.

Nights in Vietnam were the only beautiful part of my time there: the sounds, a mixture of animals, insects, and smiling Charlie. Eyes peered at you from deep shadows, while white dancing moths migrated even to a cigarette inhaled deep inside a bunker. You lived in suffocating humidity by day, and eerie, spooky silence by night. When mortaring stopped, the atmosphere grew quiet before the silence came to life with rhythmic sounds. Guys would think they heard chamber music and whole symphonies in the night noises. This was such a night, pulsing toward dawn as mist hung in the rubber trees and crystal webs of countless insects vibrated on branches and vines. A faint glow from the east showed trees snapped off from shelling and sharply defined at the edge of our compound. Violins tuned up, each on separate scales, and the sweet, sour whine of mosquitoes mingled with the calling of monkeys in the trees.

Soon, I'd be on the trail, prepared to dress like a bride groom, following a twelve year old kid to the accompaniment of monkey calling.

We moved out at 0430 with Sgt. Fox taking the point. Later, I was to move ahead of him. My radio felt secure in my pocket, and the jacket was folded into my backpack. In the distance, I thought I saw arc light, but heard no rumbling. Heat lightning from the gathering morning clouds may soon settle over us and bring on the humidity and the cicadas that sawed as the heat rose. I watched the flicker of light over the horizons and the building of thunderheads.

"Monsoons," muttered Fox, as he headed over the wire.

Melea skipped along. I concentrated on the direction we were headed and watched my compass. One of my fears on the trail was becoming lost, separated, disoriented, losing contact. Having to sit out there in the shit. Shit was a constant companion. The place sometimes smelled like it. I thought about playing Boy Scout and marking a tree, tying apiece of string so someone could follow my trail. Stupid. I swear to God we passed some VC graves, one dug up recently. Damn, they stank.

We scrambled down an embankment toward the edge of the forest, passed through a stand of elephant grass, then found bamboo, and soon were engulfed in Indian Country.

"I am Melea. We travel together. I will make you o-key guide," she said. Her eyes curled in a childish grin, her voice like a doll's. Despite my reservations and galloping heart, I grinned at her and followed. I had put the radio on our frequency, and it made low crackles. The shadow team was doing its radio check, and would do so every thirty minutes.

In silence we walked for an hour, a winding route full of double backs and up-and-downs, humping through the bush. I signaled every half-hour.

How Fox followed the kid and me, I'll never know.

As the first light began to appear, I noticed the thick canopy above us. We passed places where the jungle had been scooped up from shelling, a broken, jagged landscape. I swear to God, we passed more VC graves, little mounds of earth piled up, wild orchids heaped on top, brown from the heat and humidity. It made my groin contract and my nose itch.

When Fox and I switched off, Melea moved out swiftly, knowingly. She turned only to glance at me and motion us forward. I tried to pick up the crunch of other troopers behind me. Impossible. That was a good thing.

When Melea paused and squatted, she motioned to me and smiled reassuringly. "No hurt. You talk." She pointed to my radio. I used the code, 6-9er-2, then, "Porridge, 6-9er-2." In response came a crackling voice. I stuck the radio back in by shirt pocket. Didn't fasten the flap well.

"Porridge is warm, 6-9er-2," came the reply.

Melea smiled confidently at me. We resumed our hike.

Late in the day we reached a clearing and crept up behind a tree with low branches that spread over the ground. Melea crouched and grinned.

"My house," She whispered. "Melea's ville!" She punctuated her whisper with a gesture, then put her finger to her lips. We took a long look at the hooch, a straw and cane hut with some corrugated tin leaning against the siding. A rope looped over a flap that could be raised slightly to emit air. The thatched opening revealed a cooking pot over a smoldering fire. Scrawny chickens were pecking around outside. A basket woven from bamboo leaves contained what looked like seeds drying in the sun. At the side of the hooch grew stringy plants and what looked like marijuana plants. Vietnamese like their bong. No other sign of neighbors. It was a dilapidated hut hidden in the jungle.

I lay, feeling my legs throb. Melea's smile twinkled up at me and her nose curled.

"My father come soon," she whispered. "He checking. We wait. You do radio now. O-key!" She always said, "O-key!"

I nodded, sipped from my canteen, and offered her a drink. She refused, shaking her head vigorously.

I felt my shirt pocket to give the radio a click. I wasn't there. I scanned the ground around me from the way we had come. Nothing. My panic rose. My security was gone. How could it have slipped out of my shirt without my knowing? Damn it. Nevertheless, it wasn't there. Frantically, I scraped the soil around me. Nothing there. Gone.

Now I was out of contact, even with Fox, who was about 40 meters behind me. He needed to know I had screwed up. The thing must have slipped out after the last call at least forty minutes back. Could I have let it slip when I stuck it back in my shirt, not my pants? I didn't button the frigging lapel flap.

"You hang on to that prick! It keeps you alive," he had preached.

Damn it.

Now, if this mission didn't go right, and we got separated from the shadow team....

"Stupid!" I muttered

Melea put her tiny hand on my knee. She thought I was frightened.

"You no be fright," she said in a whisper. "No fright, o-key?"

She didn't know the half of it.

It seemed like we must have lain there for two or three days, long enough for the clouds to roll in and the evening to approach. I had no security, no radio, a pistol, my weapon, the C-4 bag, and a bunch of silver chains. If we were hit and I had to scramble, only that radio could save me. We were in deep trouble. Fox had the fire power. We were in slow motion, dragging shadows into a changing light.

At 0530 I heard squeaking sounds, creaking like machinery, then the crackle and pop of a large object pushing its way through the underbrush, probably on top of Fox and his team. I buried myself in cover beside the tree. I anticipated Fox opening up, but only the squeaking and rattling continued, then some low conversation. Not Vietnamese, not a language that I recognized at all.

Melea suddenly jumped up and down.

"*Pere! Pere!*" she exclaimed. I thought Fox might open up right then, but he didn't. He was watching what I was watching. The girl bounded out into the grassy clearing, waving her arms and bouncing in the direction as the rattle-trap rolled into my view.

A bicycle wheel-barrow affair burst from the jungle with two antennas from a tactical radio sticking straight up. They whipped the air. We carried EE-8s with the unit, or 312s. I wasn't sure. I was the dumbass who had no radio.

A stout woman pushed the wagon. In the bed, between the large bicycle wheels, sat a small white man, wearing a jungle helmet with a yellow envelop sticking out of a yellow hat band. He was a thin little man wearing a dirty white jacket and fatigue pants like mine. His pants were tied in large knots where his knees ought to have been. He appeared to be sitting on a pallet covered with a pillow. Animated in the dim light, he squirmed in his place as Melea climbed the side of wagon, giggling and laughing, muttering a mixture of French and Vietnamese.

The woman danced in her place with light steps. Her mouth curled up, revealing her distinct resemblance to Melea.

A reunion.

I extracted the white coat, pulled it on, the best I could, and lay still. No sounds, but Fox had to be watching this show. I didn't move.

I might have jumped at Melea's call, but we might also be blown into the trees. I had to trust her. She led me every step of the way through the boondocks. I was lost, and without a radio. I tried to step where she stepped, watched for soft places, booby traps, toe-poppers (small mines) under petals, punji sticks, pit vipers, and other snakes. It was psychedelic. All the way, she had been certain, "O-key."

She pointed and beckoned me into the open space. I could do nothing but obey. Stiff legged, I showed myself and adjusted the white trader's jacket over my shoulders, where I had slung the explosives and the pouch of silver. I held up my palms, so the family could see that I was not armed. My M-16 lay in the crotch of the tree. I'd get it later.

I swung the leather pouch of silver loot in front of me so the Frenchman and moma-san could see it.

Silently, he stared at me as I approached. I towered over them. As I stood there, I was totally exposed. I knew Fox had to be covering me, wondering what the hell happened to my radio communication. As far as I was concerned, I had punched a really big ticket!

The family appraised me, and the chickens returned to their pecking.

We stood, staring at each other for a few moments.

Then, the woman bowed very low, so I did the same. The man whooped in loud laughter and beamed at me.

"You like the music of New Orleans?" he asked

"The what?" I asked in French.

"Jazz of New Orleans? You like it? Count Basey, the Louis Armstrong?" His English was halting. "Al Hirt, big strip joint, o-key? Clarinet of Pete Fountain. I know French Quarter. New Orleans French Quarter, man. At night club they play much good jazz. Be-bop. GI know fine music, yes? The rock 'n roll no good" His voice was nasal and creased with a heavy accent.

"Yes! I know," I said in English. He knew my cover too. No pretending anymore.

"Good. Good. We listen to fine New Orleans jazz, then good Vegas show band, and we drink. I have much good wine. Not VC wine. Fine French white grape."

He gave a gesture to the woman, who went into the hooch. Melea jumped to the wagon, and lifted up the push-bar, slipped under it and strained against it, gesturing me to follow her forward to the hooch where she pulled her father.

I glanced back at the jungle out of which I had come and prayed Fox was watching all of this. In front of me, the moments danced. Maybe I'd get this

French guy's address in my red book and Melea's too! The happy family in the middle of a strange war! We all could meet after it ended and listen to New Orleans jazz.

I swear to God, I went into the hooch where he had this goddamned electric generator vented out the back of the hooch, and a Sony hi-fi unit with tweeter and woofers, the good stuff. The moma-san spread a cushion over a mat for me to sit, and lay my coat in the corner. A pho pot sat on an open fire steaming in the low light. One wall had shelves on which were at least fifty or more skulls, dried heads on display. I guessed they were little monkey skulls from hunts. In the midst of that display was a framed photograph of a young man, not the French/Vietnamese, but a relative, maybe, who wore a military hat and uniform. The red star of North Vietnam was prominent in the picture. Could it be a son, who had fought in the mountains. Viet Minh? I didn't know. My first visit inside a Vietnamese hooch gave me shivers.

Two hammocks were slung from poles which supported the cane-woven roof. A large rectangular floormat lay nearby. Obviously the family slept in hammocks, hanging from the ceiling and sat on the floor, which was hard clay.

Moma-san noticed my leather pouches. I pushed the C-4 pouch beneath my leg to hide it. She took the pouch of silver and lay it nearby, then turned to producing two short, fluted glasses and a bottle of white wine. Not saying a word, she poured the wine as the old man pushed himself to an amp beside a turntable. He produced a 33rpm recording of Al Hirt and brandished his record collection with gestures and words spoken in French I didn't understand.

"*Chacun a son gout*" he said, and placed the recording on the turntable. "You will listen well in my home to the chef *d'oeuve*."

We listened to Al Hirt, "Honey in the Horn," a trumpet collection so fine it could make you cry.

Melea's mom swayed to the music as it floated out over the jungle to Fox and the other guys from two big speakers. I sat there sipping the wine, feeling warm all over. Absurd freaky, weirdo stuff.

Mama-san filled my glass a second time and prepared food, dumping chopped vegetables with noodles on a griddle and stirring them, sloshing some kind of juice from the pho pot over them. I guessed fish was bubbling in the pot. She took a second handful of noodles mixed with chopped leaks and made them steam, watching, smiling and nodding at me the whole time.

Melea sat watching her father and swaying to Al Hirt's horn. They seemed to be waiting for an overture. I didn't know who was to bring up the purpose of my visit, so I said nothing. I didn't give too much thought to Fox outside, who was watching this go down.

When Al Hirt finished playing, "Laura," we listened to the Vegas show band and Sinatra's, "A Swinging Affair." Moma-san served up the pho in a bowl, sprinkled with vegetables and noodles. It smelled strongly of soy and fish. No telling what else was in that pho pot. Monkey meat? Old bones? Overcooked vegetables? The wine made me mellow and warm. We were swinging with Frank, all right, a nice mellow, warm, genial affair.

To drink with a Vietnamese family was special, to eat was more special. We were, after the third glass of wine and the food, sort of drunk. The Frenchman's eyes drooped on his third glass. He ate little. The all-day march had made me tired too.

I ate the porridge from the pot. It tasted surprisingly good, despite the fact I thought of old socks, but Vietnamese don't wear socks!

He reached for the bottle again. "Monsieur, you drink with me *tout a fait!*" He gave the wine bottle a shake so I could see the fluid level. About one-quarter of the bottle to go. I slowed my pace, letting him take a fourth glass before I emptied my third. Despite the food, I was feeling a little numb. Outside the insect rhythm band began making an accompaniment to Sinatra.

A few times I thought I should ask the old guy when he planned to show us where the VC supplies were stashed, but I didn't. I let Sinatra croon. He was giving his best shot on "I Got It Bad and That Ain't Good," when the mood struck me as very funny.

Here I was in the middle of the God-only-knows-where, surrounded by jungle and men with loaded weapons, killing machines, listening to Sinatra, as I sat beside an amputee, and drinking wine, eating monkey meat, and God-knows- what-else, preparing to commit bad acts. My legs felt warm, and my lips had tingling, numb sensations. The old man with shaded, thin, narrow eyes let his head move in rhythm.

When the recording ended, he motioned for Melea to flip it and reset it. I had left wine in the glass.

"*Monsieur*," he said suddenly, "you have come to assist me. We deliver the *coup de grace. Ha*! Death to the motherfuckers!" He gave a little toast with his glass. "I have been waiting for soldier to come, *denier cri*. You have friends with you, but you will first trade with me, then we see if we can make bargain. You have lovelies for my wife." He nodded toward the satchel that lay within reach. "The payment you have, before the final one comes tomorrow, yes? You deliver me silver. I deliver you VC motherfuckers. *En rapport* we shall fuck them, yes?" His little eyes danced maliciously.

The hooch smelled of the cooking pot and smoke. It was stuffy. Moma-san had lit several short, yellow candles. The flickering and our shadows on the wall and ceiling appeared grotesque.

I reached for the pouch of chains and drew out several, letting them dangle over my fingers and glitter in the candlelight. Moma-san's eyes grew large, and the Frenchman smiled, revealing fine white teeth.

"*Beau monde, ma bell, tres bon*," he whispered, taking them from me and gesturing to his wife. "Death to VC motherfuckers!" he said in a low, sinister tone.

She placed the silver chains about her neck, and another about the neck of Melea, who was grinning. Neither spoke.

"Comme il faut!"

I offered more. The family lavished themselves in silver chains. The moma-san placed more of them over Melea's head, letting the long, unclasped strings loop over the little girl's face, cascading down her neck onto her chest. She became a tangle of silver chains, and her eyes danced. The old man beamed and patted the stumps of his legs in a rhythm to "The Stars Fell on Alabama." I filled another glass and prepared for a long night.

Sgt. Fox had dug in to await my signal. I was cooking on the wine until Moma-san served up more fish and rice balls. Rice was great. Can't say much for the fish. I hate fish sauce! My host opened a second bottle, a chardonnay, and we ate again. I was hungry. I didn't hesitate, though the pungent taste of the food was strange. It didn't matter. No one spoke until half the wine was gone.

I felt better, except I needed to take this enormous crap, so I was shown a slit trench in back of the hooch, the family crapper. At least it had a rail to sit on. I sat down for business and noticed a five gallon plastic bucket full of water. I figured it was to wash stuff into the ditch. When I finished, using handy GI sandpaper to clean up, I picked up the bucket and noticed a live fish swimming in it.

My God, had the fish I had eaten lived in the crapper can?

I didn't bother to dump water in the ditch. The stench was terrible. I fled back to the house, feeling sort of nauseated.

Sgt. Fox had dug in to await my signal, that never came. I had been cooking on the wine until I saw the crapper fish. The jazz music still played. I gazed over the perimeter of the yard, hoping Fox could see me. I gave a thumb's up. I wiped my mouth and ducked back into the hooch, sat down, and took my last sip of the wine.

"Quelle here est-il?" my host asked.

I signaled seven with my fingers.

"You must hear the plan. You leave a *mintij* midnight. Go quietly through the bush to place beneath the mountain where there is friend waiting. Up wire path, steep climb, to rocky ledge, you find. There you meet Bo An, who waits. You must say to him in French, *'Voulez-vous bien m'y emender,'* which mean, 'Please take me there.' He show you tunnel into ground. It not occupied till sun up. Much supplies there."

What the hell was a wire path? Later, I learned he meant a path with a cable attached to trees to assist with climbing up through the rocks.

He said the cave was not occupied until dawn.

"Down there you will find much supplies. At first light, motherfuckers return. You can do business quickly. Get out. O-key?"

I listened. I didn't know much French, but I sure as hell memorized that phrase.

This whole thing was insane. I had to communicate with Sgt. Fox, give him the same intel the old man had given me. We had to find a way to get explosives into the tunnel. A delay fuse, a lot of plastic C and the Claymores. I knew I could get that stuff up there easy.

"I need to contact my people," I said in English.

"Qyui!" Henri (the old man's name) didn't hesitate, but gestured to his wife, who pushed back the drape covering the opening to the hooch, and ushered me outside, then took me by the arm and led me to the back of the hooch into the trees.

There was enough twilight. I could crouch and give the low whistle and move parallel to the hooch until I heard the low signal back.

Fox whistled twice, and I found him along side my M-16, leaning against a tree.

"Goddammit, Peterson, where's your radio?"

I told the truth. "It fell out of my pocket," I whispered.

"You numb-nut! How you going to complete this thing without keeping up?" he hissed.

As I turned, I saw a shadow creep along the edge of the tree line, moving low, and fast, hurrying toward the side of the clearing nearest us.

"Hurricane" Fox snatched me into the bush. I grabbed my rifle. "You take Ferguson's radio. He can shadow me. This is a fuck-up son, but we can tell TC (Tactical Command) the porridge is still hot. TC has been lighting up the channels cursing you. You can't be no numb-nut on this. Gotta be done. At least we ain't an abort."

All I could do is nod. "Yes, sir!" I said.

Ferguson gave me his EE-8. I stuffed it deep into my pants, but also clipped it to my cartridge belt.

I explained the plan about the rendezvous with the guy at the rock ledge, who would show me how to get into the tunnel. I checked the C-4. Fox handed me five more shape-charges.

"Don't let that radio out of your sight, or you're in deeper shit than the crapper you used back there. Don't want to be no lonely motherfucker out here, Peterson."

He got that right!

"Keep contact tight. You fucked up once. Don't do it again. It'll work out."

The talk went from the radio call to the TC post and back to the mission. We had about two hours before midnight. A real cowboy mission. I just needed a good horse to ride. I'd enter, set the charges, then would pull back at least 500 meters, wait until the explosion and pull out another 400 to the LZ (landing zone) and meet the others. I'd use the compass. Night tracking was a specialty I had learned and used. No other choice, now.

Honestly, I didn't know about Melea, but I figured she'd do the leading. The old man couldn't make it through the bush at night. I was a speed guy. We'd haul ass up and down with limited time to make the contact. Move at midnight. We agreed to continue the same radio call as before. I swore to that one.

Luckily, the night was dark and clear with low clouds. Rain didn't seem to be a threat. I'd just as soon it had rained. Water in the trees concealed movement. I didn't want to move out with a load of clanking supplies to carry anyway. I had my camouflage tape, so I quickly strapped down my pouch of explosives, the grenades, the extra bandoleer Fox handed me. I gave him the fucking trader's jacket. What was that? I put an extra strip around my leg to hold the radio steady as I moved.

We were zipped up.

I walked casually back to the hooch and entered. Nodding to the family, I sat down and tried to sleep a little. Turns out I was pretty tired. We let the music play.

I had set my watch alarm for 1140 hours.

The candles burned low, the odor of smoke still filled the place. It wasn't bad. I slept a little, one eye open.

Melea touched my arm at 1130. Her father had rolled himself close by me and whispered in wine tainted breath, "Melea will lead you. O-key. She know the way of no mines, no booby traps. You come to gorge where many fallen rocks go off to right, and tall mountain trail left side. Trail wind 'long edge of several gorges, (he said 'gore-jars') to large tree. Beneath tree you find man and say password. You must speak now like this, *'Voulez-vous bien my' emender.'* You say words now."

Peering into his bleary eyes, I said it. *"Voo-lay-vo-b-yuan-mee ah-mnya."* I would have no trouble remembering. I said about ten times to him.

"Man lead you up slope to rocky ledge. You enter tunnel. Down short rope. You find tiny space for only one. Tunnel ten meters into storage area. Much guns and ammo, large supplies. You do business. Guards out for two, three hours each night. No problem. Give me pleasure to hear sound of your work and know many of the motherfuckers die this night. Ha!

"I will piss in their mother's pussy!"

I knew he was not kidding. It never occurred to me I should wonder where he got his information. I only wanted to know who the guy was that I was meeting, a guard, Bo An, bribed for silver, I guess.

"It be o-key."

Melea imitated him. "O-key!" she said, emphatically, "O-key, o-key!"

"O-key" I said and bowed. Nothing casual.

I had my doubts about this whole affair.

Old man Henri put his hand on my shoulder, gestured to moma-san to bring me the leather pouch. From it he drew a long silver chain for his wife, an ankle bracelet for Melea, and handed me the pouch. "Give to contact, Bo An. It is bargain. He awaits you."

Melea snapped the chain about her ankle, but her mother demanded that she not wear it. She pointed to me. No trace of involvement was her point should we be intercepted. I didn't want to think about it.

The radio popped. I knew it was Fox waiting for me outside, ready to get underway. Everyone was anxious to get under way.

Get on the trail. Get this mess over.

Henri looked at me and gave out the longest, loudest belch I ever heard. It was personal punctuation.

I nodded to Henri, bowed to his wife, picked up the pouch of silver chains, and followed Melea out of the opening of the hooch into the night.

At the edge of the bush, we rendezvoused with Sgt. Fox. Together, we checked the new radio I carried, C-4 plastic, beehive rounds, and shaped-charges.

"This is a T-4 timer for the explosive's delay. You know how to use it," Fox hissed. "Now, do it. We are behind you. Don't fuck up."

I nodded, "Affirmative."

"Make her stop when you get 100 meters from your contact. She gets it. Give us time to set a perimeter while you go to work. Put her in good cover. Pick her up as you pull out."

I nodded again.

He traded my pistol for a loaded .45, a K-bar knife (I had one; now I had two), and a second bandoleer. I taped everything down again, even the frag grenades. I felt like a damn mummy. Face black and everything. Bad ass, dude!

"Security belt check, Peterson. If you need something, click that radio. Go hunt 'em."

Fox was wearing burnt cork on his face which off-set his weird eye. He had taped himself up, pants, blouse, ammo, grenades. Maximum stealth for night movement.

I heard the radio pop and someone say, "Porridge is hot, 2-9er-6!" I felt hot, like hot stuff.

I moved out, feeling the drunk Boy Scout stuff again. I rubbed as much dirt on my pants to darken them even more. Didn't work all that well, and stunk of wine and sweat. Maybe fish. I thought of the fish in the bucket by the crapper. That was me, fish in a bucket.

We moved out. The first 100 meters were tough, as I considered the risk of this mission. I shook, all my parts quivered with adrenaline. I breathed deeply to suppress fear and excitement. A wrong move would be disaster. I got nauseated, so I breathed more through my nose. Damn wine. Vietnamese shit-food.

Melea touched my arm. She had a sixth-sense. "You no be fright. O-key. I know secret way. Come with Melea." She had that great little voice, like small bells tinkling. Her grin like a moonbeam, and her little curled up lips made her the elf. Her eyes were dark like black pearls. She was an electric angel.

We moved out.

She had circled the clearing and slipped into the jungle, down a path that led to a slope. She peered over her shoulder to keep me close. I was breathing like an elephant, damping down nausea. While the going was tough, she moved quickly and easily, beckoning me, reminding me of a ghost in the mist. Her movement helped me to calm down.

Our pace slowed when the climbing began. I heard this voice playing in my head, singing, *"Voo-lay-vo-b-mee-ah-mnya. Voo-lay-vo-b-mee-ah-mnya."*

I noted the time. Dawn came at 0500. I needed to go in-out, and get it done. We had the time.

The climbing grew steeper. We paused to catch our breath. I listened for Fox and others, but heard only engulfing silence and the rhythmic noises of night bugs. Whining mosquitoes flitted around my ears. I brushed at them. It did little good. Just part of the symphony of the night.

Put the breath of fish sauce on them.

We pushed up a steep grade and down a slope.

Melea had on a little sack dress, tied at the waist. She was barefoot on the trail. It didn't matter. *How could she do that?* As she moved, I memorized how thin her little ankles were, the curve of her tiny neck and her boney arms. Like a Barbie doll.

We hiked for another hour. 0200 hours.

I thought she had not slept for nearly twenty-four hours! How could she keep going? She had sat quietly in the hooch as we ate and drank. I didn't see her sleep. *Kids go forever, then they drop.*

Another half hour, and we rested. I thought I heard the distant sound of music. My neck froze and hair crinkled with excitement.

Melea heard it too.

We scrambled off the path and took cover in a bush collection of vines. I could hear Melea panting softly. She put her hand on my arm, and looked wonderingly at me.

Guitar music, maybe a radio.

I remember another time when I was hiding in a thicket near a lake at home, hearing music in the trees.

Plunky guitar music and an American voice sang, "Billie Joe McCallister jumped off the Tallahatchee Bridge."

I'd listened a hundred times to it, a soft, sexy female voice with low resonance, sultry, mournful and crazy, singing how this boy had jumped.

The mystery of it mingled with what I was doing, lying under the bush vines with a little kid, ready to jump off my own bridge. Bobby Gentry, right there in the middle of god-forsaken Vietnam, singing, "Ode to Billy Joe."

The sound couldn't have been more than one hundred meters away.

We still had another thirty or forty meters to climb where the grade would level off and turn into a short trail. I could barely see.

Motioning to Melea, I pointed upward, so she could crawl softly. I followed, figuring when I reached the top, I could peer up and over to see if I could locate my contact, old Bo An. *Or would it be some other VC bastard, listening to a transistor radio he had taken off a dead GI?*

Go around him, I thought.

The final climb took time and care, placing knee or foot, trying not to slip or make a sound. In my head I kept repeating my password, *"Voo-lay-vo-b-mee-ah-mnay. Voo-lay-vo-b-mee-ah-mnay."*

All the French I had ever heard suddenly came back to me out of a well of brilliance. My mind became a French book collection. I saw myself asking directions of this little man with the radio. *"Voo-lay-vo-b-mee-ah-mnya-ah-li-hotel?"*

"Je voudras use chamber au lit, av sale de bain, un sans repas."

For a second, I was fluent. *"Parle-vous? Je Parle un peu...Ya-t-il quelqu un lei qui parle anglais?"*

Melea reached the place where the slope leveled. She waited for me. I was a stealthy bastard, a long way from Cochran, Georgia, lost and praying Fox didn't choose this time to make a radio contact. I felt he was close. He had to hear the music. Old Billie Joe McCallister was doing it again off the bridge, jumping his ass. Breaking Bobby Gentry's heart.

Melea gestured to her mouth with her fingers for me to speak the French password. Obviously, the guy had not heard us. We were very close. She must have known him. I wanted to be closer, so I crawled, keeping the ledge on my right.

I paused. In a firm voice, I said, *"Voo-lay-vo-b-mee-ah-mnay."*

The music stopped.

I spoke again firmly, *"Voo-lay-vo-b-mee-ah-mnay."*

I saw his movement ahead of me, and unsheathed the K-bar knife at my side. If it wasn't him, I would hit him as hard as I could. It had worked before. *Get up under him hard before he could see me.*

Melea sensed my tension and moved behind me.

Then a reply came, *"Voo-lay-vo-b-mee-ah-mnay."* A scratchy voice.

I stood up and gave a bow. He returned it. I nodded. He nodded.

We stood bobbing heads. He motioned with an AK-47 to follow, and we slipped off the trail into a bower of trees. As we walked, I took the pouch of silver off my shoulder, then remembered I hadn't paused like Fox wanted.

Shit, maybe I did pause.

It was not a time for regrets, now.

My heart became a machine gun.

We crouched in the bower beneath the bo-trees, hundreds of roots like fingers, where everything that could bite and scratch hid.

Soon enough for Fox. He was a savvy guy. He'd see I was dealing.

The man took the pouch, opened it, and studied the stuff, smiled broadly, and nodded several times. I could see his rotting teeth in the dim light.

I nodded back and gestured upward.

He had terrible complexion, shining eyes, cropped hair that stuck up oddly, and his black pants and tee shirt hung off him. His breath was like nothing I ever smelled. Staggering odor. Must have been eating rats or something worse.

He gestured down a trail where the path turned sharply upward. Secured to a tree root was wire cable that looped over rocks and fallen timber. Climbing the side of the mountain using the cable for balance was the order. He pushed Melea back from my side and motioned for her to sit or lie in a depression made by the roots of the tree. He gestured upward with his rifle. I had to climb. I didn't know if he would follow.

I glanced at Melea, put my hand on her thin face. She didn't smile. Her lip quivered. Taut face and serious, she was cold to my touch. She crouched into the slot in the roots of the tree to wait.

Turning to the cable, I began to climb.

The way was not too difficult, the turf soft and loamy. I made little noise. My radio fit snug. I had my rifle, the sack of explosives, and the grenades. The guy had to know my intent. I focused on the climb and not the destination. Work is a great help controlling tension and apprehension.

In minutes, I reached a ledge where boulders made a nice redoubt, concealing the entrance to a cave, a black hole in the side of the mountain, which loomed above me. The view over the gorge was obscured by heavy foliage. Nice cover.

Enter the hole, Emmett.

I had no light.

Shit!

How stupid! How can I do anything in a pit without light!

Only flares I had were for signals for the extract. *Nothing! A black hole. Hopeless.*

I almost descended, then grew disgusted, slapping myself mentally.

Come on! Screw the whole thing! Just screw it! Come on!

My mind went raging at my stupidity. Just a fucking flashlight.

Beside me a flicker of light, like neon flashing on, the shaft before me glowed. Inexplicable light, glowed, fluttered and lit the dark hole.

I stepped quickly behind a rock and eased against the side of the opening. breathing like a greyhound.

Son of a bitch! I had been betrayed. People were waiting on me. The bastard below had warned them. That little, snaggle-toothed son of bitch!

A thousand thoughts flashed. My mind went bawling from fear, wine, record party, trusting an old Frenchman, even the little girl.

A fucking screw-over. Sucked and fucked, Peterson!

I pulled out three of the shaped charges. At least I'd fire a few of those mothers.

Yet, something made me pause. I held the charges and waited. Something was coming, a sort of scraping, clawing up the cable. I lay the charges at my feet and pulled out the K-bar again. The little guy was coming up. He'd want to see the spoils of his little trick. I positioned myself to lunge the moment he stuck his head above.

He popped up, smiling. I saw his crooked, rotting teeth emerging from his grin. He gestured to the tunnel, nodded as he had done below, jumped over the edge of the tunnel opening and caught a thick rope I had not seen. He shook it, looked at me, then eased himself over the ledge and back out into the night.

I almost scrambled after him. What the hell! I knew by now Sgt. Fox was in position down below. I stopped, looked into the hole, stuffed the charges back into the satchel, slung it across my back and went down.

The drop was not more than six or seven feet to where three bulbs connected to a wire dimly lit up the tunnel. They showed a small opening just large enough for one short person.

 I stooped over and wiggled through.

There it was. The real deal. A stockpile in a cave. I entered the crawl space and pushed myself forward. Just enough room for my weapon, my satchel and me. One wild deal. I didn't think about it. Automatic pilot. Excited, hoping that at the other end I would spill out upon a whole room of NVA. I almost enjoyed the slithering down the tunnel to surprise them. Freak 'em out. Blow them up. Splatter 'em against the limestone and mud, and explode the whole mess. It occurred to me I was not going in the front door. No matter how small Charlie was, this was no space for speed. There had to be another way in. The thought gave me some satisfaction. The Frenchman had known his stuff. If there was a guard at the back end, there must be another at the front. I crept a few more feet to a place where the space widened into a kind of doorway.

I crouched, took out my .45 and a grenade, then peered into the dark cave quarters. Breathing hard, I made a conscious effort to slow everything down, to size up what I was about to see and do.

I'd roll out into the other room. Staying low could buy me time if there was a room full, but I heard nothing.

I made my move.

I rolled over my shoulders, turning the room upside down - lights, boxes, flooring. I remember feeling the unevenness of the flooring, the crunch into the small of my back my weapon made, as the radio swung by its strap in my pocket.

The room appeared small, unoccupied. Light illuminated two rows of crates and several bags. The crates were Chinese. A small place, loaded tight, with clothing, food, ammo, and weapons' crates. Mortars maybe. And mortar rounds. A crate open with half dozen shells removed!

I traversed the back wall, thinking it safer should someone burst in on me. Down the wall to the aisle between. I paused to listen - no sound. I wanted to pry open a crate, but knew I shouldn't take the time or make the noise. At midpoint of the aisle, I found a cache of shells. Boxes stacked four high. I placed C-4 in the middle. Reaching the end of the aisle, I made my way across another entrance to discover at least fifty rifles leaning against the cave's wall, four light Chinese machine guns set up on the floor, and stacks more of ammunition boxes. Maybe grenades. I placed two charges there and made my way up an opposite wall, which appeared to be food cans and rice bags. I slit the side of one bag to reveal about fifty pounds of prime hashish, the mother-load. I could have been a millionaire in a day by hoisting one bag out. I guessed the rest of the bags contained similar material. I slit another, the same thing. On down the aisle, I slit a carton bag open to find American field utilities marked with North Korean labels! The bastards! It was a chance for me to get off my own soaked stuff, so I shed my pants, ripping through the cameo tape, slinging my clothes on top of crate. For a momento I took another shirt, and a dark green teeshirt to conceal me when I reached the jungle.

Quickly, I worked, taping my pants, the vest of grenades, and the radio.

God, get that radio. Dressing room of the North Vietnamese Army! Fabulous, if I was caught half-naked, pants around my ankles, I'd fight in my skivvies! A farce.

I moved toward the other Chinese ammunition and mortar shells. At least a hundred. In their midst, beneath a crate under the straw, I planted my last two charges, the one with detonator and timer. I put the shaped charges to flare over the entire stash of ammo, right and left. I set the detonator timer for maximum time, fifteen minutes and made my way to the rear of the room, sticking C-4 plastic along the way. When the place blew, the entire mountain would go with it.

Time to make tracks. No sound. Little fear. Goddamned jungle cat.

I wanted my friend at the entrance below the ledge to cut the light now, but I had no control. I slung my weapon over my shoulder, made sure the radio was secure and crawled toward the exit.

A few feet from the opening, I heard the popping of light weapons. I crept on, anxious to reach the exit and freedom of some clear cover. Reaching the rope and about to climb, I heard a clear burst of fire outside.

I began my ascent, fearing I may be headed into a trap. I had little choice but to try for the exit.

Automatic pilot. Seven, eight feet. No problem. I knew that I could take cover in the rocks.

Wondering if my contact had been discovered, if Fox had mistaken him for the point of a VC patrol, I remembered Melea hunkered down among the roots of the tree. The firing grew more intense. Mostly AK fire, I thought.

Lights suddenly went out. Whoever was doing the firing had reached the switch, wherever that was. It could mean that the friendlies below me were in deep shit.

With a grenade in my hand, I scrambled onto the ledge to discover the night seemed more bright than before.

The firing became intermittent as I pushed myself between two boulders in the redoubt, trying to remain invisible. I waited. Firing stopped. Only the buzz of night insects resumed.

I risked a radio call, nothing. Again. I prayed Fox heard me. I cursed for having lost the first radio.

God in heaven, help me now.

Descend. The detonator on a timer, stupid! How many minutes had passed since I set it? Did I check it with my watch? No choice but down.

The entire mountain could blow any minute.

I made my way to the cable for the descent, using both hands. I paused, counting to ten, thinking that deliberate descent may not be a good idea.

I had made it this far.

Roll down the second slope. Find Melea, and drag her along with me. The master plan.

How cool I was. A Night Ranger! No idea of what I might find below. React. Move. Press forward. Night crawler. Ghost runner.

I grasped the cable and barreled down the slope, expecting a burst of fire, the whiffs of hot air, the zinging shots around me.

When I hit the bottom and found level ground, I made a darting run, and dove into the brush. My breath came in sobs. I waited.

This couldn't be happening. I listened, panting, waiting for my eyes to focus, my breath to return. No sign of Melea.

The firing started again off to my left. Bursts of M-16 fire, the steady rattle of AK-47's. It had to be Fox buying me time. I gauged the distance of the firing. Several more bursts, then silence - I thought I would hear shouts or voices. Nothing. I decided to move. With the fire fight up the trail, I decided that I should back-track the way I had originally come.

Lifting my head, I looked for a break in the trees. *A low run for the trail. Estimate where I could go down past the tree's primary turn.*

I lifted up slightly and saw a stark thin leg, inching out from behind the trunk of a tree. I darted with my K-Bar ready to strike around from the opposite side and caught Melea as she was coming around.

She didn't recognize me, but grabbed my neck, tying to strangle me. I couldn't be sure of her. Might have been pure terror. Dropping my knife, I tore at her arms, but she held tight until she recognized me. I clasped my hand over her face and mouth to prevent her from making a sound and drug her down beneath me into the crotch of the tree. The wind went out of her. She gasped, staring with terrified eyes not my face, but gasping at something invisible, and sucking hard for breath. I caressed her forehead and tugged at her dress, lifting her waist up and down pumping breath into her until she managed a mighty gulp and breathed. Her eyes were frantic and wild. She gestured at me. Something she saw had terrified her.

It was my contact. His stomach was ripped open. Bullets had sawed him in half. His rifle was flung to his side. Silver chains spilled from the open pouch. I grabbed his rifle and the bandoleer of ammo, two weapons in case one fouled up. I slung it across my back. They made an awkward cross.

Adrenalin kicked in hard.

I picked up Melea by the arm, gesturing in the direction I thought we had come. She shook her head fiercely, and pointed in the opposite direction. I took her will for my own, grabbed her by the waist, hauling her onto my back, and burst out of the trees down the trail, zigzagging, feeling her climb over the weapons and the radio. In a few meters, the firing resumed. Bullets kicked up behind us. I dove off the trail to my right and tumbled down over rocks and small trees.

I lost my grip on the girl, or she lost me. We fell, whirling down a slope, tumbling forward, knees to my chest, then flailing outward, reeling amidst weapons and bandoleers, gathering speed as we flew down.

The firing raged in hot flashes. Bullets hurled in the air. Buzzing and sawing the limbs of tree branches and bushes.

I stopped suddenly. Felt dull pain in my side as breath went out of me. The thump was like being hit hard with a very heavy pillow.

The firing ceased. Numb silence. Charlie's voices shouted above me. Another brief burst of fire, then nothing but leaves fluttering down.

I struggled for my breath. Felt dizzy and sick. I wasn't hit. My knee hurt, not from a gunshot wound, but bruising and having been twisted. My side ached where a sharp object poked me. It was the radio.

Melea. What happened to Melea?

I had only one weapon. The M-16. The AK-47 had been torn away in my fall.

No firing now, only my own rising breath. No distant voices. No Melea.

I felt with my hand, seeking her. She lay unconscious beside me, her leg warm next to mine. I dared not move for fear the VC were descending. Lying in the grass, itching, and feeling sore, I knew her leg was next to mine. I strained to hear her breathing.

No sound came from her.

For a long time, I waited, aware of the need to move, yet not.

Finally, I rolled slowly to my side. I reached to feel Melea. She was motionless on her back, her head turned to one side, her eyes closed. Her hair fell across one eye. She appeared asleep. Her right leg was crooked so her knee gently touched mine, while her left hand lay across her stomach, a sleeping child.

A low, misty moon sliver arose giving me just enough light so I could rise up slowly, look over at her, reach across, and feel her face and her pulse.

I saw the back of her neck gone. Her head was turned away, and her spine stuck out where the nape of her neck ought to have been - her face was turned away. Her lips were closed. From the corner of her thin mouth came a tiny trickle of blood.

Outraged, my mind went clicking. Snapshot after snapshot, burning images into me. Her knee against mine. Hand resting across her stomach. A sleeping child, facing away. Her spine. Her closed eyes. A tiny trickle of blood.

Madness. Wild rage overwhelmed me, pulling me.

Rise up. Charge back up the hill.

I found my rifle. I didn't think to use the radio.

Lunatic anger.

I bolted up, dashing through bamboo, a wild run, flailing the air in front of me until the terrain turned downward at the verge of another stand of tangled jungle. Into a wild collection of rubber trees and elephant grass, I crashed and stopped. I saw Melea's tiny face, the trickle of her blood. Shaking my head to get the image out, I gasped. Trying to breathe slowly, taking stock of where I was, using the moonlight and the haze. Where was my damn compass?

Think. Think.

I was cut off.

The radio. I still had the goddamned thing.

Thank you, Jesus!

Pushing my way into the jungle, I found cover.

A call. Risk a fucking call.

"Goldilocks. 2-9er-6. Come in, Poppa Bear. Do you copy?"

I fiddled with the volume, waiting for a contact.

Three tries.

Blessed Mother of God, answer me!

"Goldilocks, 2-9er-2. Poppa Bear. Do you copy?" The answer. I fiddled with the volume.

"Yes! Copy," I whispered.

"How's the house?"

"Full!"

"Can you walk?"

"Negative!"

Silence.

"Say again. Can you walk?"

"Negative!" I responded.

I didn't know what to do. No compass. How could I report where I was? The code wasn't going to allow it. I looked at my watch.

Ten minutes. Hadn't Fox and I given each other coordinates earlier? Why had we not discussed coordinates? A compass!

"Contact. 2-9er-6. Out for five."

"Copy," I said.

At least they knew I had lit the place. They knew the fuse time. I had to get away. I had to leave Melea. Find a way. When I set the fuse, I had checked my watch and shocked myself. Only nine minutes had passed since I lit the charge in the cave. It seemed like two hours.

With my knife, I cut several large leaves, stuffed them around me and crept back 100 meters to where I thought Melea lay. Quarter moon. Not looking at her face, I covered her with leaves. As I lay them over her, I thought of her impish grin. In my vision, I saw the blood trickling from her lips, felt her knee resting against mine.

Forcing myself to forget the sight, I bolted again back into the cane break and rubber trees. I didn't stop until I slid down another slope, dragging debris with me.

The vision of her. The noise of sliding. The coming explosion. Soon.

I plunged on for some time, then stopped and listened. For at least a minute I waited.

Had to risk another radio check. Same code. Same conversation.

I broke the code to say that I was below the mountain at least one click. Then, I got the worst message.

The voice told me a night pick-up was impossible. They couldn't track my radio signal. The canopy was too thick. They'd have to look for me in the area at first light, using the sun on the horizon as reference. I'd have to set flares and hope the Huey could spot the smoke and not NVA.

The news sent me into a rage. Fear and rage. I don't remember what I said. I do remember the sudden firing I heard on the other end. Gunfire and profanity, a spewing sound. The radio went dead. My mind spun. My damn brains almost came out my ears from the pounding of my heart. Storming out of my head, I looked about wildly.

Was the radio guy hit? Cut off, too.

How would the chopper find me?

I felt like cursing God, running in circles, the whole fucking war down in a storm sewer. I wanted to beat the butt of my rifle into the ground and cry, but I couldn't do that. I sat there and shook all over.

No noise, damn it. No noise. Almost 3AM. Wander around in the fucking dark for two hours alone, place my flares, hope that some stiff in a slick would spot me. Needle in a fucking haystack.

My head as talking, pounding, cursing.

Fuck the radio goons, fuck Fox with his blue, god-damned eye; the god-damned captain, the entire fucking chain of command; the fucking Viet Cong; the little French bastard with no legs; his god-damned fat, waddling wife; stupid-assed-bicycle-wheel wagon she pulled him in; fuck the French language, and the whole fucked up operation. Just fuck all of it!

I cried for the first time since I was ten. The jungle, all the damn mist and fog around me moaned.

I moved out again. Running, staggering like a psychopath.

Blast away with my weapon, turn the whole mountain into an unhinged freak show, light up the jungle. Fourth of fucking July. Turn it all to red Jell-o. Fuck Frank Sinatra and the whole state of fucking Louisiana. I hated jazz, the god-damned Tallahatchee Bridge. Jump off the motherfucker. I hated the United States of America, Westmoreland, and LB-fucking-J. Lost in the stinking jungle. Swimming in a shit pot like a fish.

The whole thing sucked.

I floundered into the dark recesses of jungle in the middle of the night.

Vegetation ought to be ripped up by the roots. It was growing down on top of me, shoving me under its stinking weight.

Tear up the whole god-damned jungle, set it afire, blow it to the moon, grass, vines, bean roots, elephants, elephant-god-damned-grass, and Charlie in his black pajamas, squatting silently, waiting, sucking on his rotting god-damned teeth.

Melea. Melea.

Magnified in my mind was clutter and jibber-jabber.

Blow them all to hell and to the fucking moon.

I blasted along like I had no legs. I could fucking fly. God-damn. I could fly. Lifted up on soaring rage and terror. Hell broke loose and ran with me.

Run the whole god-damned night, until I reached Cambodia, if I had to. Run across the rest of Indo-China to India, up the goddamn Himalayas. Be the first GI to run his ass out of a war! Jump the hell in the fucking Mediterranean.

This was me.

Hauling ass, feeling no pain, moving as possessed, my legs suddenly quit. They became bags of rice. I went reeling and staggering like a drunk off five bottles of the Frenchman's wine. Bombed, I went down hard on my chin. My breath ripped out of me, pasty vomit rose in my throat. I lay retching, heaving, trying to get gulps of air, trying hard to hurl my guts on the ground.

With my head down, I lay on this slope and refought every inch of the war. Relived the entire tour, jerked my way through every fire-fight, every mission, every conversation, every dawn, and every dusk. The night patrols, guard duty, the latrine tours. I burned the shit for days. Every stinking, damn shit-trench.

I saw the two glassy-eyed lieutenants, who were hit in my first big unit action. I fired my weapon the first time at trees and shit, knowing Charlie waited for us. Innocent eyes, glassy from fatigue and fear, white faces, black faces in the night; bunker quakes from close shelling, a moma-san picking up a little kid in the first village we lit. The shot-up point man on a patrol I drug out.

How quick the hooch exploded in flames, the feathers and sticks floating in the ash, chickens running everywhere. Wailing and screaming wounded people. Sick afterwards, knowing that we burned somebody's house.

Laughing maniacal boys. *"No prob-lem-o, Peterson. Burn the mother down. Torch that fucker."*

Eyes of Sgt. Hurricane Fox, "rock vet." *Lightning in a bottle, Peterson.*

Charlie hung on the wire, torn up by .50 cal. machine gun fire. I saw it all.

Not people, but pieces of people, hands, arms, legs and faces. Torn like rags.

And little Melea. Melea.

I saw her darting through the bush. I wanted to call out to her.

She always smiled, always looked back. I heard her say, "Hey, GI, you no fright. You big man! You o-key. You o-key."

She ran off hand-in-hand with the Hag of Vietnam, a drooling old bitch-ghost with candles in her eyes. She was laughing at me. Melea flailed her arms and was whisked away.

I lay on my back panting, full of crazy visions.

The first explosion wasn't very big, but it made me jump. My visions vanished. I rolled over to prone, ready to fire my weapon, then realized it was my C-4 doing its job, not shelling.

In the Tomb of the Soul 343

Wide awake, aware for the first time my brains had not spilled out of my head, I heard a second explosion, a third, and a fourth. A cold-blooded rumble, thrilling in its flatness, grew into a series of detonations, short and definite, a prelude to a gigantic discharge, shaking the ground.

Behind me the night sky lit up, a furious volcanic storm of raining fire. The roar was an extravagant, long, monstrous convulsion. Leaves and water rained down on me. Rolling thunder. Whistles and screeches pierced the night, howling and echoing. Flares like a late afternoon sun firing upward, above the trees, above where I lay.

I was transfixed. Everything stood at attention, tree branches lifted to witness the grand spectacle. I felt detached. Wonderful, complete denial. Night fire.

The ammo continued to pop off - hundreds of firecrackers. Fourth of July picnic. Flares shot into the sky. Commendable, wonderful, terrifying blasts of fury into the night sky. The whole country paused to watch it blow. The sap in the fucking trees boiled.

The second roar was as grand as the first, a great baritone sound that ended in a cry of destructive might.

I began to scuttle away.

Get away. Put time and distance between the next moment and the sound of it.

I didn't think much about the sight. I tried to focus on moving, retraining my eyes, and keeping balance and my mind on moving out. Move on down the mountain because the explosion was so riveting any enemy in the area would take cover.

Let the clamor continue. Hurry.

When I had covered another five hundred meters, I decided to find a clearing, and hide at the edge of it until dawn.

It worked.

At first light, I lit flares. A good idea. I was exhausted. I glanced at my watch. Only 0445. I could still hear occasional explosions.

I found low branches at the edge of some bamboo grass. *Why did everything in Vietnam hang down?* Nothing lifted up. Several large, overgrown mounds, probably termite mounds appeared at the edge of the clearing.

Now with first light, I thought I heard a Huey in the distance. A distinct throbbing of its rotors.

Cover. Crawl to the middle of the field, set a flare and scuttle back.

I lit the first flare and waited.

I was thirsty. I hadn't thought about thirst at all until I stopped. It was violent thirst. Somehow my canteen had been torn off. I licked dew off the leaves. Good moisture. I was scared, jumpy at every sound, every movement, even the calling of the monkeys I couldn't see.

I tried to think of football.

Not the same. Good tired. Classes at Longstreet. Major Burke. He would never excuse us to go for water. Tough it out. We always did. This was worse, but it was for Major Burke I would make it out.

Moisture on leaves was like good wine.

My legs hurt. Cold sweats. Shivering. Shaking. Sitting with my hands around my drawn-up legs, my weapon across my lap.

I remembered Melea. Her tiny arms, her thin legs.

The chopper sound faded.

I kept looking at my watch, hearing lids of powder still popping off in the distance.

The sound of the chopper rose again, closer. I decided to risk another call and give them some idea of where I was. Three or four tries until I received a distant voice.

"Copy, 2-9er-6. Goldilocks," the voice said.

The sound was as sweet as water to drink. I told them I could see the mountain; the sun was rising to the left of it. I must be south. The explosion had been clearly visible. I described the clearing, the stand of trees I was under. I must be south of the mountain. I could see the sunrise.

I had only four willipeters (white phosphorus flares).

Fuck the VC if they heard me. I would wait twenty minutes and begin setting flares at ten minute intervals, then switch to yellow smoke, and finally red as a last resort.

This is madness. Berzerko!
Had to be done.

A long wait began. On my third willipeter, the sweet sound of a slick made me sob. As the chopper's throb came nearer, the face of Melea appeared, the trickle of blood from her mouth, the impish grin, blue in the early morning light.

Her little voice called and her hand beckoned me. "O-key, GI. O-key. Hey, you no be fright." Melea lay under elephant grass at the base of the mountain.

The little girl had got me out.

The chopper swooped in low, and I made my last run of the war toward freedom and home. Away from Frenchmen, silver chains, and flashes in the night.

Melea lay buried under elephant leaves.

At the wide door of the chopper, a strong arm dragged me in. I retched. Dry heavings came hard. A guy thrust the canteen into my hands, grabbed my weapon and strapped me in. I was too sick to swallow the water. The surge of the lifting chopper tagged me to the bird. Throb of the rotors swept us from the clearing, as I clung to the webbing of the chopper walls. The jungle disappeared in a smear of green.

"Swallow a little more water, soldier, then try to drink," the gunner said. "You blew shit out of 'em, man!"

"Goldilocks secured! Goldilocks secured! This is Red Chief One. I say Goldilocks secured." The pilot gave me "thumbs up."

The noise was deafening sweetness. I forced a smile and took a long drink. Below the jungle transformed into a long, deep chasm of avoidance.

I was exempt from feeling anything about the night. I had to file a report.

Fox had been hit in the shoulder. He was okay. Only two of the group made contact with Poppa Bear. The firing I had heard was from my contact at the base of the mountain. The body I saw when I found Melea must have been enemy, not the guy with bad teeth and breath, the guy who had stolen Bo An's silver chains. Apparently, a VC patrol had come up quietly and surprised Sgt. Fox. For whatever reason, my contact had cut him down, then been hit himself. Melea stayed tucked in the root of the tree during the firefight. Fox had called for help as he was being overrun. Third platoon had engaged, and the VC broke contact. They pulled Fox and the others out. Mission complete.

Whoever fired down on me, VC or friendlies, must have hit Melea. I never knew.

I filed my report. Cold turkey for me. Just words on paper, numb-in and numb-out.

I tried to be exempt from feeling anything. I had gotten a child killed.

"Drink up, Peterson. Eat steak, have a few beers, then see the Captain. You're a fucking hero."

Melea was dead.

I got a medal.

Twenty-Five

In all my dreams, before my helpless sight,
He plunges at me, guttering, choking, drowning....
— *Wilfred Owen*

At five in the morning, Emmett finished reading the diary to Barbara Lynne. He had forgotten so much. He felt drained, and she sensed it as well. He lay the notebook aside, and they slept on the sofa until mid-morning. When they awoke, the sun was shining.

Barbara stretched and stood up. "You are," she said, "without a doubt, a good person. You need to embrace that goodness. You served your country so well. I love you." She brushed his forehead with her lips.

He admitted to feeling a little better, though in the back of his mind lay the thought of the windbreaker and the gnawing question of what to do next.

They had breakfast and didn't speak of the Kuballes.

Later, he said, "I might go talk to Mr. Sam. He won't say a word to anyone. Maybe, he can guide me a little." Barbara Lynne agreed. She also worried, unable to imagine the magnitude of Nathan's deeds and the horror of it.

Emmett didn't wait long to visit Burke. He called Sam, and drove to his home, where he told him the story of the windbreaker discovery, and about Evelyn's having consulted him about Nathan's behavior. He didn't go into details about her having been beaten, but he did say she reported the fights between them that were fairly regular. "It got physical," was all Emmett said. It was after learning about their fights, he had decided to check the locker.

Be sure about everything before proceeding was Sam's advice. Consider speaking to Dan Jeter.

Sam did not tell Emmett that Nathan had come to him earlier in the week to tell him that Evelyn had left him, and that he felt angry about it. Sam could see too much information sharing could be destructive to a lot of people.

Emmett decided to wait and see before going to Dan Jeter.

Days passed. Evelyn made an appointment for Nathan and her to have a session at the Office of Family Counseling at the Medical Center. She had not consulted her husband. When Nathan learned of it, he glared at her and stalked out of the house.

Evelyn yelled after him, her voice as raw and threatening as she could make it, "If you can't face this, then I know for sure you are a queer, worthless bastard! Do you hear me you queer! I'm leaving you! I'm not coming back!"

He didn't turn back. Her shouting echoed over the neighborhood and pierced his soul. He was finished with her too.

Nathan drove to Davis Wallace's home, an apartment above his sporting goods store.

"God," Davis exclaimed, "you alive?"

"Not sleeping too much," said Nathan.

Davis rarely saw him in the middle of the week. He reached over and pecked Nathan on the cheek. "Come on, sit down. You had the spring game the other night, didn't you?"

"Yeah."

"Was it okay? Your team win?"

"Of course, my team won. I'm tired from all of it."

Nathan appeared wild-eyed, a bit more than 'tired.'

"Well, its sort of early, but you want a drink, beer? Hair of-the-dog?"

"Sure," said Nathan. "I'm ragged out. I got end-of-the-year papers to grade, averages to do, and football uniforms to inventory. Just a lot of dull shit."

Davis brought him a beer and sat it on the coffee table.

Nathan looked at him with forlorn eyes.

"Evelyn left me today," he said flatly.

"Oh, wow!" Davis said. He waited before speaking. He had not picked a beer for himself, but poured a cup of coffee. "I don't know whether I'm shocked, or not," he said. "What set that off, buddy?"

Davis had taken to calling Nathan "buddy," a label that annoyed him, but Nathan tolerated it. He knew it meant endearment, but it sounded so superficial. He wasn't Davis's buddy, not in the cheap sense.

"She tried to schedule a session with some doctor shrink at the Medical Center, a family counseling guy," said Nathan. "She didn't even ask me ahead of time. Just did it. It pissed me off. I don't need some psychiatrist probing around me for anything for any reason?"

"We've had a lot of fights, but this was...the worst." His eyes were like stones as he stared at Davis. "I sort of slapped her around."

Davis was visibly shaken. "What do you mean, you slapped her around?"

Nathan's stare became a glare. "I mean what I said. I slapped her around. I'm not having her scheduling me to see a doctor just because we don't agree on some stuff, or my schedule doesn't suit her, or my friends at school aren't her friends. *You know what I mean?* Certain things are fucking forbidden, private!

"So, I'm not going with her to any doctors or shrinks! I left the house. When I came back later, I found a note. 'I'm gone. You know where. We can't live like this,' it said."

He swigged his beer. "She should know now I can't put up with any more of her shit!"

"So, what does that mean?" ask Davis, obviously fumbling to understand. "You getting out? Slapping her is serious."

"How the fuck do I know. Divorce, I guess. She can have the whole frigging house, as far as I'm concerned. I just want out of there."

Davis stood and walked to the window, watching Nathan the entire time. Inside, he felt a mixture of sadness and pleasure, sadness for the suffering his friend was feeling, and a peculiar selfish pleasure. He'd have Nathan to himself.

"You got your job to take your mind off that stuff, don't you?" he said suddenly shifting the subject, "Hey, Alan McConnell came into the store a day or two ago, looking for longer cleats for his shoes. What a specimen that kid is. I like the way he looks."

Nathan smirked. "You would."

"He's very personable, nice young guy. He's good-looking."

Irritability rose in Nathan almost instantly. Veins in his neck seemed to swell. "Don't get any of your faggot, fancy ideas, Wallace!" he exclaimed.

The threatening response surprised Davis. "Look, I'm not saying anything more than the fact that he's an athlete. I don't dig high school guys. I do like to watch 'em play ball. That's all. Take it easy, man! God almighty, you got the edge."

Nathan backed down. "Just don't get funny with me on kids at the school. You should know that."

"Hey," said Davis, "you know that night we had was nice, you and me, after Carl Desmon left, and the last one we had. It was nice between us. Didn't you think? You're my guy, Nathan, a special guy. I told you that a few weeks ago."

Nathan looked sullenly at him. "Don't get off on that 'special' talk, either. I got a wife who likes to do that." He took another drink of beer.

"I thought you needed me," Davis said. His voice was soft, almost cloying.

"Maybe. I do that sort of thing from time to time." Nathan sounded snide. His eyes were like marble.

"So it wasn't a problem when Desmon was here?"

Nathan thought Davis looked like a sad puppy.

"No, sweetheart," he said, "it wasn't a problem. I needed a confessional booth, I guess."

Davis thought he might be breaking down some of Nathan's defensiveness.

"You know what I think. Kuballe? You need a diversion. I'm not talking about sex, or late-night partying, but some new vistas."

Nathan smiled at him. "I do need another beer."

"Sure." He had stocked his refrigerator, so he handed him another beer.

"I'm here to help you, man. School is out in ten days. You and I can hit the road for a few weeks. Maybe drive out west somewhere. Grand Canyon, Vegas, or California. Get outta town. Be free. It might get you over the funks. Hell, Evelyn might even have time to rethink the whole thing."

Nathan's face reddened at the mention of Evelyn's name. "Sure," he said, "if I don't kill her first!"

The comment made the hair on Davis Wallace's neck stand-up.

"Oh, come on, man! Don't talk shit like that. You scare the hell out of me."

"You know what I think," exclaimed Nathan in a very even, but angry tone, "I think you can fuck Evelyn and the whole Hilliard crowd, especially that goddamned coach and the collection of friends he has, from that fat-assed Harry Parsons to that guy, Burke. Fuck 'em all.

"And don't mention the McConnell kid to me again!" He was fuming.

Davis's eyes grew large. "Okay, man! Okay! I was joking. Poor idea. Sorry I spoke. I just want to help you."

"Look," said Nathan. "I don't need any goddamned help. Evelyn says that. I don't need her! I don't like you using her words on me. You got that? Buddy!" His voice conveyed a snide, grotesque tone.

Sure, sure!" exclaimed Davis. He began to think he just wanted Nathan Kuballe out of his house. The conversation was turning very dark.

"Let me tell you another thing. Set the record straight! Buddy! Hal Rivers wasn't queer. He was a pure friend, true, dedicated to me - to me. But, he wasn't a queer. I was the queer!"

Davis was on the defensive. "Did I say he was? I never said that. I did ask."

"You sure as hell did ask. He was as pure as driven snow. I'll tell you another thing about Hal Rivers. He knew things about me he'd never tell or discuss. He knew I was queer, but he didn't care. He knew I was married. He knew I was scared shitless a lot of times. He knew about Rondell, and the others. Hal didn't give a good goddamn about them.

"You want to know what happened to Art Rondell?"

Davis backpedaled, stunned by the outburst.

"Art Rondell! A guy in Vietnam that I slept with!"

"No! Not really! Do I need to know?" Davis was inching toward his front door.

Did he intend to run?

"He was shot in the back of the head in a latrine at Dak To. He was fragged because he was a super queer, and others knew it. He scared hell out of me because he blabbed all the goddamned time. Sort of like you, Davis! So don't blab. Why do you think I transferred to Long Binh?"

"But, Hal...," said Davis.

He knew immediately he should not have said a word.

"What about Hal? I told him. He didn't give a damn, even if Art's brains were splattered all over the toilet hole."

Tears filled Nathan' eyes. "Hal didn't gave a good crap. Evelyn called me queer!"

Nathan shook his head. Everything was silent.

"Damn," muttered Davis.

Sorrow was palpable. Davis's fear was in the open. "Look Nathan, I...." He never finished.

"Nobody gets it! Not you! Not Evelyn! Not Sam Burke! Not anybody!" Nathan swayed unnaturally.

God, he was imagining the issue with Art and Hal, even with me.

Finally, Davis spoke. "Why did you come over here?"

Nathan looked at him, his face drawn with fatigue and anguish. "I wanted to talk."

"Oh," said Davis.

Nathan swayed like he was a little drunk.

"I shouldn't have said anything," Davis said, softly. "I'm usually a good listener. I'm sorry if I upset you, buddy. One thing I'm not sorry about. I'm not sorry about loving you." He was really scared.

Nathan noticed as Davis's voice break.

"Don't," he hissed, "come at me with that 'sorry' crap. Do not go moralizing about you and me. And, don't mention McConnell or Rondell. Everyone knew Rondell was weird. No one knew I was as weird as he was. Art's chicken-shit blabbing got him killed. I met another guy, so Art died. Then Evelyn starts."

Davis looked at him, trying to understand. This wasn't happening, was it?

"Tell me you didn't shoot that guy?" he said.

Nathan gave a visible jerk. "That's a good one, Wallace! You think I shot him? We're just talking here, Davis. Just talking."

"Yeah," said Davis, "I guess we are." It made no sense.

Nathan went to the refrigerator and got his third beer. "Just talking," he said, as he popped the top. "A lot happened in Vietnam, a lot." He sat down for the first time. He took several long breaths. Tension seemed to leave him.

"I thought you'd understand," he said quietly. "You need to understand."

Davis stood. Nathan's mood really frightened him. "I guess I do," he said with a slightly awkward laugh. "I do know the war is over, man. It's done. And Evelyn…"

Nathan glanced up at him. "Yeah, man," he said, "all done. But…the hiding ain't done, is it?"

Davis had to find a way to get him out of his house. He started inching toward the door. His truck was right at the bottom of the steps. He could dart out quickly. "Hey, why don't we go for a walk, or over to the pool? Take a swim. Why don't we do that?"

Nathan took a step toward him. It was menacing.

"Did you hear me, Wallace. I said the hiding ain't done. Maybe in a little while, then it might be done. Just one thing. You got all the answers, don't you? Just one more thing, *buddy!*"

The label sounded ugly to Davis. The relationship with Kuballe was becoming something he couldn't recognize.

Nathan's eyes were glowing. "Tell me one thing." He paused and spit out the question. "How do I tell Evelyn anything? I've shot that wad. Blown it to hell. She called me a queer!"

"You don't have to tell her a *damn thing!*" Wallace blurted. "You told me everything. Isn't that enough? It should be. She's made her move. She left you."

"Did I ever tell you that she called me 'queer'?" Nathan remained calm when he said it.

Davis did not dare to speak. He just watched Nathan carefully.

"Well, she did," Nathan said. "Right to my face. So I hit her. What was I supposed to do?"

His voice shifted to a mocking, high-pitched tone. "Yes, Evelyn, I'm queer. I made love to a couple of guys in Vietnam, and even before that. Hal Rivers was my friend. He wanted to get me straight until I fucked up. Wanted me to be a nice, regular, straight guy. I fucked up with him. It was me who fucked up! He had to kill himself because of me. Now I'm fucking Davis Wallace."

His words filled the room, then he was silent.

He sat forlorn and empty. "How is that one, Mr. Wallace, old *buddy?*"

Davis took a cue and walked out the door, saying. "It doesn't matter a damn bit. Not now." His voice was loud and emphatic. He headed down the steps toward the truck. Nathan followed Davis Wallace as he struck up a brisk walk down the block past his truck. They walked for nearly two hours saying little.

"I'll see you later," Nathan said finally, and turned back up the street toward his car. "I'm going home and get a few things."

Nathan picked up his Camaro from Davis's apartment and drove home, parking his car on a side street. He sat at home until 8pm.

He didn't know that Evelyn had not gone to Houston, but to a friend, who helped her draw up divorce papers. She knew the spring football season had ended, and Nathan would spend long hours doing inventory and storage for the next season.

Evelyn thought she could slip into her house while he worked, load up a U-Haul and be out before Nathan got home from school. She'd leave the papers on the counter. She didn't count on him not having gone to the school. If he came in, she would simply tell him she was finished with him. To hell with him and the house.

He could throw a fit, but he wasn't going to beat her ever again.

She told her friend she would call just before leaving.

If the call didn't come, her friend was to contact the police.

She was afraid of Nathan.

Nathan waited at the house. He heard Evelyn's car in the driveway and the U-Haul behind it as she got out and opened its rear doors. The sight of her blinded him.

He grabbed a knife, crawled beneath the kitchen table, and watched her enter from the garage. She placed an envelop on the counter. She was scribbling a note on a piece of paper, when he grabbed her from behind. She presented him no difficulty. He had her on the floor before she knew it. The knife he used came from the kitchen sink.

Twenty-Six

What foul beast slouches
Toward Bethlehem....
— William Butler Yeats

A LITTLE AFTER MIDNIGHT ON THE DAY EVELYN DIED, EMMETT drove to The Hilliard School to check Nathan's locker. If the windbreaker were there, he would have evidence. He could speak to Jeter, and they'd figure what to do. If he found nothing, he'd talk to a doctor and get himself some help with his nightmares, a good plan.

The night was clear with a brisk breeze. Trees rustled beside the gymnasium. Entering through the glass doors by the pool, he picked up keys from his desk, and crossed the basketball court to the locker room.

In the dim light cast by an exit sign, he unlocked the door to the locker room, thinking he heard the clink of metal from inside the weight cages. He paused and listened to the silence. Two hundred lockers, lime green, spread before him as he went down the steps. With his heart beating curiously fast, he smelled the pungent air, tainted with a faint burning odor. His senses heightened. His eyes ached. He wiped them with his fingers. It was perfectly quiet.

Why did he hesitate? Go on. Center aisle. Locker #121.

The floor had a sickening glow. Dampness lay everywhere. A bitter odor bit into his nose.

Nathan's locker was center aisle. Emmett had to switch on one panel of lights. *What did it matter?*

The lights flickered on. His heart beat in his chest. He could also feel the blood in his ears.

What was this apprehension? Just search the damn locker, and leave. Nothing there but dead socks and a soiled jock strap, probably.

Quietly, he walked up the center aisle.

What if Kuballe locked his locker? You stupid-ass. You didn't think of that.

Emmett lifted the latch. It was loose. The door swung open. The gym shorts hung on the hook, a rain cape and pile of unwashed stuff lay at the bottom. He lifted the rain cape and stuff. There it lay, the brown windbreaker and the black wool cap. It was just as he thought.

His heart sank.

Kuballe was the gunman! Why shoot at Evelyn?

Shoving the locker door with a bang, his head grew light. With revulsion, his breathing became heavier. He set on the bench and stared at the green slats of the locker door, surrendering to the weight of his discovery.

Trouble. You asked for this.

Clink of metal from the weight room cage startled him.

A hateful gnawing gripped him.

He wasn't alone. His mind kicked into another gear.

'Nam time. 'Nam time.

He listened, forcing himself to spread the sounds as military training taught him to do: weight room noises to his right, water dripping, ceiling lights humming. He suspended his breathing. No other movement was detectable, only his breath and his heart beat. He slowed it all down.

Easing to the floor and digging it with his fingers, he waited as the door to the locker swung open again about to bang against more metal. He stopped it, and the air handler fan unit kicked on.

More metal clinked in the weight room. Sharper this time.

Like a spider, Emmett walked backward on his hands and toes to the end of the locker rows, making no sound at all.

Hesitant footsteps came toward him, and a shadow lengthened in the aisle. He scrambled on his hands and feet around the corner before the other person peered down the aisle where he had been.

The footsteps stopped.

"All right! This is Coach Peterson. Who's there?" he demanded.

A tall, thin, figure with blond hair that Emmett recognized appeared, Nathan Kuballe.

Emmett stood up. "You are working late, Coach," Emmett said.

They stared at each other, but the glow of the exit light obscured Nathan's face.

Nathan didn't answer him, but stood impassively. He shoulders sagged.

"I forgot some papers at the office," Emmett said. "I thought I heard something, so I decided to go out the back way through here. I didn't see your car."

Nathan only stared at him. "You should leave." Nathan's voice was husky and dreamy

"I was. Are you okay?" Emmett asked. He strained to see Nathan's face a few feet away.

Nathan seemed to list from the weight of a silver revolver dangling from his hand.

"You aren't needed here." Nathan's words faded as he spoke. He didn't raise the revolver.

"Let me help you, Nathan," Emmett said.

"No! No help!" He took several steps back and leaned against the wall.

Emmett ventured toward him.

"Don't come. Leave! You don't belong here." Despite his order, Nathan didn't move or raise the gun.

"I'm not going to leave you. I want the gun. Let me help you. Give me the gun." Emmett's voice was firm and steady. His mind focused on his next move.

In one quick motion, he snatched at the gun, slapping it from Nathan's hand, sending it clattering and spinning down the aisle. Emmett grabbed Nathan before he could react and drove him to the floor, ready for a struggle. None came.

Nathan crumpled with a moan. Blood streaked the wall from Nathan's shoulder.

"Take your fucking hands off me," he said weakly.

Emmett held him until he stopped struggling. He watched Nathan's fainting eyes flutter.

Nathan was losing a lot of blood. On his forehead under his hairline was a red streak that continued below his left eyebrow, as if someone had hit him with something. He was full of sweat and blood.

Nathan's eyes rolled as Emmett left him to call for help.

Returning with towels, he rushed to stop the bleeding. The bullet had entered Nathan's left shoulder and blown out his back. A pool of blood gathered on the floor.

Sirens whined in the distance. He held Nathan and gave compression to the wound as best he could.

You know what this is, Emmett? Arms and legs. Heads and ears. Queers and tears.

The Hag sat on a bench beside him.

He was covered in Nathan's blood when the police entered the locker room with medics and rushed around him. His head pounded from their shouting. He was helped up.

"Here, here's another one," a voice said.

Inside the weight room cage, Emmett saw a body slouching on the weight bench, as though studying the yellow gymnasium wall.

It was Davis Wallace.

"What is this, Coach?

"Somebody turn on more lights!" a voice yelled. "We got a corpse in here! Are you fighting in here, Coach? What is this?"

The Hag's candle eyes burned inside Emmett's head.

"I came to check in a locker when I found Kuballe shot in the shoulder. I called you. I got towels. Didn't know about the other guy."

"Little late at night to be in a locker room."

"I know. I know. I can explain."

"You better do that." They pulled him away from the scene.

Medics loaded Nathan on a gurney. They swarmed around the body of Davis Wallace.

Leading Emmett to a chair in the office of the locker room, an officer with a notepad sat across from him writing as Emmett gave an account of what happened. He was shaking.

All the while the Hag watched them until Dan Jeter entered.

The light in the office was killing him. Emmett covered his eyes to blot out visions, the flurry of activity, and bright lights.

"Tell them everything, Emmett," Jeter said. "Leave nothing out. I'll call the school attorney."

Emmett began again. He had never quarreled with Nathan and barely knew Davis Wallace. He didn't know Kuballe was in the gym. He knew Kuballe was having severe marital trouble, that he owned a brown windbreaker and a wool hat, like what the Ware's Cafe shooter wore.

They found the evidence in Nathan's locker.

The gun was Nathan's. Emmett had knocked it from his hand, when Nathan collapsed.

No, he had not seen Davis Wallace in the weight room cage.

Barbara Lynne came to him from out of nowhere.

Tell us about Evelyn Kuballe and your conversation with her. How well did you know her? Why do you think she chose to talk to you?

Are you having an affair with Evelyn Kuballe?

God, no!

How did you know she was in Houston?

"Why don't you just contact her?" Emmett shouted at them.

They had dispatched a car to the Kuballe house because they had gotten a disturbance call at 11PM.

An hour passed like a stone as he was questioned.

He wrote out a statement for the police, answering their questions.

Mel Perkins arrived and took charge.

Forensic people worked.

"There's been some kind of fight here."

Emmett's knuckles and hands were not bruised.

A medic gave Emmett Aspirin for his headache.

All the while the Hag leered and grinned. She was in him.

Emmett paid no attention to the sudden flurry of activity erupting among the investigators standing by the weight cages separating the locker room from the standing weights and the body of Davis Wallace.

A detective came into the office. "Mrs. Kuballe's body has been found at their home about twenty minutes ago! Her throat has been cut. Many stab wounds. We have the knife."

Everyone was startled.

"You finish your statement, Coach. You can leave. We aren't holding you."

When Emmett stood, he only noticed the green and gray floor coming up to meet him. He waved his hand toward Barbara Lynne before he collapsed.

In his head the Hag cackled and candles flared making acrid smoke. Panicky chatter began. Flashes of light popped before his eyes. An elevator clicked. Silver-white movement waved in the air, sheets and towels. Smells of smoke and alcohol.

Wild images whirled, overwhelming his better vision.

Paramedics were on him immediately. Emmett was transported to the hospital emergency room. Barbara Lynne had ridden beside him in the ambulance.

At the Medical Center, Emmett was placed in an induced coma. The psychiatrist told Barbara that Emmett had to rest undisturbed for several days. "He has suffered acute mental trauma. Let him rest."

She would not leave Emmett's side.

～

While Emmett slept, sedated at the hospital, Dr. Childs explained to Barbara Lynne why her husband had to rest.

"His trauma is great," the doctor said. "These things take a lot of time. *A person who has experiences of this sort of trauma may go for years with no problem, then one day the psychosis occurs. It could be post-traumatic-stress syndrome, or a condition we call psychorrhexis, a kind of malignant anxiety, or extreme nightmares. We are just learning about it.*

"He's not exhibited violent behavior, but he has been a witness to shocking events lately, as well as in his military past. I think that could do it. What he's been through in the last month is enough to traumatize him. We'll let him rest for a couple more days, keep him under, then we'll see how he is feeling. He's a strong guy and should be fine with some help."

Barbara remained with Emmett, going out only with her Aunt Maggie. Britches stayed close-by when Maggie wasn't there. Harry and Sam Burke remained in close touch.

Nathan Kuballe was placed in isolation in the hospital, pending the investigation into the murders.

School was suspended for two days. A letter went to parents of the boys. Emmett slept.

In the evenings Dan came, slipping in the door of Emmett's room at the hospital, giving Barbara Lynne hugs, patting her hand, saying little. He thought it best not to share Nathan's condition or discuss the determinations made regarding Evelyn's situation.

In the Tomb of the Soul 365

Twenty-Seven

This is the way the world ends
This is the way the world ends
This is the way the world ends
Not with a bang but a whimper.
— T.S. Eliot

Later, Mel Perkins, the school's attorney, met Dan and Maggie at the headmaster's office with the news of Nathan's death. When a nurse came with medication to his room, she found him, hanging in the shower.

The guard at the door outside had heard nothing.

They found a note, scribbled on a paper towel, a confession to the shooting at the cafe, and also of the murder of Davis Wallace at the school gymnasium weight room.

It contained recriminations against Evelyn that concluded. "Of course, I killed her. She drove a stake into my heart."

At the Kuballe home, police found a long, rambling description of Nathan's involvement with Hal Rivers, professions of his love, and his erotic desire. Nathan suspected Hal took his own life purposefully because Nathan had unsuccessfully tried to force himself on him.

The note said, "When Hal Rivers said he was going to the school authorities about their relationship because he was mortified, I threatened him. He hit me, so I beat him. You don't know what it is like to beat the man you love. Go ahead and walk out on me. Walk away. Do it your way, betray me.

"So he did ... onto the goddamned track."

Scrawled below these remarks was one word, "Coward."

Mel looked mournfully at them. "So, Nathan hanged himself." He lay his notepad down with resignation. "That's the story for now. Out of abject mortification, Hal intentionally walked into the path of the discus. The worst suicide I can think of.

"It was an act of spite, perhaps. It drove Nathan to his death." he said.

The story paralyzed Maggie and Dan.

"My God in heaven," Dan said quietly. "I had no idea, Mel. No idea at all."

Maggie sobbed quietly.

As Dan put his arm around her, Mel Perkins said, "We have to believe that love and guilt affected Nathan's marriage and all of his behavior after Hal died. Nathan was a gay person. Because Evelyn seemed close to the truth of his identity, he hated her. He had been hiding all his life. So, when she got too close to the truth of his homosexuality, he killed her. Not so much a crime of passion, but of pain."

Dan simply shook his head. "You mean his whole life was a charade? I never considered anything like this regarding Nathan."

"It appears that way. Tragedy. I hate it for the school, our football coach who stumbled into it, and for all of us."

All Perkins could do was stand there.

"The pain and the waste," mumbled Maggie. "Dan, you realize this has gone on for ten years? We didn't even know. Never talked about it. We were silent."

Dan was incredulous. "I don't know how we sat by as we did."

"You sat by," said Perkins, "because you focused on your school business and the kids. You trusted your faculty. The Hilliard School is about the boys, the kids, and how they grow. It's about trust, Dan, you got to have trust in the people who work for the school. It can't be otherwise."

Dan looked at him. "I didn't know the Wallace man. I didn't know Kuballe either. Jesus help us!"

"He was a sporting goods rep the school used from time to time. He and Kuballe became friends."

"Or more than friends. Or lovers."

"I expect so," said Perkins. "It is hard to understand. In his note he said he was Wallace's lover, but also called him a 'nebbish,' a word I never heard. It's Yiddish for a 'clinging vine,' someone who is constantly hanging around, but serves no meaningful purpose. It's an insulting word. Kuballe grew to hate himself, and apparently everyone else, especially his wife, who called him out." Perkins looked tired.

Maggie went out to Miss Lillian's desk and got Kleenex and dabbed her eyes. Her mascara was running.

Dan gazed out the office window.

Mel continued. "He and Wallace often came to the school to work out. On the night he killed Wallace, he also killed his wife because the note he left saying he did. He wrote, 'She deserved it.' Coach Peterson must have entered minutes after Nathan shot Wallace. They must have been fighting over something. Maybe Nathan was too stressed to tolerate much from Davis Wallace. The gun got fired in a struggle, hitting Nathan in the shoulder.

"Somehow Wallace got knocked over a rack of weights. His blood and hair were on the bars. Ballistics shows two shots were fired, and the only fingerprints on the pistol were Nathan's, so Nathan must have shot Wallace in the head after he fell."

"Mother of God!" muttered Dan. "I never thought, or dreamed this. None of us. God help us!"

"Minutes later Emmett must have arrived. In his statement he says he had come to the locker room because he suspected Kuballe of the cafe shooting. He was checking on a jacket and hat he recognized in Kuballe's locker. He wanted to be sure. He discovered Nathan wounded. He briefly struggled with him for the gun, but Nathan was too weak to resist. You know the rest."

The two men could only look at each other. Maggie stood in the doorway.

"I'm going to the hospital to speak again with Barbara Lynne," Mel Perkins said. "We will figure this out, Dan."

Dan Jeter could only nod.

Outside, the Texas breeze blew in the cottonwood trees. Maggie stood weeping.

~~~

Barbara Lynne stared into her lap as she listened to the account of Nathan's rampage and death. Emmett had been so close to the situation.

As the attorney finished, Maggie and Dan came into the waiting area. Dan, looking drawn and tired, watched his niece closely, noting how she brought her hand to her lips and blew warm breath into her fist. Her eyes glistened.

"Once," she said to her Aunt Maggie, "when Emmett and I first met, he took me to see a terrible movie. At the end of it, he asked me, 'What was the point of that?'

"'Point?' I said to him, 'There's no point to that movie I can see. None at all. Just a bad movie!'"

"'There ought to be a point,' Emmett said to me. 'Without a point, it's a complete waste. Things need to have purpose.'"

Barbara Lynne looked at Maggie with empty, sad, teary eyes. "This whole thing is just an awful waste. No purpose, but waste, and tragedy. I don't understand anything about why or how. I just…" she sobbed, "want Emmett to wake up and be well."

~~~

The day before his death, Nathan had been interrogated in the psychiatric care ward at the hospital, while the wound in his shoulder stabilized and healed. He had lost blood. He had stopped eating. His temperament became increasingly more sullen.

Nathan sat and stared out a barred window onto a small courtyard. His mind was blank. His face reflected no emotions.

Not far from Nathan's room, Emmett Peterson had slept behind a guarded door attended by only his wife and an occasional visitor from the school.

Nathan's only visitors were police and a psychiatrist. He had refused to speak at length to anyone, having written his statement.

In the early afternoon, after not eating for the fourth day, Nathan had left his chair by his window and gone into the bathroom. He stood before a sink and peered at a dissolute creature staring back at him from the mirror, a marble-eyed beast with a laceration from its hairline to its ear. Its thick, blue lips puckered. A gray sheet looped off its shoulder, revealing a grape-like wound. The beast wagged its head from side to side, swinging its long blonde hair.

Nathan knew it to be himself.

He imagined another face with sagging jowls, which floated in the mirror just behind the beast. It was dark eyed, the clerk of all his sins, who carried a bouquet of yellow flowers. "Buy her some flowers. Women *likes* flowers." It was the face of Hal Rivers.

The beast spoke in bubbles of despair, saw bloody foreheads and knees in a stinking latrine, and heard weak female whimpers.

Out of its dark eyes came tears rolling off the jowls, and bruises blooming across its face from a dent in its forehead.

The sheet draped over Nathan's shoulder dropped. Thick-lipped and sobbing, he quaked.

Once, soft, smooth hands had stroked him, given him pleasure. Now, yellow wreaths and pungent, rotting flowers draped around him. Bowl-eyed Hal Rivers, deft and caring Christopher Aston, and easy, compliant Davis Wallace, all watched him. A blonde American GI with a single bullet hole in his chest smiled at him.

He heard Evelyn's footsteps in the garage, her repellent voice, her tiny shriek as he grabbed her, and her weak submission to his knife thrusts.

When the faces faded and disappeared, Nathan knew only one could save him from himself. For so long, too long, his soul had been a tomb of buried longing and anguished secrets.

Did I hear the shots in the cafe and glass breaking? Who was that?

"You useless queer! You sorry bastard!" Evelyn said. "Useless. Who are you?"

He hated her. The beast grew again and shivered.

She ravaged your home, the beast said. *Disrupted your peace-of-mind, your sense of self, your manhood. She has siphoned off your pride and burned you to the core of your heart.*

You're a useless bag of shit! she called.

"She judged me," Nathan said to the beast in the mirror. "You see that?"

She passed judgment! She's a bitch! exclaimed the beast.

Nathan hugged his shoulders until the grape wound throbbed, burst open, and bled. He made Evelyn scream for her life under his knife.

The beast quivered and staggered, but didn't leave. Pain pierced Nathan's heart, making a hole in it. He wound the sheet into a coil and knotted it at one end.

In the mirror, he saw an orange ski rope slithering and slapping water. .50 caliber machine gun fire rattled the area, chipped wood shards from the boat sides were flung into the air. The boat's sharp, swerving, careening, tossed him into the boat's gunnel and onto the floor into a corner, where debris and bilge water, mixed with blood, covered him.

Into the shower stall in his bathroom, Nathan took the sheet. Beneath the stinging water, he fumbled with it, looping the sheet over the shower pipe and nozzle.

"God in heaven," he prayed, *"I'm damned."*

As he secured the sheet to the water pipe, he wrapped it around his neck and mumbled, "You should have known, Hal, how much I loved you. You didn't give a rat's ass until the last day. I wanted you so much, so very much. You should have known, you stupid bastard.

"I knew you didn't know. I loved you more than you loved me."

Standing beneath the hot water, he heard Hal's scornful rebuke. *What in hell are you doing, Nathan?*

Water beat off him, sending up scalding steam clouds. He choked and merged with the beast in the mirror, globe-shaped head, sad-eyed, elliptical face with blue, sagging lips. As this face turned blue, it faded into a boy with blonde hair and a faint smile. The boy was waiting for him as he went limp.

The sheet, saturated with steaming water, tightened with his weight. Around his purple neck, over the grape-like wound, it went. He went limp. His weight strained the narrow water pipe.

Nathan Kuballe hung there, covered with his own crimson sorrow.

Twenty Eight

Why, hapless man, have you left the light of the sun?
And come here to see the dead in a joyless place?
— The Odyssey, Bk. 11 (92-93)

In Emmett's hospital room, the Hag of Vietnam with shinning eyes camped in Emmett's mind and leered at him, commanding a sea of faces in a luminary chamber of lost, crippled, and dead souls. Smells of rotting flesh and earth rose from smoky ground, a pit, in which lay the remnants of Emmett's wretched, festering soul. Clawing over sharp rocks, ruined and twisted metal, the stumps of blown trees and jungle vines, Emmett crawled toward the Hag. She turned her head, and the ground heaved, vomiting the litter and debris of war: rifles, big guns, transponders and hand-held radios, tangled-flesh-ripped razor wire, torn shelter-halves, boots, smoldering weapons, and ponchos. Forlorn, dented helmet liners strew the ground. In the distance, half tracks rumbled, turning up reeking soil, bodies blown apart, bursting and popping guts, bringing with it the crying of wounded men and women. Shrieking and howling punctuated all the confusion and waste before him.

The Hag showed him the wares she had kept in a pit of horrors, the wasted remnants of his lost, ravaged life from firefights and explosive exploits in dark jungle forests. She spoke to him in gibberish, and around her was wicked light.

The shades of lost comrades came up to dance, wounded comrades wavering in the gloom, bold blood-soaked reminders. Colonel Rodman's hush money, cat glasses of Gloria Evans, nude pictures of Jane Mansfield, brown dead boys, a smoking machine gun, and the head of a dead VC soldier. Emmett's youth spilled before him, then flowed into his mouth, mingling with the nausea of panic, pain, and despair.

The Hag cackled.

Peterson, you Fool. I have loved and licked your tear-stained face, my slave boy.

Her wrinkled breasts shook, as her face, scarred and battered, became Evelyn Kuballe, bruised and weeping in her car.

From the Hag's twisted mouth came dead bodies: the VC guard at a mountain cave, a dead companion with cropped hair, his insides spilling into his own hands, a crippled point man staggered toward Emmett. Five shivering souls, huddled together, blocking their own ears from the hideous crackle of gunfire - lost, found, lost again.

Step carefully. You tread on Racine. He's in shreds. All abandoned boys now dead. Tread carefully.

Emmett didn't know.

"That isn't true," cried Emmett in confusion.

The wailing waitress from Ware's Cafe, in a bloody green uniform, her thigh mangled, her shoulder slung to one side, approached him. She was pursued by Nathan Kuballe, who suddenly sat upon the ground, wrapping a towel around his neck. Beside him lay a gun and a bloody knife. Both Nathan's hands bled.

The ghost of Nathan reached for a man that Emmett did not know, a fat man with bloody cheeks and a dent in his forehead. The ghost's mouth frothed with blood as he sought to kiss Nathan. The air was putrid with the smell of dead flesh. Crushed flowers lay about all of it.

The Hag sang, a wailing and high-pitched keen, that pierced Emmett's ears. It mingled with pigs screaming, which Emmett had heard once. All the phantoms danced to the wailing of hogs and the Hag. Among them dropped a legless Frenchman. He was weighed down by ropes of silver chain. Beneath his arm, The Hag carried the severed and bent leg of Melea that she lay before Emmett.

Peterson, you let the girl take a bullet meant for you, a silver bullet in her little neck.

In the dream, the Hag inclined her head toward him. It fell off her neck, revealing her spine, and becoming Melea.

You not o-key, GI? Not o-key. You have other woman now, who is lost like you. Older girl, you marry her.

In his delirium, Emmett squirmed. He knew Barbara Lynne was alive.

That girl not Melea. That girl love, but not like Melea love.

Melea's eyes were lit by candles.

You kill Barbara Lynne. Make you feel good. Feel o-key. Be killing machine. Be Death-giver Man.

Emmett screamed. It made no sense.

Melea melted into a weapon that lay on his lap.

Barbara Lynne is alive.

The Hag cackled inside his head.

Pick it up. Do it. In the woods, you shoot her. No one know. Float beneath the water in her lake. Come back to me. Do it, Peterson. Pick up the weapon. Lock and load. Fire. Kill Barbara Lynne Jenkins and love me. Death-giver. Life-taker.

Barbara Lynne sat at Emmett's bedside where she had been for four days. Her face was the color of apricots. Her soft hands stroked Emmett's face, and she breathed on him.

In his traumatized state he felt the breeze and the flutter of wings. He looked at the rifle lying on his lap. Grasping it by its muzzle, he hurled it away into the dark pit.

The Hag's cheeks expanded and her eyes popped, as hot liquid poured from them. It splattered on him.

Do it, Peterson. Spread the death on the bitch like you spread it over Melea.

Light as air, the weapon floated back to him and came into his hands. The place smelled of gun smoke and vomit.

He held the rifle over the odious pit, holding back the Hag. He didn't want Barbara Lynne to see the horrors there.

You are a helpless man, Peterson. You left the light of the sun long ago. Now you in realm of the dead. You drink my blood, you know the fates of those whose lives you took.

He took the rifle and fired at the wavering figures. It fired itself, spraying the scene, spraying hot fire. Melea spun away from him. He fired at Colonel Rodman, then Gloria Evans. They faded.

Melea, headless, and grotesque, waved past him. Evelyn Kuballe, naked and sobbing, watched him. The air thickened. The man he killed reached for him. As he fired at it, the guttering body flew back into the pit. The weapon breathed and glowed with the heat of his firing.

Barbara Lynne waited quietly, anxiously, just on the other side of the long white, picket fence were Emmett had come to meet her, just out of reach, as in the movie with Holden and Novak.

You kill Barbara Lynne. Make her dead. The Hag cried.

Melea's voice rang in his ears. Her breath stirred in him.

He turned the weapon toward the darkness where the voice resided, toward what seemed to be Melea's voice. He fired. The white-hot tracers ripped Melea. They blazed at the Hag, sawing her image, blasting them both away, leaving the scene fluttering. The Hag's cackle fluttered and faded.

Shoot. Light it up, boy.

He fired at the grotesque debris of hair, candle eyes, and gnarling bones, blasting the whole scene, that was memory-made. The weapon, hot in his hands, shook his body until it rattled his heart, shaking, searing every part of him.

Explosions from the mountain's detonation echoed.

The Hag exploded into melting candle wax. The grease, hissing and splattering, disappeared.

Emmett began to claw and climb from under it all, groping, tearing his way to Barbara Lynne. He dug toward the place where swallows swooped and skimmed, to the place where Barbara Lynne's kisses were. Her soft hands came to him. Pushing up next to her, she lifted him back into life.

> *First there was rowing, and after that a fair breeze.*
> — The Odyssey, Bk. 11. l. 640

Twenty Nine

*Had anything been wrong, we should
certainly have heard.
— W.H. Auden*

Several days later, Sam Burke and Dan Jeter sat at the coffee table in Dan's office. Ordinarily, it was a school day, but the school was empty and cheerless. Outside, storm clouds skidded against blue sky. The coyote on the pedestal stood before the window, posing in a ghostly hue of silver light that made him glow.

"Now that I think on it, Nathan hadn't been himself for three years, not since Hal Rivers died," said Sam. "I thought once upon a time he was an extrovert. I've watched him for more than a year turn down chances to be happy. He became a morbid man. I should have known something wasn't right."

He clasped his hand over his mouth and sighed.

"I should have guessed. Emmett came to me three days ago to say he'd found the windbreaker evidence. I advised him to see you. He wanted to be double sure. Maybe I should have sent him to the police right then."

For Sam, this was a confession. He continued, "But, I don't know anymore. Was that good or not? We can't get far on hindsight, Dan. Maybe I should have told you."

Dan listened and said, thoughtfully, "Emmett should have come to you. He loves you, Sam, like a father. Who knew or even mentioned Kuballe's being a gay man? Not in our vision anywhere was it?"

Sam shook his head. "I don't know as much as I thought. At one time, I guessed I had seen every ordeal a school could bear. The news of Kuballe's situation and the killings were out of my ken."

Dan sat down, letting his long legs stretch out. Then, he pulled them back and stared at Sam. "Well, we got to think about this. What now?" he asked in a glum tone. "This school could close down. This could do it."

Sam looked at him. "I don't think we let it, no matter what!" Sam exclaimed, after a time. "Simple as that. We don't let it. You run the place. We do it together. We move on. We listen more. We be more sensitive, more careful and discerning."

He stared long and hard at the fast moving clouds. "I believe that tragedy is part of life.

"Close the place, or leave, and the darkness wins. That's what I think in my heart. But, we must be more thorough and sensitive."

Dan shook his head. His glum tone did not change. "Move on, you say. To me, right now, that sounds like what I'd like to do. Just go the hell off and forget about it. Tell the Board and be done with it all.

"I also know thinking like that is complete bullshit. It's what got us in this place, ignoring pain."

The storm clouds seemed to break open suddenly, and a shaft of light beamed into the office.

"It's like a Greek tragedy, isn't it?" Dan said, and continued, "News articles will say The Hilliard School is supposed to be a safe place and secure, yet people shooting each other, dying on the school track, people hanging themselves. Questions everywhere.

"How do you overcome that?"

Sam suddenly turned to his young friend and placed his hand on his shoulder.

"You don't," he said. "You bury the dead. You restore the order. Schools renew themselves every year, don't they? New kids, new parents, new personnel, more openness and caring.

"Somehow, we lift up the good."

Sam began to pace.

"Maybe, Dan, we blow on the ashes. It's what the Biblical Job did. He rekindled his home fires, and he was blessed. We have to do that, tough as it seems."

On the night of Hal's death, they had been sitting with Alan McConnell and thinking Hal would tell them, when he awoke, why he had walked out of the woods that afternoon. He had not awakened. Now, Kuballe was dead, and his wife. Also dead was some stranger, who was Nathan's companion.

"I can't begin," said Sam, "to comprehend what was in Nathan's mind or in Hal's for that matter."

Dan didn't respond.

"The meaning of utter loss is never knowing. You read it at Hal's funeral," said Sam. "The golden thread gets broken. Got to have strength and power to fix it back somehow.

"Hemingway said it, '...stronger at the broken places.'"

Dan was perplexed. "We'll never know. I'll tell you, Sam, it riles me up. This is going to affect enrollment, faculty recruitment. The whole package. Landslide stuff. I'd like to kick somebody's ass!"

"Or feel sorry for them," said Burke immediately. "If Nathan was sick, we didn't know it. If there was something there that gave him love for Hal, we can't know that. He held pain close to his chest, and deep secrets. We just didn't know, or chose not to know."

"You know what I think?" Dan asked, "and I've been reading about this. I think there was some love there neither of us can relate to. To them, it was a desperate and lost kind of love. When the anguish broke lose, as it must have broken in Hal Rivers, it reaped a whirlwind, a Jeremiah. We certainly weren't ready for it. I feel somehow like Nathan has to be pitied more than scorned, though I'd like not to feel that way. Something in me makes me want to kick his ass. Something makes me want to be more insightful."

The remark didn't surprise Burke. He had thought the same, but he said, "Well, plenty of people will scorn them both, and pity Evelyn, who is a tragic waste, like Davis Wallace. We didn't know Evelyn. Didn't try to know her. She could have been a bane in Kuballe's heart, a reminder of what he could never be. He never shared her with us. She didn't come around much at all. We saw some good in Nathan, I think. We didn't recognize the core of his pain, or what it was made of.

"What I do know is playing the judgment game is not my style, Dan. Not at all. It serves for nothing. It's way beyond us and what must not be studied now. We got to be more careful, more thoughtful, maybe, more loving."

Dan was lost in his thoughts for along time.

Finally he said, "God's business."

Sam smiled. "You read the Bible, Dan. Don't tell me you don't. I'll never forget the rare verse you read at Hal's memorial. You can't second guess the will of God, or know much about it. In this life, no prompt-book exists for the players when the stage turns into mumbo-jumbo. We have to blunder along. So we get the note from Nathan Kuballe, written when he is standing at death's door. How do you analyze that, and if you do, what do you have?"

"Yeah, the note," said Dan. "I'm bewildered by the note."

He peered out his window, and saw himself staring back. "We have a job. You are right. A big job. A colossal re-build."

"Yep," said Sam. "It's very hard. Sometimes I think we are souls struggling outside the tomb, trying to live, and all we do is make messes and struggle to fix them. Do you think the dead laugh at us after they die because of our living consternation?"

Dan was surprised. "If they do, then we are all cynics or idiots. We should not be in the business of being cynics and call ourselves school people. We should build on reconciliation and restoration. The Hilliard School cannot go through the next decade trying to pry open dead men's tombs to make inquiries, can it? We got to live in the present. Pick up the pieces. Embrace each other, even in new ways. We do, like you said earlier, move on. That's it, if the world will allow it."

"Yes! If the world will allow it!" said Sam Burke. He stood next to Dan.

Together, they seemed suddenly insightful and less whipped.

They looked at their own reflections in the window. More light flowed in.

"So, where should we start?" asked Dan Jeter.

"We start with what's good," said Sam Burke

"And, now, what would that be?" Dan asked.

"That Emmett's young and alive," said Sam.

An Loc, 1996, Epilogue

What place is this?
Where are we?

I am the grass.
I cover all.
– C. Sandburg

Emmett and Barbara Lynne arrived at Tan San Nhut Airport at night and found a Toyota taxi to their hotel in mid-town. They had taken the first direct flight to Seoul, Korea, on Delta, eighteen hours non-stop from Dallas. After a four hour lay-over in Seoul, they flew Vietnam Air to Saigon, recently renamed Ho Chi Minh City. Emmett had been repelled by the name change, which came as a surprise even after the Communist regime had taken over and reunited the country.

Hitting the night air, they were stunned by the enormous humidity. The taxi weaved and honked its way to the Rex Hotel. The constant stream of mopeds puttering along, ridden by men and women, were like so many ants seeking a destination. It was 11:30 PM, up-side-down time from east Texas.

They arrived at the Rex Hotel and were greeted by a smiling Vietnamese night clerk and a woman to carry their luggage to their room. Both travelers were haggard from their twenty-two hour flight. They rested for two days, recovering their sense of time and adjusting to the food, which was decidedly excellent and extraordinarily cheap. The Vietnamese had adopted the best of French, Thai, and Vietnamese hospitality. On the one trip Emmett had made to Saigon during the war, he had made a mental note that the food was exceptional, remembering the tease he got from comrades about his "having gone native." The next evening they found a French restaurant and had the works, good wine and five courses. It seemed the war had, at least, given the public an appreciation of pidgin English. Speaking was not a problem, and Emmett's French served them, as well.

On their fourth day after resting and shopping downtown, they embarked on a road-trip to An Loc, a 130 kilometer drive on Highway 13, northeast from Ho Chi Minh City to the village in the mountains near the Cambodian border. No one appeared to object to seeing an American man and woman. In Saigon they saw French, Australian and South African travelers, but no Americans. The countryside was far different from what Emmett remembered.

The road was narrow and winding like a snake. Heavily loaded trucks, high with a variety of material from bundles of bamboo to stacks of feed sacks, cattle, pigs, and farm equipment, rumbled along, dodging the myriad moped stream. No rules for the highway. Everyone weaved in and out. The southern mountains of the Central Highlands loomed in the distance like arthritic knuckles sticking up against a brilliant sky.

Their driver was Mr. Chung, a stout man from Da Nang, who worked for a touring company, called Vet Tours, specializing in driving returning veterans through the country side. He was friendly, exceedingly courteous, asking immediately if Emmett had served in the "American War."

"I did," Emmett said, wondering if the guy might put them out on the road.

"I adopted by Korean family in Da Nang," he said, in passable English. "I educated in Hanoi, but live now in Ho Chi Minh City. My parents die in American War."

Barbara felt a twinge of guilt. They had discussed how to approach the people when the war was mentioned. In Houston, where they had to appear to apply for their travel visas, they were told most Vietnamese were content after nearly thirty years, to go about their business. Treat the subject as history. "Don't express your sense of guilt, and above all don't engage them in conversations about their own past unless they initiate it. It should be natural."

Emmett had thought of this advice a good bit over the years as he worked through therapy and conversations with other vets. His decision to return was the last phase of his doctor's recommendation.

"You must lay down, once and for all, your fears, guilt, and resentments of your time there. The Vietnamese people will share as they will, but their suffering and yours are mutual, believe me. Research tells us that.

"When you study-up on your trip, be sure to read Carl Sandburg's poem, 'Grass.' I used it a lot with veterans who struggle with post-war trauma. The process of reconciliation is different for every guy, but I think you will grasp the central intention of Sandburg's little poem. He was reacting to World War I's impact, but it applies to veterans in any war. Let me know."

Emmett read it to Barbara Lynne. He had thought the first line said all that needed to be said: "The grass covers all."

As they drove along in their Toyota, the city turned into country-side, vast rice fields, set against distant villages. In April the fields were deep green with rice plants, and here and there, farmers stood in the fields, bent over tending to their crop.

"We stop soon to rest, and you can go into rice patty, see how they gather grain. See big buffalo. Vietnamese family use rice for more than food. They burn rice, how you say, 'shocks,' for fire, make broom, eat, make more plant. Many things. Feed family.

"You like Vietnam?" He smiled at them. "You in war?"

"Yes," said Emmett, "for fourteen months. In 1969 and 1970."

"I not born, then," he smiled. "You older man, now. You from where, USA?"

Barbara piped up, "We're from Texas."

"Ah," Mr. Chung said. "You Dallas Cowboy."

Emmett laughed. "Yes, I am."

"I Cowboy like. Aikman, a tall man."

"Yes," said Emmett.

"I watch many games. You like basketball? I Kareem fan. Much basketball."

"I am more football," said Emmett.

"Emmett played football," said Barbara Lynne. "He was good."

"You married man?" Mr. Chung asked.

"This is my wife," he said.

"Ah, she have many children. I know. Very nice, lady." He smiled.

"We have two boys in high school," said Barbara Lynne.

"They not come with you?" Mr. Chung said.

"No," they both answered.

"You at An Loc?" he asked.

Emmett felt something peculiar. *Mr. Chung* must have known.

"Only for one day," he said.

"Many battle at An Loc." Mr. Chung stared at the roadway that had thinned of traffic. "Americans want to see battle places. I drive, they look."

"That's why I want to go."

"O-key," he said.

Emmett smiled and answered, "O-key."

Barbara Lynne touched Emmett's hand. "Emmett wants to go up into the mountains east of town," she said.

"Ah, very dangerous. Many mines. I help you. Both go?"

"Yes," they said.

"I take you to fine place. Tunnel there."

"I know. I want to go near there." Emmett said.

"You know tunnel? Very dangerous rocks."

"I know."

What if Mr. Chung knew? What if his...

A voice inside Emmett told him not to go there. *Bullshit.*

They were all quiet.

Emmett knew An Loc had been the site of a decisive air battle, one that would decide the future of helicopter warfare for all the Armed Forces. US forces had lost a dozen birds at An Loc, long after he did his dirty work. He had read of the battle in the war journals as he prepared himself for the return to the mountains.

In the moment he decided he would not tell Mr. Chung he had been there before 1972 to blow the mountain ammo dump. He had sought information to learn if his early mission had prepared the way for the later battles. He had found nothing. Chung's caution only made him more intent on what he had to do.

In the distance they could see the string of mountains rising in the mist, like a jagged rows of blue knuckles tinged with lacey mist. With each kilometer, they drew nearer. Emmett's mountain was called 835. He mentioned that.

"Yes, I know good place. We eat on roadside. We stop soon," he said. He pulled off at an intersection onto the road to Bien Hoa at a little shaded stand where a man and his wife had set up a sugar cane juice business.

"Very near 835," he said.

We stopped the car. A man with a machete was shucking cane. For a few dong (currency), she would squeeze the stripped cane in her metal machine by running it through a mechanism that reminded Barbara Lynne of a clothes wringer her mom had used when she was very small. The woman, wearing a cone shaped hat, caught the squeezed juice in a pan, tossing the spent cane stalk into a pile on the ground. She poured the juice into a metal pitcher and transferred it to three paper cups. Two stalks of cane produced at least six ample cups of sweet cane juice.

"You like fresh coconut milk?" Mr. Chung said. "They have coconut."

He gestured to the older man with the machete, who picked up a coconut next to his cane pile, and deftly whacked off the top and handed it to Barbara Lynne.

The man gestured to her to drink directly from the hole in the chopped coconut and chase it with cane juice. She tried it.

"This is incredible," she said, bowing and smiling. The woman squeezing more cane gestured to mix the two, which Barbara did.

"You like, much," the Vietnamese woman said nodding amiably. Immediately, the man chopped another for Emmett and another for Mr. Chung. The people smiled constantly.

Everyone was very happy. Mr. Chung paid the man. He offered coconuts for them to take with them, but they declined.

The couple had provided plastic chairs, like children might use in a kindergarten classroom, for Emmett and Barbara Lynne to sit. She and her husband squatted and smiled at them. It brought a vague memory to Emmett of Melea's hooch and her mother.

"This is great," exclaimed Barbara Lynne. "I never expected a picnic in the jungle. It must be 98." She was perspiring.

"It's hot like this all year," said Emmett, who ate the snacks they had brought along.

Mr. Chung was pleased they enjoyed their lunch stop. It was only 10:45AM. The sun was brilliantly hot.

"It make cooler in the mountains soon," Mr. Chung said, as they went on their way toward the misty mountains.

As they drove a short while, Emmett muttered to Barbara Lynne, "I wonder if that fellow who cut the coconut fought in the war?"

Mr. Chung overheard him. "He did," he said.

"Oh, really! South Vietnamese Army?"

"Viet Cong," came the reply.

"Gosh," muttered Emmett. His feelings were odd.

"War over for Vietnamese," Mr. Chung said.

There was a pause.

"And for me," said Emmett. He thought he meant it.

They drove into an undistinguished village of old store fronts and rusting awnings. Lots of patchwork hung from the sides of the building, and people plied the streets, carrying loads of sticks of cinnamon and baskets of vegetables. They paid little attention to the vehicle traffic. The village seemed as sleepy as any old town in Appalachia with only the constant stream of people in doorways and bicycle riders being dodged by ever-present mopeds.

Outside of the village the road narrowed into a bumpy country lane with occasional farmers with their buffalo prodding them along or turning into the expansive rice paddy that ran to the edge of a mountain range appearing suddenly to block their way.

Emmett watched the green jungle with a concentrated stare. Barbara felt his tension. He had waited so long. Beside him on the car seat, he had a small satchel of things and four bottles of water he intended to take with him.

Mr. Chung pulled the car to a small road like a cattle path and inched along.

Emmett saw the sign in Vietnamese and English: "DANGER PROCEED CAUTION. UNEXPLODED MINES."

Barbara saw it, as well.

"We here, sir," Mr. Chung said. "You follow foot-trail. If you go off, you in great danger. I wait, yes?" he asked.

"Yes," said Emmett. He signaled three hours pointing to his watch. "Three hours. Maybe not as long."

"She go, too?" Mr. Chang looked at Barbara's hiking boots.

"Yes, she go too," said Emmett.

Barbara Lynne noted the seriousness in his face.

"O-key," he said. "You no go boom." He did not smile.

Emmett nodded, "10-4."

He took Barbara Lynne's hand, and they began their trek, moving from emerald sunlight into humid shade.

Barbara said nothing, but thought the air felt heavier with humidity than earlier. There was no breeze.

Emmett hiked resolutely up the path. For a time everything grew downward. It was eerily quiet, no sound at all, except their own breathing.

The pathway moved through foothills with no breaks for a view eastward. They paused to rest. Emmett consulted his compass and an old assault map. He pointed the way forward, remembering Melea, how she danced along in her bare feet, seeming to twinkle over the ground. He had been told the area had been defoliated and reclaimed in the last ten years. It appeared thick and lush.

Emmett hiked in silence, careful to keep to the trail, but cautious about unusual debris over the pathway. *Surely not.*

Dr. Childs said to face the fear with no hesitation.

Emmett felt no fear, just heat. He had swallowed apprehension long ago. He wanted to see it again in the daylight, how the mountain turned upward into the rocks.

Had bombs and explosions obscured the cave's mouth, or the cable wire upward he had climbed in the dark?

Had he climbed this way in the dark?

He paused again to study the coordinates and the map. They drank from the same water bottle.

Where had the coordinates been that night when he was cut off? In a knapsack in his hole at the firebase. Dumb ass.

The area was over-grown with elephant leaves, and the greasy water rolled off into their faces like rain. The sun was barely visible.

They hiked several hundred more meters when the trail stopped and suddenly turned upward into rocks. A soft mist fell, like gentle rain, and it covered the rocks, making them slick. He cautioned Barbara to wipe her boots' bottoms and tie up her pants to avoid catching them as they moved. She used scarves she had tied about her neck. Both were wet with perspiration.

Emmett felt compelled to be silent, but there was no reason.

"We can speak, can't we?" she asked.

"Of course. I was taught not to speak in this terrain. Just training," he smiled at her.

It gave her reassurance he was with her. "Our only company are the mosquitoes and monkeys, believe me," he said.

"I hope they don't hurl apples," she muttered.

"Not Vietnamese monkeys. They use coconuts. Just duck."

She laughed.

As they hiked, he watched Barbara Lynne place her feet as he had showed her, trying to fit her steps to his longer ones.

An hour had passed. The rock climb began to be arduous. Somehow trees had forced their way through the rocks to tower above them, making the canopy shady and humid. The light was dim, though it was mid-day. Mosquitoes came out to greet them. They rubbed citronella on themselves and dropped the veils concealed in their bush hats. Emmett slapped them as they fed on his arms, otherwise he ignored them.

Barbara Lynne watched Emmett's back and his steps. *How did he fight in this place? How desperate this must have been.*

The climbing seemed endless and became less stepping up, but pulling up, until they arrived at the top of the slope where it became level. They paused as he surveyed the area, looking intently up and down the trail and consulting his compass. More water.

Did she lead me up this trail or down?

He thought he saw remnants of an old trail, leading off into deep overgrowth. Melea had led him there. He pushed into it holding Barbara Lynne's hand and proceeding cautiously. The wet air was sticky to breathe. He was drenched with sweat. In five minutes he saw the bo tree with its wide roots, cutting ruts in the jungle earth, hiding lizards and snakes.

"This is the tree," he whispered, "where Melea hid. Maybe the cable is still here."

She looked at the root system, extending like layers of snakes clutching each other, making nooks and crannies large enough for small animals, even a child.

"She hid here?" she said. "In these roots?"

"Yes, and waited for me." He didn't mention the firefight or the dead soldier, who Fox's men killed.

He saw the rusty cable still winding through the trees and over the rocks after nearly thirty years. It was the one clue that he had found the spot he wanted to be. It felt sacred to him.

"I'm going up to the tunnel mouth. Up the cable. You wait for me here."

She nodded, not divulging the horrible thoughts she was having about his falling out of the rocks and not returning. *If Melea can wait in the dark at night. I can wait in the daylight. I have to trust him like Melea.*

He slung the satchel over his shoulder, and tested the rusted cable. He had been smart enough to bring leather climbing gloves. He put them on and began his ascent.

The cable looped over and around the rocks as he remembered. Half-way, he paused and looked back, down and out over the jungle's expanse. He was twenty-one when he last climbed like this. He was winded.

The view east of where he stood on a boulder was vast, stretching for mile after misty mile down a gorge and out to rice farms and beyond. He reckoned the view was five miles or more. It was beautiful. That night long ago he had been oblivious to anything but the next moment.

The words, *"Voo-lay-vo-b yan mee ah-mnay,"* sang in his mind as he worked the old cable. Mounting between two boulders, he saw it.

The cave mouth, still in tact. A black hole below the ledge were he stood, a hole filled with debris, vines and rock, utterly impassable. It was not his intent to enter the tunnel. For it to be there was remarkable.

Quickly, he slipped off the ruck sack, unbuttoned his wet shirt, slipped off his soaking pants, pulling them over his hiking boots. The air was hushed and humid, not too hot, and a warm breeze cooled his sweating back and shoulders for a moment. Bugs found him quickly. He slipped on the old, dirty jungle fatigue pants, too tight for his waist now, and the torn, stained, ripped combat teeshirt he had taken from a bag in the cave. It smelled of mildew and age. He had kept it for thirty years.

Leaning against the largest rock, he closed his eyes and allowed the moment to absorb him. He was back beside the opening in the mountain, the place where Melea had led him. His mind folded and unfolded upon itself. He waited and listened. Nothing came, but the sound of tree monkeys, cicadas, and calling birds.

After a few moments, he found a silver chain in the satchel, engraved by a Dallas silversmith, and added onto in Ho Chi Minh City by a very happy Vietnamese jeweler, who seemed to know what it was. It read in Vietnamese, "You be no fright, GI. You o-key?" He made sure it was spelled just as she had said it.

Momentarily, his eyes misted over as he kicked dirt and debris into the cave's mouth, listening to it clatter, which very quickly got absorbed by the calling of a chorus of tree monkeys. Like a kid, he picked up one large stone and let fall, rattling and banging down the opening as it shredded its way through a sea of jungle green and disappeared.

"Boom!" he said, aloud. The monkeys answered with laughter...not demons...but monkeys, real ones.

In a few moments he had his civilian clothes back on, and stuffed the silver locket into his pocket. With a shoe string, he tied up the old combat fatigue pants and teeshirt, and the tossed them into the cave, watching them flutter into the darkness.

Then, he descended, much more quickly than he had climbed.

At the base where the climb had begun, he found Barbara Lynne waiting with tears in her eyes. They held each other for a long time. She studied his face and wiped it with her fingers, took a handkerchief and wiped his forehead and perspiration.

"Almost done," he said.

He fished the silver chain and locket from his pocket, stepped up on a root as large as a man's leg. Inching his way to the trunk, he found split bark and wedged the chain into a crevice and kissed it, then let it hang there. It glistened in a tiny sliver of light.

Jumping off the root, he caught Barbara Lynne's hand and led her down the mountain.

Note: In 1996, Emmett and Barbara began preparing for their trip to Vietnam by taking the $3,000 Colonel Rodman had given Emmett as cover-up money for their having discovered him with Gloria Evans. They used it as a down payment for their trip to Southeast Asia and to An Loc, Vietnam. Emmett also received notice from an alumni newsletter from Longstreet Military School that Colonel James Rodman had been killed in a helicopter crash in 1985 in Central America.

Glossary of Terms and Phrases

.50 CAL - machine gun that fires .50 caliber ammunition.

5-2 & 4-2-5 - football defensive terminology, 5 down lineman, 2 linebackers.

5-STEP DROP - number of steps a quarterback takes before launching a pass.

90-DAY-WONDER - derogatory term for a new lieutenant who spent 90 days in Officer Candidate School or "OCS," then shipped to Vietnam.

AK-47 - standard, Chinese made rifle used by North Vietnamese and Viet Cong.

AN LOC - Vietnamese Village, north and west of Ho Chi Minh City (Saigon) on the Cambodian border at the base of the Ho Chi Minh Trail in the foothills of the mountains.

BARRACKS BOY - any military student who lives in the dormitory of a military school.

BONNIE PARKER - infamous bank robber and gun-moll in the 1930's. Killed by the FBI.

BULLRING - a large circle on asphalt at a military school, used for marching; usually punishment for cadets who make mistakes. They had to "walk the bullring" for a designated number of hours for their mistakes.

CALLAWAY GARDENS - known in the 60's, 70's, & 80's for it's water-skiing show.

CAMP HOLLOWAY - a helicopter staging camp in Vietnam in the Quang Tri Province.

CAMP JACKSON - one of several Army basic training posts for new Army recruits in South Carolina.

CHARLEY'S ANGELS - a popular crime thriller TV show starring three women.

CHOPPERED IN (AND OUT) - flown into an area by helicopter, or pulled out of an area.

CLYDE BARROW - infamous bank robber and murderer in the 1930's, lover of

Bonnie Parker, also killed by the FBI.

DAK TO - a village in Vietnam where notorious battles were fought.

DOGPATCH - a village outside the city of Da Nang where many Marines were billeted or passed through to go in country.

DONG NAI - river near Long Binh, running inland. Dangerous up stream.

DMZ - "De-militarized Zone" refers to the imagined border between North Vietnam and South Vietnam. Actually, the 17th parallel.

ETA - "Estimated Time of Arrival" for removal of troops carried into battle by helicopters.

F-105 THUNDERCHIEFS - US fighter jets. Suggests pilot training.

FISH - slang nickname for first year cadets at Longstreet Military School.

FRAGMENTATION GRENADE - a hand grenade containing explosive that would send metal shards upward when detonated. Infantry soldiers carried them as standard equipment.

GENERAL GAIP - a highly skilled North Vietnamese general, who led the Army of North Vietnam against the US Army in the south.

GI - "Government Issue" GI became a slang term to denote any American soldier.

GI BILL - federal money made available to veterans for school after enlistment service. Extended after WWII to all veterans.

GUADALCANAL - a strategic island in the Pacific, WWII, where Americans fought the Japanese.

HAG OF VIETNAM - an apparition of Emmett's, signifying the horror of war, death and destruction. Part of his PTSD imagination. (Not to be confused with the Vietnamese stock trading group.)

HENRY V - a play by Shakespeare about a young, wayward king, who is forced to grow up quickly.

HILL 835 - mountains were assigned numbers on maps in Vietnam because of the difficulty of names spelled in Vietnamese. 835 was the mountain at An Loc village.

Ho Chi Minh - Revered president of North Vietnam who led the reunification battle to reunite north and south Vietnam under a Communist regime. Died in 1967. Capitol city of S. Vietnam, Saigon, was renamed Ho Chi Minh City after him.

Independent school - a private school that is not affiliated with a public school or school board. Also a school not funded by taxes collected by the state.

IOS - "Infantry Operations Specialist" highly trained in tracking, reconnaissance and close combat.

Iwo Jima - a strategic island in the Pacific taken from Japan late in 1945.

Johnny Mathis - famous pop star and singer in the 1950's and 60's, whose hits included the love song, "Chances Are."

Key to the flagpole - imaginary term used as tease for new cadets at a military school.

Kick-back play - an illegal football play where a punted ball is caught and immediately punted back to the opposing team in the hopes of recovering it for an advantage.

LBJ's jail - slang term for the stockade at Long Binh, Vietnam, (Lyndon Baines Johnson, US President).

Long Binh - the largest supply depot in South Vietnam, located south of Saigon. Also the induction point for most new recruits arriving in Vietnam, and the home of the Army's stockade.

LZ - "Landing Zone" for helicopters.

M-16 - Standard issue rifle for infantry in Vietnam.

Master Teacher - honorary title bestowed on an especially gifted teacher, like Sam Burke, usually found in an independent, or private school, or university.

MP's - Military Police.

PBR 119 - anachronism for "Patrol Riverboat," 119 was the PBR unit out of Long Binh.

Pivot shoes - imaginary type of shoe used as tease for new cadets at a military school.

The Phantom - a daily cartoon adventure hero, called also, "The Ghost Who Walks."

Pho pot - in Vietnamese culture a pho pot is kept on a cooking fire. Mixture of ingredients are tossed in randomly and constantly cooked. These pots are never cleaned or emptied, but constantly simmering. (In Hanoi one can see a pho pot that has been used for 130 years!)

Prufrock - fictitious character of indecisive nature featured in a poem entitled "The Love Song of J. Alfred Prufock," written by TS Elliot.

PTSD - "Post Traumatic Stress Disorder," a clinical term for psychological disorders among combat veterans, often brought on by what they have seen and done.

The Rockpile - a strategic observation site for US forces along highway #9.

Roger Ranger - an early kids show TV character, a sleuth.

Santayana - a Spanish philosopher, 20th century.

Smiling Charlie - slang for Viet Cong.

SVN - South Vietnamese Army personnel.

The Stones, man - reference to the rock band, The Rolling Stones, who are associated with the Vietnam War.

TAC or CP - "Tactical Command Post" or "Command Post."

Tennyson - Alfred, Lord Tennyson, English poet laureate in the 19th century, who wrote Morte de Arthur, "The Death of Arthur" (King Arthur).

Toe poppers - small mines, or booby traps, set off by tipping a detonator, resulting in severe leg and hand wounds.

Trip wires - detonator wires that troops might trip over setting off explosive devices, like Claymore mines.

VC - Viet Cong, Army of North Vietnam, usually recruited in the south.

Viet Minh - rebellious Vietnamese that fought against the French in

Indochina and in northern Vietnam in the 1950s.

Ville - slang term for "village".

Willipeter - white phosphorous smoke set off by use of a flare, ignited by pulling apart, used to signal the location of troops on the ground. Phosphorous smoke could be used in different colors, i.e. red meant a "hot" zone or enemy filled area.

Acknowledgments

Thanks to the following folks who were invaluable as friends and guides through the reshaping of the manuscript:

Sarah Marley and her husband, David, for invaluable advice and help in the early going.

Thanks to Georgia Military College at Milledgeville, Ga. who honored my classmates who died in Vietnam.

Thanks to Rachel Myers and her husband, Danny, for their restaurant, Rachel's Southern Style, for allowing us to commandeer a booth for editing at noon, and Suzanne Spencer, for serving up a lot of good food.

Thanks to Felix Moring, friend of my youth, and Vietnam veteran.

Thanks to Ed Robinson, shepherd of many GMC reunions and friend, who initiated my renewed interest in my finishing up this book.

Thanks to Jim Schwender, friend and Vietnam veteran, who read and commented on the manuscript.

To my teaching colleague, Jack Kridler, Vietnam veteran, who named Melea in the novel.

Special thanks to Bowen Craig and Bill Bray for their constant interest in publishing this novel, for editing help and invaluable discussion of the content and development of this project.

A special thanks to Jeffrey Meyer and Reyna Larzaru for hosting me to their home in Vietnam in 2014, and hauling me around the country on a motorcycle to visit camps and battle sites, where so many good people fell on both sides.

To Mr. Chung of Hanoi, who was our constant and able guide up the Ho Chi Minh Trail over to Hue and down to DaNang.

Special thanks for cogent and well expressed critiques of the book by son, Jeffrey Meyer.

To the editors of *Vietnam Magazine*, as I've read every edition of that publication since 1995.

Thanks to my veteran Air Force son, Kenneth, in Florida, who has constantly cautioned me to be careful with the book, reminding me that veterans of Vietnam are very special folks. "Get it right, Dad!"

To the men and women of the Armed Forces, who sacrificed life and limb, and go unappreciated.

Remembrances of those veterans who suffer from PSTD, who have been overlooked or forgotten.

To those brave gay men and women, who fight and struggle to be free to be themselves.

Thanks to Phyllis, my wife of 50 years, who endured patiently sixteen years of my preoccupation with this novel and the other two books I've written.

Herb Meyer
Spring 2017

Biography

Herb Meyer, a retired teacher, lives in Athens, Georgia. He has written two other novels, *Slow, Slow: Quick, Quick* and *Launching*, both juvenile fiction books. *In the Tomb of the Soul* is his first adult fiction book. Meyer is a graduate of Georgia Military College (high school), and holds degrees from Emory University and Middlebury College. He has taught in Georgia and Texas. He is a student of Vietnamese military history and has visited in Vietnam extensively.

www.ingramcontent.com/pod-product-compliance
Lightning Source LLC
Chambersburg PA
CBHW020922090426
42736CB00010B/995